W9-CJF-372

Audubon
Nature
Handbook

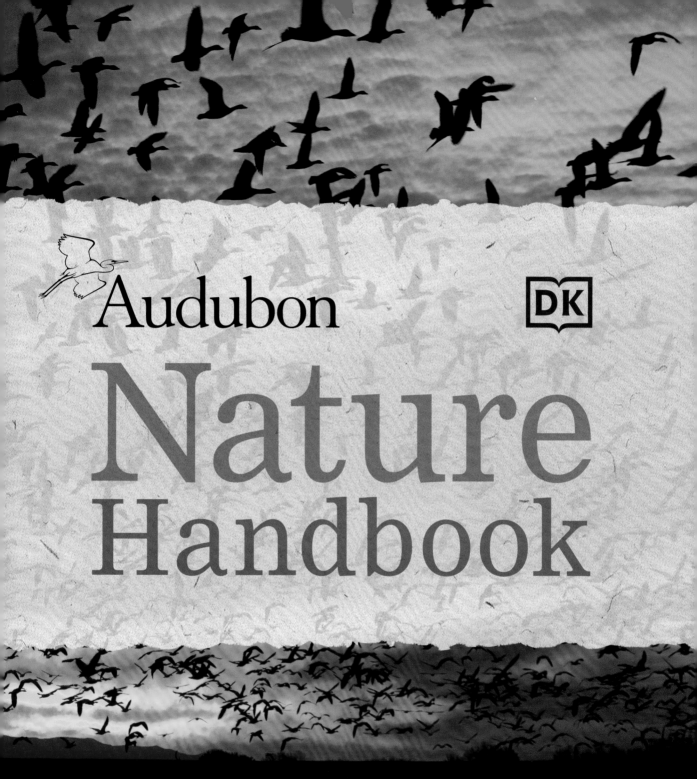

Audubon

DK

Nature Handbook

DK | Penguin Random House

REVISED EDITION

Senior Art Editors Ina Stradins, Pooja Pipil
Senior Editors Rob Houston, Dharini Ganesh
Editors Tim Harris, Shambhavi Thatte
Designer Simon Murrell
US Editors Lori Hand, Mika Jin
Picture Researcher Laura Barwick
Managing Editors Angeles Gavira Guerrero, Rohan Sinha
Managing Art Editors Michael Duffy, Sudakshina Basu
DTP Designers Vikram Singh, Anita Yadav
Senior Jacket Designer Suhita Dharamjit
Jacket Designers Stephanie Tan, Tanya Mehrotra
Production Editor Kavita Varma
Production Controller Laura Andrews
Pre-production Manager Balwant Singh
Production Manager Pankaj Sharma
Jacket Design Development Manager Sophia MTT
Editorial Head Glenda Fernandes
Design Head Malavika Talukder
Art Director Karen Self
Design Director Phil Ormerod
Associate Publishing Director Liz Wheeler
Pubishing Director Jonathan Metcalf

FIRST EDITION

Senior Art Editor Maxine Pedliham
Project Editor Ruth O'Rourke-Jones
Editors Martha Evatt, Laura Palosuo, Cressida Tuson
US Editor Jill Hamilton
Designers Rebecca Tennant, Silke Spingies, Simon Murrell,
Stephen Knowlden, Elaine Hewson
Illustrator Dan Cole/The Art Agency
Production Editor Tony Phipps
Production Mandy Inness
Creative Technical Support Adam Brackenbury, John Goldsmid
Jacket Designer Duncan Turner
Picture Researcher Laura Barwick
Managing Editor Sarah Larter
Managing Art Editor Michelle Baxter
Reference Publisher Jonathan Metcalf
Art Director Phil Ormerod

This American Edition, 2022
First American Edition, 2010
Published in the United States by DK Publishing
1450 Broadway, Suite 801, New York, NY 10018

Copyright © 2010, 2022 Dorling Kindersley Limited
DK, a Division of Penguin Random House LLC
22 23 24 25 26 10 9 8 7 6 5 4 3 2 1
001–327085–Aug/2022

NATIONAL AUDUBON SOCIETY™ and AUDUBON™ are registered
trademarks of National Audubon Society, Inc. All rights reserved.

A National Audubon Society licensed product.

All rights reserved.
Without limiting the rights under the copyright reserved above,
no part of this publication may be reproduced, stored in or introduced into
a retrieval system, or transmitted, in any form, or by any means (electronic,
mechanical, photocopying, recording, or otherwise), without the prior
written permission of the copyright owner.
Published in Great Britain by Dorling Kindersley Limited

A catalog record for this book
is available from the Library of Congress.
ISBN 978-0-7440-5211-4

DK books are available at special discounts when purchased in
bulk for sales promotions, premiums, fund-raising, or educational use.
For details, contact: DK Publishing Special Markets,
1450 Broadway, Suite 801, New York, NY 10018
SpecialSales@dk.com

Printed and bound in China

For the curious
www.dk.com

MIX
Paper from
responsible sources
FSC™ C018179

This book was made with Forest
Stewardship Council™ certified paper –
one small step in DK's commitment to a
sustainable future. For more information
go to www.dk.com/our-green-pledge

Consultant Editor

Chris Packham developed a fascination with wildlife from an early age and studied zoology at Southampton University, England. He has written several books on wildlife and has hosted many nature-based TV shows for the BBC including *Springwatch* and *Autumnwatch*. Chris is involved with many wildlife conservation organizations including The Wildlife Trusts, The Wildfowl and Wetlands Trust, and The Bat Conservation Trust, and is a Vice-President of the RSPB.

US Consultant Editors

Stephen Kress is founder of the National Audubon Society's Project Puffin and visiting fellow at the Cornell Lab of Ornithology. Dr. Kress received his PhD in environmental education from Cornell University. He is the author of numerous books and articles on seabird restoration and gardening for birds.

Elissa Ruth Wolfson studied environmental education at Cornell University and worked as a naturalist before becoming a science journalist, editing and writing for environmental, botanical, ornithological, and veterinary publications.

Contributors

Steve Backshall (Mountain and hillside) is a naturalist, author, and television host who has traveled to more than 100 countries, discovered new species, and climbed some of the world's highest mountains.

David Chandler (Web of life; Lake, river, and stream) is a freelance writer and environmental educator. David's books include the *RSPB Children's Guide to Bird Watching*, *All About Bugs*, and *100 Birds to See Before You Die*.

Chris Gibson (Coast) is a lifelong naturalist who writes, teaches, and broadcasts about the natural world. He is a senior specialist for Natural England.

Robert Henson (Weather) is a meteorologist and science journalist based in Colorado. He has worked as a tornado researcher and written extensively on climate change.

Rob Hume (What a naturalist needs; Forest; Consultant) worked for the RSPB for 30 years, editing *Birds* magazine for 15, and has written around 30 books.

James Parry (Tropical forest; Scrubland and heath; Grassland; Desert) is a writer and lecturer who has traveled widely to study wildlife and different habitats. He has written several books on natural history.

Dr. Katie Parsons (Close to home; Farm and field) has a PhD in animal behavior and ecology. She currently lives on a 30-acre farm in the Devon countryside, which she manages for both wildlife and vacationers.

Elizabeth White (Tundra and ice) is a documentary film-maker for the BBC Natural History Unit. She has a PhD in animal behavior and has filmed wildlife across the globe, including Antarctic and the high Arctic.

Audubon

Contents

DISCLAIMER
Always remember to keep safe and be sensible when exploring an unknown terrain. The Publisher has set out some basic guidelines on safety on pages 40–41, but it is the responsibility of every user of this book to assess the individual circumstances and potential dangers of any habitat they wish to explore. The Publisher cannot accept any liability for injury, loss, or damage to any user following suggestions in this book.

The Publisher would draw the reader's attention to the following particular points:

• plants may be poisonous or protected by law from picking or uprooting

• fungi and berries should only be collected for consumption at reader's own risk since many fungi and some berries are poisonous

• wild animals may bite and/or sting–take suitable precautions and a first aid kit.

ABOUT THIS BOOK

This book is an inspirational guide to exploring and observing the natural world, wherever you may be. The species included are examples of wildlife in each habitat, wherever they occur in North America, and occasionally elsewhere. Not all examples shown for a given habitat will be found together or in one specific geographical location.

Foreword

After the day she discovered the black rat snake coiled in a fish tank in a corner of our basement, my mom descended the steep staircase leading down to that dimly lit set of rooms with a bit of trepidation. Unbeknownst to her—or the rest of my family—I had captured the critter while exploring some recess of a local park and brought it home to study and nurture, thinking it best that I keep that information to myself (lest I be told I was not allowed to keep it). Mom was not thrilled by her discovery; she immediately knew which of her three children was responsible for it, and without discussion made me return the snake, which I had already named Slinky, to "wherever the heck I had found it."

I was that kind of kid—excited by the natural world and compelled to explore it and, yes, sometimes bring pieces of it into my own world to learn more about (just to be clear, I am not endorsing secretly stashing snakes or other wildlife in basements!). And I know I'm not alone. Not everyone may be as obsessed with studying and understanding the natural world as I was—nor as lucky to be able to grow up to study zoology and work for the National Audubon Society, helping to protect birds and the places they need—but research and experience suggest that the human desire to connect with nature is deep-seated within us. The late biologist and naturalist E.O. Wilson coined and popularized the term biophilia, meaning an innate human desire to

connect with nature, and the benefits that accrue from that connection. Ongoing research continues to show the benefits of spending time in nature—including improved mental health, reduction in stress levels, and better attention and ability to focus. And of course, without everything the functioning natural world and its ecological processes provide us, we would never have evolved on this planet nor could we continue to live on it. Nature truly is everything to us.

Appreciating nature may be straightforward but understanding nature, the vast array of its biotic and abiotic components, and their complex connections, is another story—a story that has been critical to humans for the entirety of our species' time on Earth. When humans lived closer to the land, in-depth understanding and appropriate stewardship of the environment and its processes were critical for survival and was passed down through teachings and cultural traditions. As our species has developed from our primordial hunter–gatherer lifestyle to where we sit now in the 21st Century, we are less intimately connected to nature but are still reliant on, and beholden to, its processes. Sadly, through our own activities we interfere with, alter, and disrupt natural processes at our peril, as evidenced by the impact that climate change is having on our world.

How can we create more and better opportunities to understand and connect with the natural world,

benefitting ourselves individually and even, through improved understanding, to instill a stronger conservation ethic across the landscape?

First, I would encourage everyone to put down their technological devices, disconnect from the constant inflow of information, and go experience nature. This doesn't necessarily mean trekking to a national park or wildlife refuge (although if you do have access to parks or refuges, go for it!). Parks and green spaces in our cities provide a respite from the modern world and can be vital portals to the natural world, hosting wildlife and plants that can surprise, delight, and restore us. Slow down, take a breath, listen to the sounds, look at what's around you, and let your mind and senses take it all in. If you have a notebook, take a few notes or sketch what you're seeing; listen to your curiosity. What is making that noise? Is that bird a permanent or transitory resident here? How do those dead leaves become soil?

Second, indulge your curiosity and explore! Asking and investigating questions may satisfy one level of inquiry but will no doubt lead to other questions and other avenues of investigation that can deepen your appreciation and understanding of nature and its constituents, processes, and connections. The book you're holding in your hands will be an excellent companion in your journey of exploration of the natural world, containing an extensive variety and amount of information that can simultaneously answer questions and generate myriad more that you will want to dig into. It's also detailed and beautiful—filled with fascinating and comprehensive information that will benefit

anyone who wants to get closer to those ancestors of ours whose understanding of the natural world was deep and authentic and who quite naturally protected it.

Who knows? If I had a book like this when I was a kid, perhaps I could've saved a bit of wear and tear on my familial relationships and lowered my mom's stress levels when she thought about that basement.

Dr. John Rowden
Senior Director of Bird-Friendly Communities,
National Audubon Society

Audubon

The National Audubon Society protects birds and the places they need, today and tomorrow. Audubon works throughout the Americas using science, advocacy, education, and on-the-ground conservation. State programs, nature centers, chapters, and partners give Audubon an unparalleled wingspan that reaches millions of people each year to inform, inspire, and unite diverse communities in conservation action. A nonprofit conservation organization since 1905, Audubon believes in a world in which people and wildlife thrive. Learn more at audubon.org and by following the National Audubon Society on Facebook, Twitter, and Instagram @audubonsociety.

The web of life

The simple beauty of life can be relished on many levels. A single bright-red ladybug on a fingertip is perfect. The fresh scent of a rose is sublime. The tiny rainbows seen flashing from the wings of aphids on the rose's stem are also unexpected gems, and the marvel of a myriad of ants flying up into the summer sky creates an urban spectacle. Each is individually remarkable, but then, so are the relationships that essentially and intrinsically link them all. There is an undeniable and satisfying beauty to be found in an understanding of these webs that knit life together.

The nature of the planet

Much of the time, we are aware only of life immediately around us, yet this is only a small part of a much larger network. Life on Earth exists in many places—some very different from others, but all are connected.

The thin green line

Life in all its forms is found exclusively on the Earth's outermost layers, including the land, oceans, and the atmosphere surrounding the planet. This narrow strip is known as the biosphere—a word that literally means "life ball." Within it are millions of species, of which humans are one, with each dependent on others for their survival. The biosphere isn't uniform, however—it is a collection of different, yet interconnecting habitats, which sometimes have undefined boundaries between them.

TUNDRA
Exposed, cold, and treeless, tundra is a habitat of the far north featuring many lichens and mosses.

Key

- Grassland
- Desert
- Tropical forest
- Temperate forest
- Coniferous forest
- Mountains
- Polar regions and tundra
- Rivers and wetlands
- Coral reef
- Oceans

WORLD BIOMES DISTRIBUTION
The scientific word for a habitat is a biome. This map shows the variety of these biomes and their distribution, which is determined by climate and geology. Human impact on the environment isn't indicated—areas shown as temperate forest, for example, may now be farmland.

GRASSLAND
Grassland includes savannas, steppes, and prairies. It experiences more rainfall than deserts, but is drier than forests.

FRESHWATER MARSH
Marshes are transitional, highly productive habitats that efficiently transform sunlight to plants.

HABITAT-MAKER

Left to their own devices, some habitats are transient, changing naturally over time—a process called succession. In freshwater marshes, dead vegetation may build up at the base of emergent plants. This dries out the marsh, allowing other species to gain a foothold. Shrubs may take over, and ultimately woodland, which is a more stable habitat.

AQUATIC
Aquatic habitats include lakes, streams, rivers, and oceans. They may be saltwater or freshwater.

More than one home

Some animals have a very strong connection with a single habitat—for example, Purple Gallinules are birds found in Florida's reed beds. Other species make themselves at home in many habitats—the adaptable carrion crow can be seen in woods, uplands, and foraging on estuaries, among other places. Dragonflies make a big habitat change—from aquatic to terrestrial—when they become adults.

adult winged dragonfly emerging from its larval "skin"

TRANSFORMER
The first part of a dragonfly's life is spent underwater as a larva, yet once it matures, it becomes an aerial predator.

FOREST
Forests are highly varied and species-rich habitats. Types of forest include northern boreal, tropical, and temperate forests.

Find your own biome on the map. Perhaps it was once temperate forest.

DESERT
Deserts seem barren, experiencing almost no rain and possessing little or no vegetation. However, many species have adapted to desert life.

LIFE ON EARTH

All life on Earth exists as part of an intricate web of interconnections. These images help to put some of these into context. They start with an individual of one species, and, step by step, move on to the biosphere. Individuals of any species don't generally live in isolation—others of their kind normally reside in the same area. Together, these make up a population. Add populations of other species in the same area and this builds into a community. The community lives in a specific habitat, with a certain climate, geology, and soil—together these living and nonliving components make up an ecosystem. Put all the ecosystems together and you have the biosphere. In this way life on Earth is interconnected, and we should take care to not tip the balance.

INDIVIDUAL
As a naturalist, you might encounter just one individual of a species. However, it is likely part of a larger group.

POPULATION
The individuals of a species in one area make up the population. Different species have different sized populations.

COMMUNITY
All the populations together form a community, where population changes for one species have an impact on other species.

ECOSYSTEM
Ecosystems may be large or small, and combine the living components with an area's nonliving physical characteristics.

BIOSPHERE
This is the "ball of life." It is made up of all individuals in every population in every community and all habitats on the planet. It is the true worldwide web.

The diversity of life

The diversity of life on Earth is extraordinary. As a naturalist, there is always something new to understand, experience, and enjoy.

Scientists have identified about 1.8 million species, and it is estimated that as many as 6 to 12 million more are waiting to be discovered. Humans are just one animal species among many, but we have a unique role to play in understanding and conserving the rest.

Evolution

Just as human families exhibit variations in, for example, eye color, animals vary within a species. As differences are passed on to subsequent generations, they slowly change, or evolve, into creatures with varied appearances and capabilities. Suppose one bird has a larger bill than its sibling and is better at feeding its young so that more of them survive. Some of its chicks also have larger bills, and, with time, more offspring will acquire larger bills until they look quite different from their smaller-billed relatives. If there comes a time when the large-billed birds can no longer breed successfully with the small-billed birds, a second species has been created.

SLOW PROGRESSION
The elephants we recognize today are believed to have evolved from *Moeritherium*—a prehistoric animal that more closely resembled modern tapirs.

MAMMALS
Mammals make up around 5,500 known species, including raccoons, tiny bats, massive whales, camels, kangaroos, polar bears, cheetahs, giraffes—and humans.

BIRDS
The more than 10,000 known bird species are widely diverse, ranging from ostriches to penguins, albatrosses to eagles, ducks to owls, and hummingbirds to sparrows.

REPTILES
These are cold-blooded vertebrates, and their bodies are usually covered in scales. There are probably more than 10,000 known species, including lizards, snakes, turtles, and crocodiles.

AMPHIBIANS
These animals have adapted to life both in water and on land. There are about 5,000 species of amphibians including salamanders, newts, frogs, and toads.

FISH
Earth's brackish, freshwater, and saltwater habitats are home to almost 31,000 known fish species, including salmon.

INSECTS
Around 950,000 insect species share the planet with us—and over 500,000 of them are beetles. From dragonflies to bees, cockroaches to butterflies, insect forms seem endless.

FLOWERING PLANTS
Around 260,000 flowering plant species have been recorded, both on land and in water. These include grasses, trees, and more familiar blooms, such as these sunflowers.

TREES
The definition of what is considered a tree is not absolute, but there are an estimated 60,000 tree species in the world.

FUNGI
There are around 100,000 species of fungi. Toadstools and mushrooms belong to this group.

EVOLUTION IN ACTION

The five digits in this skeletal paw, and what looks like a thumb, belong to the giant panda, a member of the bear family. The "thumb" is actually a wrist bone, but it is much larger than that of, say, a brown bear. It can also move, is padded, and works with the other digits to make it easier for the panda to obtain bamboo, its preferred food. This appendage may have evolved over thousands of years as a trait that was beneficial to the panda's survival.

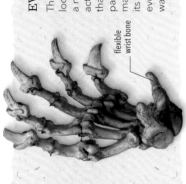

flexible wrist bone

Amazing adaptations

Evolution is about change, and if an inherited characteristic increases an animal's chance of survival by making it better at finding food or avoiding predation, for example, then those attributes are more likely to be passed on to the next generation. Within the animal kingdom, some species have, over many generations, evolved an array of adaptations to meet the challenges of life—including capabilities such as camouflage, super-sharp senses, beaks that function as specialized feeding tools, antifreeze in the blood, and feathers that repel water.

CORAL SNAKE

red touches black bands, not yellow

SCARLET KINGSNAKE

MIMICRY
Predators may keep their distance from the nonvenomous scarlet kingsnake, which has evolved to resemble highly venomous coral snakes.

PERFECTLY ADAPTED
Sword-billed Hummingbirds use their ultra-long bills to reach nectar, pollinating the flowers in the process.

Animal life

Animals occupy particular niches within the complex web of life, and have evolved various strategies and behaviors to ensure survival.

SCAVENGER

Herbivores, carnivores, and scavengers

Simply put, green plants use the Sun's energy to grow, herbivores eat the plants, and carnivores eat herbivores. But feeding relationships are often more complex. Carnivorous foxes prey on herbivorous rabbits, but also eat fruit. Crows may scavenge from the dead bodies of both animals, but also eat seeds, fruit, insects, and small animals. They are taking advantage of evolutionary niches by developing different eating habits.

HERBIVORE

CARNIVORE

Early bird or night owl?

Not all animals are active at the same time, which can reduce competition between species; for example, butterflies take nectar from flowers during the day, while most moths do so at night. Animals that are active during the day, such as most lizards, are "diurnal" and those that are active at night, such as hedgehogs, are "nocturnal" (see pp.54–55). Some animals are "crepuscular," which means you are most likely to see them at dusk and dawn.

FLEXTIME

The Snowy Owl is a crepuscular hunter that raises its young on the Arctic tundra, where, in the very far north, there is no darkness for months during the summer. At this time of year, while the female is brooding the young, the male can have sole responsibility for feeding up to 11 youngsters, the female, and himself. To do this, he adapts his usual habits, hunting in the day.

NIGHT AND DAY

Lizards are usually diurnal, day-active reptiles, relying on basking in the Sun to raise their body temperature. The opossum is a nocturnal mammal.

DIURNAL

NOCTURNAL

SLEEPY BUGS
Some ladybugs hibernate in groups, using fat deposits to help them survive the winter. One such gathering was found to contain over 10,000 individuals.

Getting away from it all

Mammals need to eat to stay warm, but in winter food can be hard to find. Some survive by hibernating. During this time their metabolisms are turned down to a minimum, and they use the fat deposits they laid down while food was plentiful to fuel this low-energy winter existence. There are also invertebrates, reptiles, and amphibians that hibernate. Migration is a strategy that is employed most visibly by some birds, but also by fish, butterflies, moths, and land and sea mammals. These creatures travel huge distances, often along well-defined routes, in search of food and breeding grounds.

LAND MIGRATION
Migrating caribou can travel over 3,100 miles (5,000 km) a year, crossing water if necessary. No other land mammal covers such a distance.

Migrating humpbacks can be seen from locations on the Pacific coast.

EPIC JOURNEY
Humpback whales migrate farther than any other mammal. Their journey, between the Central American Pacific and the Antarctic, is over 5,000 miles (8,000 km).

HOW MIGRATING BIRDS NAVIGATE

A bird's ability to navigate between breeding grounds and wintering areas, which can be thousands of miles apart, is staggering. Visual clues assist them, for example a river may keep them on track, and the Sun acts as a compass, with birds using their "internal clock" to compensate for its apparent movement. At night they use the stars as a guide. Birds can also detect the Earth's magnetic fields and use these to navigate. As they get closer to their destination smell may help: petrels, for example, find their burrows by smell.

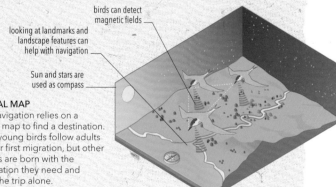

birds can detect magnetic fields

looking at landmarks and landscape features can help with navigation

Sun and stars are used as compass

MENTAL MAP
True navigation relies on a mental map to find a destination. Some young birds follow adults on their first migration, but other species are born with the information they need and make the trip alone.

Back from the brink

Human intervention in the natural world can have a dramatic impact on the lives of animals and plants.

Humans can have a detrimental effect on animal and plant populations through a variety of means. However, we also have the capacity to turn things around, and in some cases this has happened. The sea otter is one such example. Once hunted to near extinction for their fur, sea otters can now be seen in the waters off North America's Pacific coast, thanks to successful conservation initiatives. Restoration projects have also helped the American bison, after overhunting decimated herds that once totaled many millions, and the Atlantic Puffin, which was nearly hunted to extinction in the US by hunters in the 1800s, has now been successfully reintroduced to the Maine coast. Although successes like these can be achieved, many species of plants and animals remain threatened.

OSPREY
Ospreys disappeared from much of their North American range by the early 1970s due to the pesticide DDT, but after the pesticide was banned in 1972, their numbers have soared, and the birds have reclaimed most of their former range.

AMERICAN BISON
The American bison has been brought back from the brink of extinction. Over 150,000 now live on ranches and reserves.

LARGE BLUE BUTTERFLY
Reintroduction and appropriate land management has helped save the UK's large blue population from extinction.

SEA OTTER
Reintroduction projects and legal protection have enabled populations of sea otters in the North Pacific to reach over 100,000 individuals.

Weather and sky

Perhaps no greater factor has a more important or powerful influence on all life than the weather—from the very short to the very long term. Hourly, daily, and seasonal variations exert profound effects on species and their populations, and individual events can provoke catastrophe or celebration. A cloudburst in the desert, for example, is the source of an explosion of life, but the same event could extinguish it elsewhere. The impact upon all species seems set to become ever more critical as we humans pitch our predictive abilities against increasingly turbulent fluctuations in the world's atmospheric conditions. Thus, understanding weather is fundamental to understanding all life on Earth.

Climate and seasons

You can see variations of weather in daily and seasonal cycles and regional patterns. Together, these produce a climate: the norms and extremes that occur at a given place.

The Sun

Without solar energy there would be no climates on Earth. Daily cycles of sunshine and darkness result from the planet's rotation, and seasons are caused by the tilt of Earth's axis as it orbits the Sun. Because this orbit is not absolutely circular, Earth is closer to the Sun in January than in July. In about 13,000 years, however, the opposite will be true, which should warm northern summers.

POLAR CLIMATE
Some bird and whale species migrate to the polar regions, as regional sea ice expands and retreats seasonally.

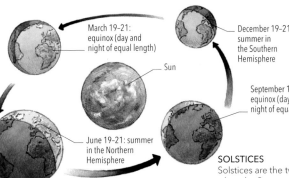

March 19–21: equinox (day and night of equal length)

December 19–21: summer in the Southern Hemisphere

Sun

September 19–21: equinox (day and night of equal length)

June 19–21: summer in the Northern Hemisphere

PORTLAND

SOLSTICES
Solstices are the twice-yearly times when the Sun reaches its highest or lowest point in the sky. Due to Earth's tilt, summer in the north will be winter in the south.

LIMA

Currents

Continents, sunlight, and Earth's rotation all influence the movement of seawater. Trade winds help drive surface water west across the tropics. The main ocean currents then move toward the poles in the western Pacific and Atlantic oceans, and toward the equator in the eastern Pacific and Atlantic. Far more heat lies in Earth's vast, dense oceans than in its relatively thin atmosphere. It is this marine influence that helps keep Portland, Maine, and equatorial Lima, Peru, surprisingly cool. Meanwhile, a broad "conveyor belt" threads through the global oceans (see map, above right).

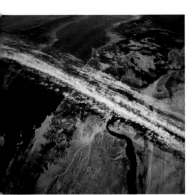

JET STREAMS
These fast-moving air currents help regulate the climate by connecting areas of contrasting temperatures and air pressure.

OCEAN WARMTH
Despite being near Antarctica, southern Chile is insulated from extreme cold by the surrounding ocean, making it habitable for temperate-zone species.

Global zones

KEY

- Polar
- Tundra
- Subarctic
- Continental
- Temperate
- Warm, Oceanic
- Mediterranean
- Semiarid
- Arid
- Subtropical
- Equatorial
- Mountain

All habitats and biomes (see pp.10–11) are affected by climatic factors such as sunlight and moisture. Earth is divided into a system of climate zones (see below), with latitude—the distance from the equator— by far the strongest influence. Ocean currents and surface types are also important. Coastal deserts get little or no rain, thanks to cool offshore waters and stable air, yet thunderstorms rage across temperate zones, where heat builds more easily and air masses often clash.

RICH DIVERSITY
Huge tree canopies in tropical rainforests serve as sunscreens, keeping the air below constantly warm and moist, which is ideal for animals such as butterflies and frogs.

CORIOLIS EFFECT

As the planet revolves, it turns more quickly from west to east in the tropics (its widest part) than in polar regions. When air currents flow from the tropics to the poles, the speed forces them to bend right over the planet's surface—a phenomenon known as the Coriolis effect. Air moving toward the equator also turns right, creating trade winds (see opposite). This effect helps explain the direction of prevailing winds and the presence of gyres, or circular ocean currents.

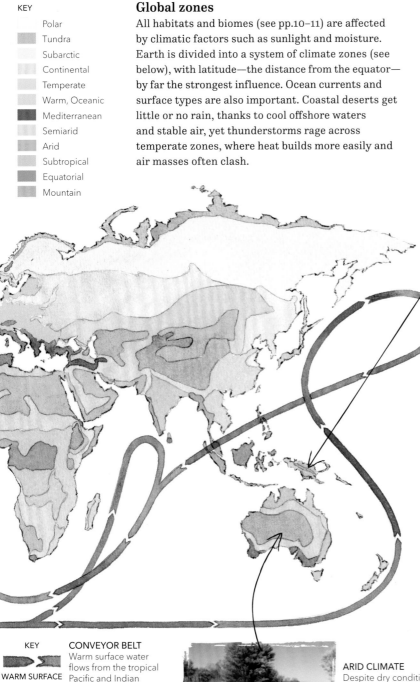

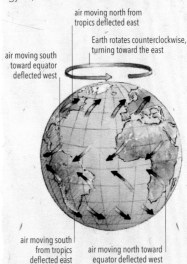

air moving north from tropics deflected east

Earth rotates counterclockwise, turning toward the east

air moving south toward equator deflected west

air moving south from tropics deflected east

air moving north toward equator deflected west

KEY

WARM SURFACE CURRENT

COLD, SALTY, DEEPWATER CURRENT

CONVEYOR BELT
Warm surface water flows from the tropical Pacific and Indian oceans around Africa, then north across the Atlantic. The water gradually sinks, forms cold bottom water, then completes the loop.

ARID CLIMATE
Despite dry conditions and large daily swings in temperature, many creatures and plants, such as lizards and cactuses, are well adapted to deserts.

Cloud spotting

Learning to read the sky's dazzling variety of clouds is useful for understanding air currents and can help you forecast upcoming weather.

How a cloud is formed

Water vapor is at the heart of every cloud. As warm air is forced upward, it cools, and the relative humidity increases. The rising air becomes saturated, and the water vapor collects around dust, salt, or other airborne particles to form a cloud. The type of cloud is dictated by its temperature, moisture content, and the air flow surrounding it.

CLOUD FORMATION
As water condenses in rising air, it releases heat. The heat warms the air mass, and causes it to rise farther until it reaches the same temperature as the air surrounding it.

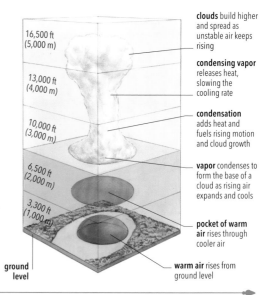

clouds build higher and spread as unstable air keeps rising

condensing vapor releases heat, slowing the cooling rate

condensation adds heat and fuels rising motion and cloud growth

vapor condenses to form the base of a cloud as rising air expands and cools

pocket of warm air rises through cooler air

warm air rises from ground level

16,500 ft (5,000 m)

13,000 ft (4,000 m)

10,000 ft (3,000 m)

6,500 ft (2,000 m)

3,300 ft (1,000 m)

ground level

Identifying clouds

The higher the cloud, the lower its temperature. Some are made of ice crystals, others of water droplets, and the composition gives each a different form. Our classification of clouds is based on one created by English pharmacist Luke Howard. In 1783, intrigued by the vivid sunsets created by volcanic eruptions, he developed a cloud-naming system, presenting it to scientists in 1802. Howard divided clouds into four types: stratus (meaning "layer"), cumulus ("heap"), nimbus ("rain"), and cirrus ("curly").

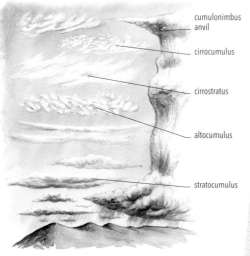

cumulonimbus anvil

cirrocumulus

cirrostratus

altocumulus

stratocumulus

Each cloud has a two-letter code— useful to note when out making observations.

Cloud codes
cirrus (Ci)
cirrocumulus (Cc)
cirrostratus (Cs)
altocumulus (Ac)
altostratus (As)
nimbostratus (Ns)
stratocumulus (Sc)
stratus (St)
cumulus (Cu)
cumulonimbus (Cb)

CLOUD LEVELS
Many clouds are combinations of the main categories. Nimbostratus, for example, is a layer of rain cloud.

SPOTTING SPECIAL CLOUDS

Some types of clouds appear rarely and only in certain areas. Noctilucent (night-shining) clouds form at heights of around 50 miles (80 km). Once observed only at high latitudes in the north or south, noctilucent clouds are now reported closer to the equator. Sometimes resembling a stack of dinner plates, lenticular clouds develop when a particular arrangement of wind layers passes over a mountain peak or range.

NOCTILUCENT CLOUD
Earth's highest clouds are most likely to be seen just after sunset or before sunrise in summer.

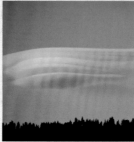

LENTICULAR CLOUD
Given their otherworldly appearance, lenticular clouds may be mistaken for unidentified flying objects.

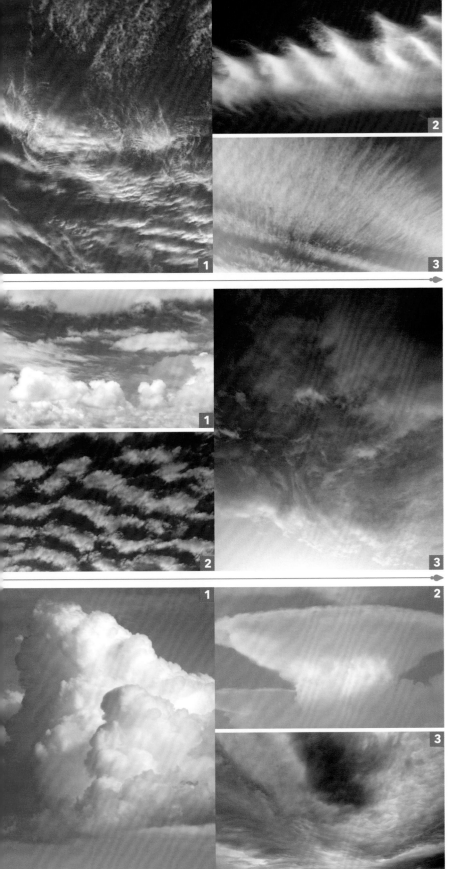

High-level clouds

Forming 3–9 miles (5–15 km) above sea level, high-level clouds consist mainly of sheets, patches, or streaks associated with cirrus formations. These clouds are often the first sign of an upcoming weather event, from a passing thunderstorm to a longer-lasting storm system. These clouds predict rain or snow within 24 hours!

1 Highly variable wind and moisture patterns can lead to a patchwork of cirrus clouds.

2 Recurring wave patterns, caused when wind blows faster above the clouds than below them, are a hallmark of Kelvin-Helmholtz cirrus clouds.

3 Contrails—narrow clouds produced by aircraft exhausts—can interact with existing cirrus clouds, or spread out to form new cirrus clouds.

Medium-level clouds

The medium-level zone, ranging from around 1–3 miles (2–5 km) above sea level, represents a transition region. Here, clouds take on a wide variety of shapes and sizes, affected by movements above and below the layer as well as within it. Most clouds in this region are preceded by the prefix "*alto,*" a Latin term meaning "high."

1 Cumulus clouds often push upward into the medium-level cloud zone. In this image, cumulus (bottom) clouds are joined by altocumulus (top).

2 Altocumulus clouds often appear as vast sheets of broken cloud, especially over the ocean. Small eddies (where wind doubles back on itself) help shape these clouds into lines or arrays of cloud parcels.

3 If more moisture is present at medium levels than below, a mid-level cloud may form rain or snow that quickly evaporates as it falls, producing streaks that hang from dark clouds. These streaks are called "*virga*" (Latin for "branch" or "twig").

Low-level clouds

Warmth and moisture near Earth's surface help make low-level clouds the most dynamic and fastest growing. Low clouds may form when conditions are calm, which can lead to fog (see p.25). In highly unstable conditions they can set the stage for cumulonimbus clouds, causing thunderstorms.

1 Towering cumulus clouds extend from a smooth base upward to heights of 6 miles (10 km) or more.

2 A vigorously developing cumulus cloud that extends to heights where the temperature is below freezing becomes a cumulonimbus cloud, with an anvil-shaped top made up of a sheet of cirrus ice crystals.

3 Stratocumulus clouds in the wake of a storm may appear ragged, as turbulence and changes in wind speed or direction eat into parts of the cloud formation.

Wet weather

After evaporating, water vapor stays airborne for a week or so. Vapor molecules condense to form clouds, before returning to Earth.

Rain

Some parts of the planet experience virtually no rain; others are deluged almost daily. The amount of rain plays a large part in the species of plants and animals that inhabit an area. Cloudy, cool areas feel more damp than their sunny, warm counterparts, which can be deceptive—on average, sunny Dallas, Texas, gets nearly twice as much rain as cloudy London, England.

1 Frontal rain occurs as weather fronts push their way across the landscape and water condenses in the air that rises above them. Intense, frontal rain ends quickly once the front clears.

2 Orographic rain results when an air mass is forced over high terrain, such as a mountain, causing moisture to rise and condense.

3 Warm, moist air topped by cooler, drier air can lead to showers and thunderstorms that may be scattered across a summer landscape or focused along a strong front. This is called **convective rain**.

4 Cyclonic rain is caused by a low pressure system. Moist air spirals toward the area of lowest pressure, producing extensive clouds and precipitation.

How raindrops form

Raindrops often start as snowflakes that grow around a nucleus of dust within high, cold clouds. Once large enough, they fall into warmer air and melt, turning to rain before hitting the ground. In warm climates, raindrops form without any ice being present: tiny water droplets collide, scooping up even more droplets and growing as they fall.

AIR CURRENTS
When warm air rises and cools, water vapor condenses to form clouds. When rain or hail forms and starts to fall, a downdraft is created by the falling precipitation.

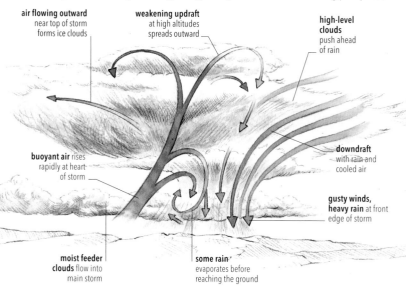

air flowing outward near top of storm forms ice clouds

weakening updraft at high altitudes spreads outward

high-level clouds push ahead of rain

buoyant air rises rapidly at heart of storm

downdraft with rain and cooled air

gusty winds, heavy rain at front edge of storm

moist feeder clouds flow into main storm

some rain evaporates before reaching the ground

Snow and hail

Many parts of the world get precipitation in frozen form. While snow develops only in clouds with temperatures that are below freezing, it may accumulate at ground level even when temperatures are slightly above freezing. Once in place, the white snowpack reflects sunlight, helping cold surface air remain. Hail forms when moisture-packed updrafts in a thunderstorm bring water to high, cold altitudes; it freezes, accumulates, and falls as ice.

SNOWFALL
On average, 1/16 in (1 mm) of water yields about 3/4 in (1 cm) of snow. The yield is usually higher for the dry, fluffy snow of cold climates.

HAILSTONES
Hailstones can be a spectacular but dangerous form of precipitation that can damage crops and vehicles. These ones are modest in size, but some can grow as big as grapefruit.

SNOWFLAKES

SECTOR PLATE

The entrancing variety of snowflakes is due to ice crystals' tendency to grow in six-sided structures (hexagons). Different kinds usually form at different temperatures. Near-freezing conditions often lead to clusters of needles or treelike branches (dendrites). Colder air favors columns.

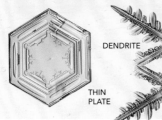

DENDRITE

THIN PLATE

Frost and dew

At night, especially when it is clear and calm, air near the ground can cool enough to bring relative humidity to 100 percent. More cooling leads to condensation on grass and other surfaces—either frost or dew, depending on the temperature. The moisture normally disappears as temperatures rise the next morning.

1 Rime frost, often very beautiful, is the result of water droplets that hover in below-freezing air and turn to ice when they encounter a surface.

2 Hoar frost is created when ice forms on surfaces, as air close to the ground drops below freezing.

3 Dewdrops are a common sight on clear, calm summer mornings. They evaporate soon after sunrise as the air warms and the relative humidity drops.

4 As surface air cools overnight, it flows into valleys and "frost hollows," where dew and frost may be especially thick.

Mist and fog

Literally a cloud on the ground, fog forms when a layer of air just above the Earth's surface cools enough so that water condenses to form cloud droplets. Even "pea soup" fog may extend only a few yards above ground level. Mist is a less dense form of fog. When visibility is more than 0.6 mile (1 km) the moisture is called mist; lower visibility is called fog.

SEA OF FOG
Cold Pacific water near San Francisco, California, leads to frequent fog, as moist, salt-laden air flows up the city's steep hills and engulfs the Golden Gate Bridge.

Stormy weather

Whether gentle, gusty, or gale-force, wind is the atmosphere in motion as it rushes toward and around low-pressure regions.

Breezes

You can feel the most reliable winds in the form of land and sea breezes found near coasts—the result of temperature differences. Asia's monsoons are caused by a season-long pattern: summer heat warms the continent, which pulls tropical moisture inland. Localized breezes create unique microclimates that affect local habitats—and people—in very specific ways.

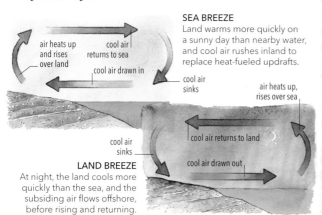

air heats up and rises over land

cool air returns to sea

cool air drawn in

cool air sinks

SEA BREEZE
Land warms more quickly on a sunny day than nearby water, and cool air rushes inland to replace heat-fueled updrafts.

air heats up, rises over sea

cool air sinks

cool air returns to land

cool air drawn out

LAND BREEZE
At night, the land cools more quickly than the sea, and the subsiding air flows offshore, before rising and returning.

LOCAL WINDS

There are many localized winds that blow in regions around the world. In North America, Chinooks are warm, dry, westerly winds off the Rocky Mountains. Nor'easters are strong winds from the northeast on the northeastern coast of the US. Santa Ana winds are dry downslope winds that affect coastal Southern California and northern Baja California.

HURRICANE
Winds pull energy and moisture from warm seas. Each year 40 to 50 of these tropical storms grow strong enough to be called hurricanes, typhoons, or cyclones— all names for the same type of storm. Many cause little or no damage, but some bring extreme winds inland, causing devastation.

Cyclones

Any area of low atmospheric pressure is, technically, considered a cyclone, although the term is usually associated with a spiraling storm. In the US, "cyclone" was once another name for a tornado, and both hurricane and typhoon are alternative names for a tropical cyclone. What we usually think of as cyclones are huge storms that generate rain, snow, and wind, and these begin as deep areas of low pressure. Winds rush in to "fill the gaps" and, due to the Coriolis effect (see p.21), begin to spiral upward—counterclockwise in the Northern Hemisphere and clockwise in the Southern Hemisphere.

Tornadoes

The world's strongest ground-level winds occur in tornadoes—reaching speeds of 300 mph (485 kmph) or more. These spinning columns—small, brief, but often violent—extend from thunderstorms. Tornadoes are most frequent and destructive in Bangladesh and the US, where temperature contrasts and moisture abound, but they occur in most midlatitude areas. Beware—if a tornado appears to be stationary but growing, it may be moving toward you.

SPIRALING WINDS
Clouds of wind-torn debris churn around the strongest tornadoes (above). In waterspouts (left), a white ring may appear where the spinning air meets the sea.

TRACKING TWISTERS

Because "twisters"—another name for tornadoes—grow and die quickly, scientists must "chase" them to gather the data for research. Truck-mounted radar, introduced in the 1990s, has allowed scientists to profile dozens of tornadoes. Storm-chasing may look glamorous in movies and on TV, but it is mostly long, hard work. An entire season may yield only a few minutes of tornadoes.

STORM CHASERS IN TEXAS

Thunder and lightning

Thunderstorms generate lightning through intense electrical fields that are produced when ice crystals and water droplets collide. Cloud-to-ground strikes are the ones that threaten people and property, but most lightning actually occurs within and between clouds. A single thunderstorm can produce many thousands of bolts in just a few hours' time. The intense heat generated by a lightning strike causes a rapid expansion of air in the lightning channel. This explosion of air produces thunder.

FORKED LIGHTNING
Cloud-to-ground lightning strikes are stunning to behold, but can be very dangerous to people and animals.

CLOUD-TO-CLOUD LIGHTNING
Sheets of cirrus clouds, or anvils, may extend dozens of miles beyond the top of a thunderstorm updraft. These highly electrified regions can generate spectacular lightning displays that you can see long before a storm arrives and after it departs.

Making predictions

Weather forecasting has developed from superstition into science. Yet with a sharp eye, you can spot the basics that drive weather—and make predictions of your own.

The professionals

Forecasters predict upcoming weather by feeding observations from across the globe into computers. Highly complex software packages interpret the data, based on our physical understanding of the atmosphere. While still not perfect, one- to three-day forecasts have become far more accurate in recent decades; extended models hint at what weather might arrive as far as ten days in advance.

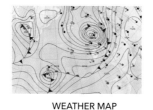

WEATHER MAP
Synoptic maps show warm and cold fronts and isobars (lines of equal air pressure).

FORECASTING
Meteorologists draw on data collected daily at weather stations around the globe.

Home weather station

If you're interested in setting up your own weather station, you can choose from a wide range of digital equipment to collect and display daily readings and store them on a home computer. Displays are linked to instruments that measure temperature, humidity, barometric pressure, wind, and precipitation. You can even upload data to public or private networks that collect observations from people all over the world.

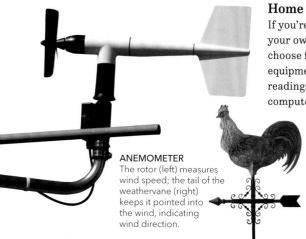

ANEMOMETER
The rotor (left) measures wind speed; the tail of the weathervane (right) keeps it pointed into the wind, indicating wind direction.

DIGITAL WEATHER STATION
By using modern equipment, you can view a detailed portrait of weather conditions, such as temperature and humidity, at a particular location at any time.

air pressure in inches of mercury

FORECASTING A WARM FRONT

In many parts of the world, you can predict a warm front by observing a distinctive sequence of clouds. As a front approaches, warm, moist air sweeps overhead, eroding cold air below. This results in thick, low cloud, and causes an overcast sky for a few hours. Steady rain or snow may eventually develop, ending with a surge of warm air.

1 Thin cirrus clouds (see p.22) are often the first sign of an approaching warm front.

2 A halo or ring may be seen around the Sun or Moon as cirrus clouds thicken into a layer of cirrostratus clouds.

3 The Sun may appear fainter as existing clouds lower and thicken, forming a deck of altostratus clouds (see p.22).

4 Heavy bursts of rain often occur before a warm front passes, but may end abruptly.

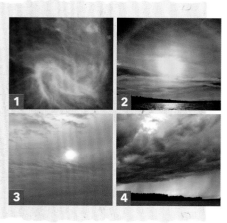

PREDICTING A SHOWER

You can spot an approaching storm by observing cumulus clouds–formed by unstable, rising air (see p.22). When warm, moist cumulus clouds rise into much colder air, they may trigger thunderstorms. Weaker showers grow and die in an hour or two; stronger storms can be set off by a cold front or embedded within a cyclone (see p.26).

1 Fair-weather cumulus often develop into small, puffy clouds that do little more than block the Sun as they pass by.

2 Moderate cumulus stretch higher into the sky, indicating the risk of a shower or storm in the next few hours.

3 Towering cumulus reach toward frigid atmospheric layers. If they keep growing, a thunderstorm may develop.

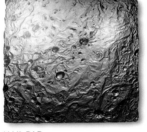

HAIL PAD
Sheets of aluminum foil spread on top of polystyrene pads make a simple way of measuring the size of any hailstones that fall in your garden.

RAIN GAUGE
This simple, centuries-old technology remains a standard, reliable method of measuring rainfall.

THERMOMETER
"Max–min" types store the day's high and low readings.

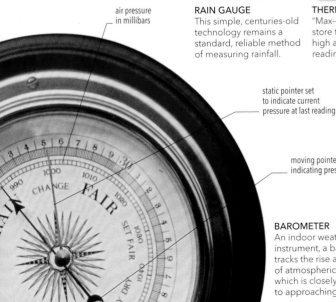

air pressure in millibars

static pointer set to indicate current pressure at last reading

moving pointer indicating pressure

BAROMETER
An indoor weather instrument, a barometer tracks the rise and fall of atmospheric pressure, which is closely related to approaching storms.

Hang seaweed indoors. If it feels moist, it might rain soon.

SEAWEED

Weather folklore

Many cultures have developed unique ways of interpreting Earth's atmospheric behavior. Common observation surrounding weather threads emerge in folklore. In many different countries, poetic sayings link the look of the sky, or the state of animals or plants, to some future weather event. And while modern forecasting has generally replaced folklore, some of these old weather sayings and practices do, in fact, work.

An open cone indicates warm, dry weather. PINE CONE

RED SUNSET
A red sunset may indicate dry air approaching from the west–hence the saying, "Red sky at night, sailor's/ shepherd's delight."

HALO
Thickening clouds ahead of a warm front produce a halo around the Moon.

SUPERSTITIONS

Unlike sayings based on atmospheric conclusions, superstitions assign supernatural meanings and explanations to what are really ordinary weather events. In some North American and European traditions, if the Sun shines on February 2 (often called "Groundhog Day"), it supposedly means a prolonged period of wintry weather. Rainbows, which are caused when sunlight refracts through moisture in the air, are especially prone to mystical interpretations.

RAINBOW
Various cultures have seen rainbows as spiritual bridges or portents of fortune or disaster.

Climate change

A global climate has evolved since Earth formed, but human activity is now forcing the atmosphere to change in new and complex ways.

Causes of climate change

Although both natural and human activity have an impact on the evolution of Earth's climate, human causes far outpace the gradual changes produced by various natural causes. Homes, vehicles, factories, and power plants burn vast amounts of coal, oil, and gas, releasing carbon into the air, where it then combines with oxygen to form carbon dioxide (CO_2). This invisible, odorless gas traps heat from Earth in the atmosphere, pushing up the planet's temperature. Atmospheric CO_2 has increased 30 percent since the 1950s and global temperatures keep rising— with potentially catastrophic results for habitats and wildlife.

NATURAL CAUSES
Major volcanic eruptions actually cool Earth's climate by releasing sulfur dioxide, which reflects sunlight.

A big eruption throws dust and gases into the atmosphere.

HUMAN CAUSES
Carbon dioxide concentrations in the atmosphere are rising primarily because of the burning of fossil fuels, such as coal.

PLANTS AND CLIMATE CHANGE

In warm regions, trees help cool the climate by shading the soil and trapping moisture. Planting trees in these areas may help offset global warming. Plants also absorb carbon, but the carbon eventually returns to the air when these plants die and decay. Conversely, trees have a warming effect in subpolar regions, where dark evergreens absorb more sunlight than snow-covered ground. Plants and oceans absorb about half the carbon dioxide emitted from human activity, but drought-stressed plants may cut their carbon dioxide absorption in half for up to a year.

SIGN OF SPRING
The famous cherry trees of Washington DC are blooming on average six days earlier than 100 years ago.

Signs of change

Many natural indicators point to a warming climate. Most glaciers around the world have retreated in the last century and the Arctic Ocean is losing more sea-ice in summer. As air warms, more water evaporates into it, so drought-stricken soil tends to dry deeper and become more vulnerable to soil erosion. Sea levels are rising, leading to expanding ocean water and increased temperatures that are causing fish to move deeper and further from the coast, making it difficult for seabirds and fishers to find enough food.

RISING SEAS
The average sea level has risen nearly 8 in (20 cm) in the last century. Low-lying oceanic islands and coastal regions are most threatened by further rises.

GLACIAL THAW
Polar bears and other creatures rely on the Arctic Ocean's sea-ice. The average extent of late-summer ice has dropped more than 30 percent since 1980.

Birds and climate change

Climate-induced threats to birds include an increased incidence of wildfires, spring heat waves that endanger nestlings, and prey numbers peaking before migrant birds return to breeding grounds. The National Audubon Society's 2018 study "Survival By Degrees: 389 Species On the Brink" examined distributions of more than 600 species of North American birds and applied climate models to forecast how each will shift with average temperature increases of 2.7–5.4°F(1.5–3°C). Many birds will breed further north, and some will suffer a sharp contraction in their range.

BOBOLINK

BOBOLINK
The Bobolink is a summer visitor that breeds in hayfields in the northeastern US and southern Canada. With a 2.7°F (1.5°C) temperature increase, it will abandon the southern 43 percent of its range as it is forced to breed further north.

KEY

● Breeding range gained
● Current breeding range
● Breeding range lost

31

STARSCAPE
On a clear night, away from
city lights, you can easily see
around 500 stars with the
naked eye—a rewarding sight.

Night watch

Stargazing stretches the imagination and prompts us to question our
place in the universe. The sky on a crystal-clear night is an incredible
sight, and it is surprising how much you can see.

*Use binoculars
to see even
more stars.*

The Moon

The Moon is a wonderful, even magical, sight.
It is our nearest neighbor in space and revolves
in time with its orbits around Earth, which means
we only ever see one side of it. It is best studied
when the low, slanting light of the Sun picks out
its mountains and crater walls in sharp definition.
A full Moon reflects brilliant, intense light and
minimizes contrast so, although you can see
the entire Moon, it may be less rewarding to
observe than other phases. The brilliance of
a full Moon also tends to overwhelm nearby stars.

Seeing stars

Stars are grouped into areas of the night sky called
constellations, with names such as the Southern Cross and
Orion. The stars in a constellation have no connection to
each other—the "patterns" are created by chance and
early civilizations named them partly to help
with navigation and orientation.
Knowing where to find
constellations will help
you understand the
night sky better. Apps on
phones or tablets can also
help identify and locate
them. Binoculars or a
small telescope will
help you see more
stars than the naked
eye, and better enjoy
the constellations and
star clusters.

MOON LIGHT
Moon phases are
caused by the Sun
lighting up the
Moon. A new Moon
is dark because the
Sun is lighting up
the side farthest
from the Earth. As
the Moon orbits
the Earth, more
of it can be seen
until it is all visible
at a full Moon.

STAR MAP
A star map is essential for navigating
the night sky. Pick out Ursa Major, or
the Big Dipper, shown on this map.

MEASUREMENTS

The size of celestial objects and the distance between them are described in degrees and parts of a degree. Calculating degrees can be done by simply using your hand as a ruler. Hold it up to the sky, at arm's length, and use these standard measurements to help make your calculations.

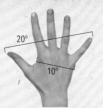

FINGERTIP DEGREE
A finger width, held at arm's length, measures about 1° across.

JOINT MULTIPLES
Finger joints are roughly 3°, 4°, and 6° across.

HAND AND PALM SPAN
An average adult handspan covers 20°; the palm is 10° across.

PREDICTED SIGHTINGS

Stars are fixed objects, but planets move around the sky. Astronomers can predict where most will be on a given night, and many resources can tell you what to look for each month, such as which planets can be seen, or whether meteor showers or a bright comet are due.

COMET

METEORITE

Planets

You can see Venus, Jupiter, Saturn, Mars, and Mercury with the naked eye or with binoculars. Venus and Mercury are best seen in the evening or morning. Planets are variable in brightness, but at their brightest, the nearby planets Venus, Jupiter, and Mars are brighter than any star. Uranus and Neptune are faint compared to Venus, and you need binoculars, a precise location, and a star chart to spot them. Unlike stars, which are very far away and appear as points of twinkling light, planets are much nearer to Earth, and sometimes have a discernible shape.

MORNING LIGHTS
Venus and the Moon at dawn make a spectacular sight. At its brightest, Venus is more striking than any star. It is so bright that it is sometimes mistaken for an alien airship or UFO.

THROUGH BINOCULARS
Jupiter is so large that binoculars show its defined shape (rather than a soft-bordered shape) as in smaller planets. Watch it on different days to see its brightest moons move around it.

Using telescopes

You can get great results from a telescope without spending a fortune. Choose a model with a wide lens or mirror—high magnification is far less important—which will gather maximum light and help you see objects such as faint stars, clusters, nebulae, and galaxies. A "go-to" system automatically points some telescopes to your chosen target. Balance cost with practicality, and always visit a good dealer for advice.

lens

eyepiece

counterweight

equatorial mount

leg and tripod

EQUATORIAL MOUNT

ALTAZIMUTH MOUNT

FOLLOW THE STARS
Mounts help telescopes follow the stars. An equatorial mount needs to be carefully aligned, while an altazimuth—such as the Dobsonian altazimuth mount shown here—moves freely from side to side and up and down.

What a naturalist needs

In these gadget-obsessed days, the excitement of preparing a tool kit that contains all the essentials for properly exploring the natural world is no longer the sole preserve of the "geek." Whether young or old, being technically prepared is part of our lives, and there are plenty of new toys available for modern naturalists. Field guides for cell phones, tiny cameras that reveal the private lives of nestlings, and chemical lures for specific moths join affordable night-vision binoculars and bat detectors that transfer recordings to your PC. But remember, the most critical part of the kit cannot be bought. It's a lifetime of curiosity!

A naturalist's kit

Curiosity, enthusiasm, and common sense are some of a naturalist's most important tools. Add a field guide and some way of taking notes, and you are well on your way.

Observing and recording

Becoming a naturalist is about becoming a systematic observer of nature. To do this, you need to have some way of recording what you have seen. It is only when you begin to log your discoveries that patterns and trends begin to emerge—which in turn make you a more focused observer. Some field guides (whether in printed form or digital) for identifying species and a notebook and pencil for jotting it all down are all you need to get started, but don't forget all the time-saving devices offered by modern technology.

DIGITAL NOTES
Modern mobile phones provide numerous ways of taking on-the-spot notes in the wild. You can take quick snaps or save observations as text messages or voice recordings. Use your phone's digital camera to create a high-resolution record of your observations during the day. Most phones will add date and location information to the image files.

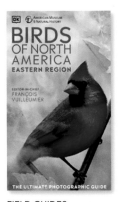

FIELD GUIDES
Either carry field guides with you, or take detailed notes of species you are not familiar with to identify later.

NOTEPADS, PEN, AND PENCIL

ADHESIVE TAPE

KEEPING A RECORD
Writing your observations in a notebook is an easy and economical way to keep a lasting record. Sketch your impressions and describe species in detail. Use tape to attach findings such as feathers and leaves to the pages.

ACCURATE NOTES
When making notes, either digitally or on paper, try to be as precise as you can to make comparisons easier later on. Always remember to record the location and date of your sightings. You may want to carry a ruler or tape measure to accurately record details such as size.

TAPE MEASURE

RULER

SPECIAL EQUIPMENT

Some animals are hard to observe well. Bats, since they fly at night, are almost impossible to identify. However, a bat detector's ultrasound microphone converts their ultrasonic echolocation calls to frequencies that humans can hear. The animals can then be identified by the rhythm and frequency of these calls. Many moths also fly unseen at night, but they are attracted to light traps, where they can be observed closely. Birds may not allow close approach, and sometimes even binoculars are not powerful enough to give good views, but birding telescopes that magnify 70x or more can overcome this problem.

BAT DETECTOR
A hand-held bat detector detects the ultrasonic calls of bats and converts them to the human hearing range.

wide lens catches light

TELESCOPE
For steady closeups use a scope on a tripod. An angled eyepiece makes it more comfortable.

ECHO METER
A device with an ultrasonic microphone can be attached to a phone or tablet so that you can record and identify bats.

MOTH TRAP
Record the moths that live in your garden with a lightweight, battery operated light trap.

USING BINOCULARS

Binoculars allow you to get close to wildlife while causing the minimum amount of disruption. To balance any difference between the two eyes, first cover the right side; use the central wheel to focus a sharp object—like a TV aerial—with your left eye. Now cover the left side; use the right eyepiece adjustment to get the same object sharp with your right eye. Look straight at what you want to see, then bring the binoculars up to your eyes. Use only the central wheel to focus on different distances.

right eyepiece adjustment

central focusing wheel

objective lens gathers light

A STEADY GAZE
Use both your thumbs and fingers to help keep binoculars steady.

COMPACT BINOCULARS
Lightweight binoculars are great, but make sure they are comfortable to use.

NAKED EYE VIEW   8x MAGNIFICATION   20x MAGNIFICATION

MAGNIFICATION
A steady view magnified 7 or 10 times shows more than a wobbly one twice as large. Choose binoculars with a magnification between 7x and 10x at most.

A closer look

In order to learn more about certain plant and animal species, it is useful to take a closer look. For some difficult groups, a magnifying lens is essential for accurate identification. Try to observe the specimen as you find it and never collect wild plants or animals. If you catch an insect for closer study, always handle it with great care, and release it afterward.

EASIER VIEWING
Clear perspex boxes are best for observing insects and other small animals more closely, allowing you to view the specimen from all sides with minimal disruption. Some containers have a built-in magnifying lens for easier viewing.

COLLECTING CONTAINERS

LOOKING AT DETAIL
Use either a loupe lens or a larger magnifying glass to record details such as whether a flower stem is smooth or hairy, the shape of a beetle's jaw, or the wing structure of a dragonfly. Tweezers are useful for holding up small specimen you may find; live animals should only be observed in boxes.

CLOTH

TAKING SAMPLES
Never uproot a wild plant—if in doubt, leave alone. Use a knife to take a leaf sample for identification later on.

LOUPE LENS

TWEEZERS

MAGNIFYING GLASS

CATCHING INSECTS
In order to catch insects for closer observation, make sure you have the right equipment, such as a net or pooter. Take great care not to damage the animal in any way and always release it afterward.

NET

ASPIRATOR

BUTTERFLY NET

Being prepared

Life outdoors is unpredictable, but a changeable forecast is no excuse to stay in. You can take simple steps to be comfortable in most weather conditions.

Evaluating conditions

For the most part, the time of year, the weather forecast, a good map, and an idea of what you are trying to achieve prepares you for most eventualities outdoors. Dress and pack accordingly, bearing in mind that you may be carrying everything with you all day. When buying new equipment, such as mosquito nets, or clothing, choose comfortable, lightweight options that allow maximum ease of movement. Your aim is to avoid getting sunburned, or being too cold, hot, or wet.

HEAD LAMP

HEADGEAR
A warm hat is invaluable on a cold day, while a cap and sunglasses provide shade from the Sun in warmer weather.

HAT

CAP

POLARIZED SUNGLASSES

LAYERING
Wearing several thin layers allows you to easily add or remove clothing as conditions change. Layering is also the best way to keep warm—the air trapped between the layers is an efficient insulator.

fingerless gloves keep hands warm while writing or using equipment

FINGERLESS GLOVES

fleece jacket combines comfort with warmth

lightweight raincoat is easy to wear and breathable, yet keeps you dry

base layer wicks perspiration away from the body

waterproof zippers ensure that gear stays dry in all conditions

external pockets provide quick access to gear

SPEED LITE

POCKET NA

PANTS

Choose pants that are both robust enough to protect you from scratches and lightweight enough to be comfortable. Pants with zip-off legs are ideal for changeable weather or an impromptu paddle.

zip-off pant legs adjust for warm weather

RUBBER BOOTS

HIKING BOOTS

SANDALS

FOOTWEAR

Choose footwear according to the terrain. Sturdy sandals can be worn on flat ground, while hiking boots are ideal for rough terrain. Rubber boots can be useful when the ground is wet or marshy.

THE DAY PACK

The best backpacks sit high on the back for comfort, have an abundance of zippered pockets, and are waterproof to keep out the rain. Like all outdoor gear, try it on before you buy it. A large fanny pack may be an ideal choice to carry small items, such as sunscreen, for short treks.

waist strap helps distribute weight evenly, sparing your shoulders

FANNY PACK

WET GEAR

What you need depends on what you're doing, when, and where. A swimsuit, mask, and snorkel are all you need to explore aquatic natural areas when the weather is warm. A wetsuit is a good investment for snorkeling in cold water, or if you plan to spend long periods of time in the water.

MASK AND SNORKEL

FLIPPERS

BATHING SUIT

Getting around and staying safe

If you're heading further afield than your local area, make sure you've planned your excursion and have the right equipment to hand.

Finding your way

Exploring a new area requires a bit of preparation and research, but need not be difficult. A map or trail guide is an essential piece of equipment—simple ones are often available online. Plan your route in advance, and carry a map even when following marked trails to ensure you make it back before nightfall.

USING A COMPASS

A compass is useful whenever you are using a map, but essential if walking on land outside marked trails. A compass, at its simplest, is an instrument that always points to the magnetic north. Use it to ensure that your map is oriented correctly, and to check your course of travel as you walk from point to point.

FINDING NORTH
Align your compass with map gridlines and rotate both until the needle points to "N."

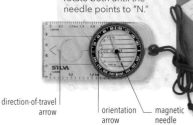

direction-of-travel arrow   orientation arrow   magnetic needle

MAPS
A wide variety of maps is available for navigating in wilderness areas. Choose a large-scale contour map for maximum detail about the various features of the landscape.

FLASHLIGHT
With no other lights around, darkness can fall very quickly. Make sure you always carry a working flashlight.

WATCH
Keep track of the time to check your progress and assess when you need to turn back.

GPS

GPS uses numerous satellites to calculate your position. It is especially useful when visibility is low.

PUBLIC RIGHTS OF ACCESS
Rights of access refer to the rights of the general public to use public and privately owned land for recreation. Access rights can vary considerably from country to country so always obtain up-to-date information from local authorities when visiting a new area. Access rights can be limited to rights of way, meaning that access to land is only permitted via a certain path or trail.

RIGHTS AND RESPONSIBILITIES
Rights of way are there to be used, but remember to close gates, avoid leaving litter, leave plants alone, and clean up after your dog if you have one.

Countryside Code

1. Plan ahead, be safe, and follow any signs.
2. Leave gates and property exactly as you found them.
3. Protect plants and animals and take your litter home.
4. Keep dogs on a leash.
5. Consider other people.

NAVIGATING IN THE WILD
It takes some time to learn to use a map and compass confidently, but it is a skill that will pay off time and again.

Staying safe outdoors

There are a few things to bear in mind to ensure your comfort and safety outdoors. Watch weather forecasts and be prepared—good conditions can turn bad quickly, especially on exposed ground and mountains. Be careful near the sea, especially on beaches and salt marshes with a large tidal range; you can find yourself a long way from safety when tides turn. Use a tide table (p.198) and watch out for strong winds. Though livestock rarely pose problems, it is wiser to avoid them if you can. Take precautions in unfamiliar places, especially if you are on your own, or as it gets dark. And always tell people where you're going and when you expect to return.

BITES AND STINGS
Spiders and insects rarely cause problems, but find out about any dangerous ones in the area.

INEDIBLE PLANTS AND FUNGI
The golden rule is, simply, don't eat anything unless you are absolutely sure of what it is.

SEVERE WEATHER
Don't venture far afield in difficult terrain if the weather looks bad—and always take suitable clothing.

SAFETY ESSENTIALS

A mobile phone is a safety essential, but you may not have coverage everywhere. Remember to program it with emergency numbers. Always pack a whistle—it can help rescue teams find you if you're unable to move. Be sure to also pack water, high-energy snacks, and basic first-aid supplies, especially if you're planning a long hike in unknown terrain.

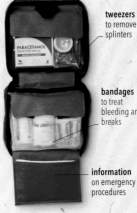

tweezers
to remove splinters

bandages
to treat bleeding and breaks

information
on emergency procedures

WHISTLE

FIRST-AID KIT

Photography

Taking photographs is a great way to record the natural world. Using the correct equipment and techniques can help you get some amazing shots.

Choosing your camera

It is the opportunistic and unpredictable nature of wildlife photography that makes capturing a great image so rewarding. Expensive gear is all very well, but being in the right place at the right time, and being alert, patient, and respectful, are key. Regardless of what you want to do, you should be familiar with your camera, and it should be comfortable to use and kept with you at all times.

With a sufficiently long telephoto lens, you can photograph birds without disturbance.

shutter — shutter dial — flash

BRIDGE CAMERA
Relatively small and light, a bridge camera enables switching from wide-angle to telephoto mode with the movement of a dial rather than the inconvenience of changing lenses.

shutter

changeable lens

DIGITAL SINGLE-LENS REFLEX (DSLR) CAMERA
The camera of choice for serious photographers is the DSLR. These cameras have a range of features that can be adjusted manually and also offer greater flexibility with interchangeable lenses.

CLIP-ON LENS
A smartphone clip-on macro lens allows you to get close to the subject and pick up fine detail. Attached to a phone, it is ideal for insect and flower photography.

lens attachment

sturdy clip secures around the smartphone's camera

CLIP-ON LENS UNATTACHED

CLIP-ON LENS ATTACHED

USEFUL EQUIPMENT

A tripod is useful when your camera needs to be stable, whether for close-ups of tiny plants or insects, or to steady your hand when using a zoom lens. You should also have a lens-cleaning cloth, blower brushes, spare batteries, and digital cards.

tripod attaches to bag

camera is protected by padding

CAMERA BAG
Expensive equipment needs protection when on the move. Carrying bags offer sturdiness, waterproofing, and balance with weight and comfort.

ZOOM LENS   **WIDE-ANGLE LENS**

EXTRA LENSES
Zoom lenses are most suitable for close-ups, while wide-angle lenses are ideal for landscape photography.

Photographing wild animals

Animals in the wild are unpredictable—you must take care not to approach or disturb potentially dangerous animals. Studying the techniques used by professional wildlife photographers can help you get great shots at a safe distance. "Digiscoping," for example, where you attach a camera to a spotting scope via an adapter, allows you to shoot close-ups without disturbing your subjects or their environment. Audubon's "Guide to Ethical Bird Photography and Videography" offers basic guidelines on capturing images and videos responsibly in the wild.

BLINDS

A blind is a shelter that offers protection for you and your equipment, and gets you close to your subject without being seen. Fixed shelters, such as a car, can be effective, but a blind built over a period of days to avoid alarming the subject is often better. Tents can be adjusted for this purpose.

Use a waterproof camera to photograph underwater life.

Light and exposure

To capture wildlife in action, and get a good depth of focus, you usually need as much light as possible for quick exposures. But don't look just for bright Sun "spotlighting" the subject; think about different types of light, the moods they create, and the effect you want. Go out both early and late in the day and observe the play of light and shadow. Try taking shots with low, raking sunshine, or with light reflected by mist or snow. A flash is useful in low light conditions, but never disturb the subject with the flash, especially at night.

1 A pheasant captured at full speed. Bright light allows a fast shutter speed to catch the action. A slow shutter speed would create a blur.

2 Bright fall sunlight has enriched this pheasant's colors. Dull light flattens color, but it can create a more atmospheric result.

3 If you can predict where an animal will be, maneuver your camera in advance to the best position for the light you want.

4 A subject, like this Northern Lapwing, can be emphasized by isolating it from its background using a shallow depth of field. Create this effect by using a large aperture.

Keeping a record

Recording your observations not only helps you learn more about what you have seen, but lets you to contribute to the data-collecting efforts of the naturalist community.

Field notes

Whether digital or hand-written, the notes you take in the field form an important part of being a naturalist. Note-taking helps focus your attention on the details of what you see—instead of a brown bird, you will learn to see a smallish brown and cream bird, with dark brown markings. Take photos or make sketches to form a more comprehensive picture, and use your notes to look up and learn the names of new species later on. A log of repeated observations allows you to link your discoveries to wider natural phenomena.

PHONE APPS

Apps designed for phones are great tools for naturalists. Apps are available that identify birds from pictures you take and sounds that you record with your phone. The Audubon Bird Guide app lets you upload your sightings. Other apps can identify bats by their echolocation calls and wildflowers from photographs.

Bolt-on ultrasound microphone device

Birdsong audio waveform

Audubon Bird Guide app shows local sightings made by a community of users

remember to note date and location of sightings

always include name and any interesting information

note colors of plants and animals

make sketches and add details for later identification

include details of environment in which each species was seen

10/12/2010
Location Ham Lands Nature Reserve, Richmond

— Rowan berries just changing color from orange to red—earlier than last year!

— Berries seem especially plentiful this year; due to wet summer?

— Gray-brown caps and light-brown stems — Grows in clumps of 2–3

Growing in the shade of trees, almost hidden by fallen leaves

Stems 4–5 inches in length, caps up to 2 inches across

pale underside

SKETCHING

If you look at something superficially you will soon forget most of the details. If you take time to observe it and draw sketches, however, it will stick in your mind for years. You don't need to be a great artist to sketch the basic shape of an animal, such as this pipit. Record the overall shape first, then add the details such as tail shape and markings.

1 Use basic ovals to create a bird shape. Get the rough shapes and proportions down, then add a basic bill, tail, and legs.

2 Fill in the general shape and revise the bird's proportions. Is it upright, horizontal, slim, chubby, or long- or short-legged?

3 Add essential details: shapes, relative proportions –do the wings reach halfway along the tail or fall short?–and feather patterns.

4 Look closely at the head and note down the colors and pattern of the plumage and the shape and relative length of the bill.

5 Make sketches from different angles, if possible. Have you labeled everything? If not, take another look. Making notes around a sketch forces you to notice specific characteristics.

Data collection

If taking notes on a regular basis, it is a good idea to transfer the data you collect in the field into a more systematic form for easier access later. Use field guides and apps to identify species and compare your observations with other people's. Don't forget to add or scan in your photos and sketches. Regular, detailed records of the same subjects can help build up a set of valuable data not just for yourself, but for the wider naturalist community. A single count of birds on a lake is interesting, but a series of weekly counts taken for a month or year can have real scientific value. Look for local or national surveys to which you can submit your findings. You can use a phone app to enter your observations to an online database such as eBird (eBird.org). Pooled data from many observers enables the production of maps of occurrence. By doing so, you are contributing to global knowledge of species' status and changing fortunes.

ORGANIZED SYSTEM
Uploading your records onto your cell phone or computer allows you to easily retrieve data collected over time. Use online apps to share your records with the wider naturalist community.

BIRDWATCHING
As well as enjoying the sights and sounds of seabirds, you can contribute to their conservation by submitting details of your observations to an online database.

Close to home

Tropical rain forests and Antarctic seas are home to many celebrity species, but it is in and around our own homes that we meet most of our wildlife. These encounters are formative at first, then ultimately much more rewarding than fantasies of exotic creatures fueled by television. To watch in "real time," to identify species that share our community, to relate to their lives and perhaps provide for them—even touch, feel, and smell them—this is the essential source of a real affinity with nature. And despite the harmful impact, so many animals and plants have managed to adapt to sharing our homes that meeting them can be an everyday event.

Home

We all have a number of visitors in our houses. Wasps, birds, and bats may nest in your loft or roof space, while beetles and termites might burrow into wood. Peer into cracks in walls and you may find mice or cockroaches. Look around to see what's sharing your space, but don't view anything as a "pest"—these animals don't exist to aggravate us, but as part of the complex system of nature.

YELLOW JACKET

BIG BROWN BATS

Local habitats

You don't have to venture far to explore the natural world. Our homes, gardens, parks, streets, and railroads are teeming with wildlife—if you know how to look for it. Many animals and plants live well alongside humans.

Garden

Gardens are great for watching wildlife, especially if sensitively managed with nature in mind. Even the smallest outdoor space—a window box, terrace, or patio—can be stocked with plants to attract insects and the animals that feed on them. In larger gardens, ponds, compost heaps, brush piles, and nature reserves provide more opportunities for animals and plants to thrive. Bird baths, feeding stations, and nest boxes attract wildlife, too.

MOURNING DOVE

GARDEN SNAIL

OXEYE DAISY

Town park

Urban parks are oases of green that provide a much-needed "breathing space," both for people and wildlife. Established parks have mature trees and may include a pond, lake, and wildlife area. Look for small mammals such as squirrels, groundhogs, songbirds, and waterfowl.

CHESTNUT

GROUNDHOG (WOODCHUCK)

Street

You may think there is little space for wildlife in the concrete jungle. However, look closely and you will see wildflowers growing through cracks in the pavement, and insects burrowing into the mortar of a wall. You might even catch sight of a rat or a raccoon scavenging in trashcans, and don't forget to look up to see birds roosting on buildings and street lamps.

BROWN RAT

CHICKORY

Railroad

Next time you take a ride on the train, look out of the window for wildlife. Some plants, including dandelions, flourish in the well-drained, gravelly conditions along tracks, and you may see mammals, such as wild rabbits. Disused tracks are often converted into footpaths, while old tunnels can be adapted for hibernating bats—but visit such areas with caution.

DANDELION

In the home

Our homes provide shelter for animals other than ourselves. We share our living space with an array of successful opportunists.

House guests

The most successful species in nature are those that can quickly adapt to change and capitalize on opportunities as they arise. As humans alter the landscape, wildlife must adapt to survive. Some animals have evolved to find their niche in our homes, which meet two basic needs—shelter and food. For example, a dry attic is a perfect place for a wasp to build her nest, while discarded food waste is a feast for a house mouse. Each species has its place in the world and many, such as spiders, provide a valuable service by keeping the levels of other house guests, such as flies, in check.

LIQUID DIET
Houseflies can contaminate food by passing bacteria from their feet and mouthparts. They suck in liquid food through a fleshy proboscis.

AN ITCHY VISITOR
Adult fleas need blood in order to reproduce. If you notice small, irritating bites, usually on legs and ankles, there may be fleas in your house. Their eggs often drop into bedding or carpets, where the larvae feed and pupate. New adults then jump on to a passing host.

GECKOS
Geckos make good house guests. They cling to walls and ceilings where they eat insects.

TAKING A BATH
Some spiders can bite if threatened, but they come inside to feed on insects, so don't harm them.

LOFTY AMBITIONS
Bats often roost in loft and roof spaces. They will not gnaw on wood and do no structural damage—their dry droppings are a good garden fertilizer.

Fleas have long back legs and can jump up to 350 times their body length.

CAT FLEA

Signs of life

Some visitors are unseen until you notice their tell-tale signs. If you live in the US, Africa, or Australia, you may not be aware of a termite invasion until you see a nearby swarm, but they could have already been at work in your home. Other visitors are more obvious, and you'll see droppings or nests. You may also hear scratching or chattering in a ceiling or wall, or smell a distinctive odor.

LITTLE NICHES
Small holes in your furniture can be a sign of "woodworm": the common name for the beetle larvae that bore into wood.

HOLES IN CLOTHES
If you see small, light brown moths in your home, check your clothes and carpets. Adult moths do not eat, but their larvae feed on natural fibers, such as wool.

BLISTERING PAINT
Bubbling paint may mean termites are around. They can cause damage to structures by eating through wooden supports.

TINY DROPPINGS
Small, black pellets in cabinets or on floors are often a sign that mice are inhabiting your home.

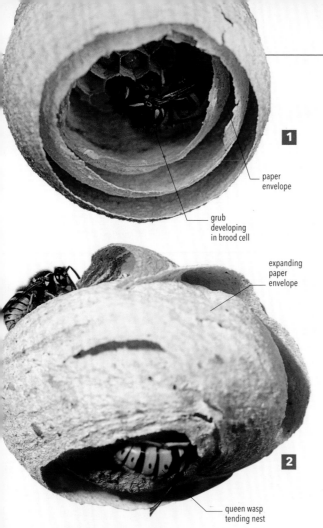

1

paper
envelope

grub
developing
in brood cell

expanding
paper
envelope

queen wasp
tending nest

2

Homes from homes

A nest is usually an indication that an animal has set up home in your house. Wasps' nests are common in attics, garages, and lofts—try to look at them from a distance, or with binoculars. Basements, garages, and roof spaces are good places to hunt for the nests of small mammals, such as mice, while evidence of nests around your house may indicate that birds are living in your roof. Swallows and phoebes build their nests outside under roof overhangs, so you can watch them as they work to feed their young. Never disturb a nest unless it is unavoidable.

LONE QUEEN
A queen wasp uses her antennae to check the size of her nest.

Wasps' nest

1 Social wasps live in colonies in nests. A solitary queen begins the nest, laying a single egg in each brood cell as she completes it. The nest is a sequence of paper layers, made out of chewed wood fibers.

2 The queen tends and feeds her growing grubs with the caterpillars she has caught until they hatch into worker wasps. The workers then help the queen expand the nest, allowing her to spend more time producing eggs.

3 The nest has a small entrance hole that is easy to defend and also helps control the interior temperature and humidity. Workers continue constructing new outer envelopes to accommodate the growing colony.

HOUSE MICE
Mice build nests out of materials they find in and around homes, such as dry grass and soft fabric fibers.

outer layer
protects nest

entrance hole
is small and
easy to defend

worker wasp
continues to
enlarge nest

3

Swallows feed their young on insects caught in flight.

MOUTHS TO FEED
Look up—you may see birds such as swallows and phoebes building nests beneath the eaves of houses and outbuildings.

HOUSE
SPIDER

Spiders

Spiders are common in homes and gardens. The best way to find them is to look for their silken webs.

More than 40,000 species of spiders have been recorded worldwide. They build their webs out of lines of silk, expelled through silk-secreting glands (spinnerets) on their opisthosoma (abdomen). Some spiders maintain and repair the same web for a while, while others eat their webs in the evening and construct a new one the next day. The intricate webs of garden spiders are a spectacular sight on a dewy morning. Search carefully among bushes and shrubs, but be careful not to touch any part of the web or the spider will hide. American house spiders do not construct such beautiful webs; look for flat, tangled webs in parts of the house that are not used very often. Other spiders you might see around your yard include wolf spiders, the females of which often carry a white egg sac under their abdomens; jumping spiders, named for their ability to jump onto their insect prey; and tiny sheet weavers, known for spinning fine, sheetlike webs in vegetation.

BANDED
GARDEN
SPIDER

TYPES OF WEBS

Different spiders spin different types of webs. Some spiders create a radial web with strands of silk extending around it that act as tripwires to alert the spider when an insect touches them. House spiders weave a tangled sheet of silk to catch insects that crawl or fly into it, and garden spiders spin orb webs across gaps to catch flying insects.

RADIAL WEB

SHEET WEB

ORB WEB

CLEVER CONSTRUCTION
Most orb weavers, like this black and yellow garden spider, take only half an hour to spin a web. They move along the nonsticky rays (spokes) of the web so they do not get caught.

Around the clock

Garden visitors change over a 24-hour period. Diurnal animals are active in daylight hours, while those awake at night are nocturnal.

FOLLOWING THE SUN

Plants that turn to follow the Sun as it moves across the sky during the day are heliotropic, and the motion is known as heliotropism. They track the Sun with their leaves to maximize the amount of light they absorb for use in photosynthesis. Sunflower blooms also follow the Sun to attract insects that favor its warmth.

Daytime

Go out into the garden at dawn, as the first rays of Sun peek above the horizon, and you will hear songbirds begin their dawn chorus (see p.98). As the Sun gathers strength, butterflies, dragonflies, and reptiles come out to bask in its warmth. Garden birds start to appear as the day wears on, you may notice them busily feeding themselves and looking for food for their young.

FIND A FOX
Foxes can be seen both during the day and at night, a pattern also followed by rabbits.

NIGHT OR DAY?

Animal behavior is influenced by a biological process called circadian rhythm, a daily cycle that provides cues as to when to sleep, wake, and feed. Many animals (including humans) are diurnal, and remain active during the day, but others are crepuscular (active during twilight hours), or nocturnal (active at night, see p.14). Nocturnal animals may have adapted this behavior to avoid competition for food with similar diurnal species, to avoid dehydration in hot habitats, or to avoid predation.

DAYLIGHT HUNTER
American Kestrels are diurnal birds of prey. They can hover for extended periods, so they can survive in a variety of habitats, including urban centers. Look for them hunting by roads.

SPOT A SQUIRREL
Squirrels are busy during the daytime, feeding and storing food for later. They are agile and very good at stealing food from garden birdfeeders.

SEE A SNAKE
Reptiles, such as black rat snakes, bask in the morning Sun to warm their bodies and speed up their metabolism.

LET FRUIT LIE
Leave fallen fruit on the ground in your garden to attract daytime feeders, such as birds and insects.

Nighttime

If you sit quietly in your garden at dusk, you might see bats. They fly and hunt insects in the dark by using sound waves to create a mental image of their surroundings. This process is called echolocation. Other nocturnal creatures often have a heightened sense of sight, smell, or hearing. Light reflected in the eyes of a fox or cat is due to a special layer in the retina, called the tapetum, which takes in the maximum amount of light and gives them excellent night vision.

BUILDING FOR BIRDS

Birds find it difficult to distinguish between window reflections and open flyway. Consequently, millions die each year because of collisions. Patterning on the window glass can reduce this danger. Artificial lights are also a problem, attracting and confusing migrant birds. Audubon's Building for Birds initiative engages with building owners and managers to keep unnecessary lights turned off.

GARBAGE RAIDERS Some mammals, such as raccoons and foxes, will scavenge in garbage cans during the night.

LISTEN FOR OWLS Barn Owls hunt over open ground at dusk and at night. Their ghostly, hissing shriek is sometimes heard.

TEMPT A MOTH Bee balm flowers remain open at night and attract moths with their scent. Other plants, such as evening primrose, bloom at night.

GO FOR GLOW Tiny lights in rough grass at night indicate the presence of glow worms, a type of wingless female beetle or larvae.

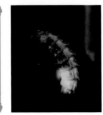

COYOTE Coyotes are most active at night. Their keen senses of smell and hearing help them find prey in the dark.

Garden birds

Watching birds in your backyard can be truly rewarding. You can encourage more avian visitors by providing good-quality, natural food.

Attracting wildlife to your garden

Sterile lawns, exotic ornamental plants, and toxic pesticides have turned many yards into unhealthy places for birds and other wildlife. But even a small garden can become a haven for birdlife if it is planted with native shrubs and wildflowers. Less mowing, fertilizing, and pesticide use mean cleaner air and water—and more birds. Why? Because there will be more insects and spiders for them to eat and, most importantly, for them to feed to their young.

AUTUMN BERRIES
Winterberry fruits in autumn are a favorite of berry-eating birds such as this American Robin, as are the berries of related species like cotoneaster.

GRAY DOGWOOD

PEOPLE-FRIENDLY
A wildlife-friendly garden is also a people-friendly garden. It is enjoyable creating it, and great fun watching it develop and attract birds and insects.

ATTRACT HUMMINGBIRDS
This Ruby-throated Hummingbird is feeding on the energy-rich nectar of bee balm. Columbines, penstemons, and honeysuckles are also good for hummingbirds.

Bird studies

Enhance your observations by attracting birds to a feeding station or bird bath. Watch quietly from a window and don't make sudden movements that might startle your visitors. Depending on your location, you may spot birds from these common groups.

Thrush family

Thrushes are small to medium-size birds renowned for their beautiful songs. Most are shades of brown or gray but some, including bluebirds, are more colorful. Thrushes eat insects, snails, and fruits. They rarely come to bird feeders, but enjoy water features for drinking and bathing.

Blackbird family

The new world blackbird family includes grackles, cowbirds, meadowlarks, and orioles. Some, like Baltimore Orioles, are very colorful. They live in deciduous forests and backyards, where they forage for insects of all kinds. These fine songsters also visit feeders, where they especially like ripe fruit such as cut oranges.

white ring around eye

plump body

short tail

EASTERN BLUEBIRD

AMERICAN ROBIN

brick-red breast

male has a black hood

bright orange underparts

BALTIMORE ORIOLE

Woodpecker family

Woodpeckers are boldly patterned birds ranging in size from small, at about 6–7 in (15–18 cm) long, to the largest species being about the size of a crow. They have sharp, chisel-shaped bills for pecking or hammering holes in trees to find grubs and make their nests. Two of their toes face forward and two backward to help them grip.

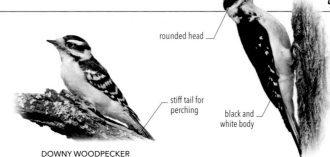

rounded head

stiff tail for perching

black and white body

DOWNY WOODPECKER

HAIRY WOODPECKER

tuft or crest

gray-edged wing feathers

white-edged wing feathers

orange flank

TUFTED TITMOUSE

CAROLINA CHICKADEE

BLACK-CAPPED CHICKADEE

Chickadee family

Birds of the chickadee family have small, round bodies and short, triangular bills. Some have crests, and some have long tails. They feed on insects and seeds gleaned from bark and twigs—or feeders.

Finch family

The finches are small birds with many plumage colors, including browns, greens, blacks, and some striking reds and yellows. Their bills vary widely in size and shape according to their diet. In addition to goldfinches, House Finches, and redpolls, the family includes grosbeaks, crossbills, and siskins.

forked tail

HOUSE FINCH

Crow family

Corvids are medium to large birds with strong, scaly feet and stout, robust bills. Many species are black or gray, but some are pied—for example, the Black-billed Magpie is white and black. Others, including Steller's, Blue, Pinyon, and scrub-jays, are brightly colored. The family also includes crows, ravens, and nutcrackers.

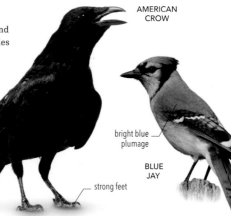

AMERICAN CROW

bright blue plumage

BLUE JAY

strong feet

BIRDS IN FLIGHT

Identifying flying birds is often challenging. However, a few clues may help you work out the family at least. Besides the rhythm of the flight, things to note include the size of the bird (often difficult to gauge at a distance), its wing shape, tail shape, color, and how it holds its neck and legs. For example, herons fly with their necks bent, whereas cranes fly with their necks outstretched.

FAST WING FLAPPING
Fast, direct flight in a straight line with rapid wing beats is typical of pigeons, ducks, and seabirds with short wings, such as auks.

SLOW WING FLAPPING
Herons, gulls, and barn owls fly with a slow, steady, almost lazy-looking wing beat, allowing them to scan for food as they fly.

wing beats

INTERMITTENT WING FLAPPING
Woodpeckers and finches show an undulating flight of flapping interspersed with pauses in which they seem to bound up and glide down.

RANDOM WING FLAPPING
Aerial insect-eaters such as swifts and swallows usually have a random flight pattern, dipping and diving after insects as they hunt.

Feed the birds

Birds eat a range of foods, according to their species and the time of year. Some feed mostly on insects, especially in spring and summer when rearing their young, while others are mainly seed-eaters. Many birds gorge on berries and fallen orchard fruit in autumn and winter. You can enhance birds' survival by supplementing their natural diet with additional food.

GREAT BACKYARD BIRD COUNT

Why not get involved with the Audubon's Great Backyard Bird Count? This annual four-day event takes place in February. To take part you simply note birds anywhere for as little or as long as you wish during the allotted period. You then report your findings back online. For more information visit http://www.birdcount.org. You can also report your bird-watching activities through www.ebird.org.

FEEDER PLACEMENT
Offer a variety of feeders in different locations around the yard. Place feeders within 6½–9 ft (2–3 m) of shrubs so that the birds can dash away if they see a predator such as a cat or hawk approaching.

bird tables can be suspended from trees by chains

low bird tables may be used by timid species, but ensure they are close to cover

tube feeders can be hung from tree branches or from brackets on walls

windows kill birds that fly into them; locate feeders either within 3⅓ ft (1 m) or more than 33 ft (10 m) away

elevated bird table fairly close to the house gives a good view of feeding birds

feeders on poles can be moved around the yard to find the birds' favorite feeding places

caged feeder allows birds to feed on the ground without predators or scavengers getting in

NATIVE PLANTS DATABASE

Audubon's Native Plants Database advises people on the most wildlife-friendly plants for their backyards, according to where they live. There are many to choose from, and goldenrods, milkweeds, and sunflowers are excellent, bird-friendly herbaceous plants. Native oaks support more than 550 species of moths and butterflies, whose caterpillars provide so much food for birds.

BIRD TABLES
Feeding tables are attractive to ground-feeding birds such as this Red-winged Blackbird. Offer a mix of cracked corn, safflower, and millet seed.

Bird-mix recipe

To make suet balls, melt one-third suet or lard and mix well with two-thirds seeds, dried fruits, nuts, and oatmeal. Allow the mixture to set in an empty yogurt carton or half a coconut shell, then hang it from your bird table.

Different bird feeders

Variety, both of feeder design and food types, is essential to attract the most birds. Some birds like to hang from feeders; some perch; others feed on the ground. Suitable foods include black sunflower seeds, niger seeds, flaked corn, peanuts, mealworms, and dried insects.

1 Small birds such as these American Goldfinches enjoy feeders with many perches specialized for holding small seeds. Nyjer seeds are small and black with a high oil content: a favorite of finches and siskins.

2 White-breasted Nuthatches typically perch facing downward, a posture that gives them a unique angle when feeding on insects in tree bark.

3 Tufted Titmice enjoy nuts. They will feed on acorns from oak trees and peanuts at bird feeders. Keep feeders clean and dry to provide healthy food.

4 In addition to visiting feeders containing a suet mixture, woodpeckers will feed on the ground or from logs drilled with holes and filled with a suet mixture, seeds, or nuts.

Do's and don'ts

1. Use good-quality bird food from specialized suppliers.

2. Clear away stale or moldy food.

3. Don't give leftover cooking fat, margarines, vegetable oils, or milk.

4. Never put out salted food or add salt to a birdbath.

5. Keep stored food dry.

Wildlife garden

However big your garden, there are many things you can do to encourage wildlife. You will make a difference and enjoy doing it.

Why have a wildlife garden?
Many suitable habitats for wildlife have been lost or degraded over the years, through changing land use and development, but with a little effort you can provide your own safe places for wildlife to breed, shelter, and find food. There are plenty of activities that don't cost much, but give wildlife a helping hand—especially by planting native species—whether you have a large garden or a small balcony or window ledge.

Lavender in flower attracts butterflies and bees.

Making a window box
If you don't have much outside space, create a mini nature reserve in a window box. Give interest and a year-round food supply by choosing plants that bloom at different times. For example, spring bulbs attract early-flying bumblebees, while summer flowers provide nectar for sun-loving butterflies. Many herbs, such as lavender and catnip, are favorites with honeybees and they also smell pleasant. Evergreens, such as rosemary and ivy, provide shelter for insects such as ladybugs throughout the winter.

1 Start by filling your window box with soil, then plant a variety of plants far enough apart to give them room to grow.

3 A very shallow saucer of water will attract water bugs and wildlife that may use it to drink or wash in. Water your window box regularly and give it some organic plant food, but avoid pesticides.

2 Cover the surface with gravel or bark to help the soil retain moisture during the summer, and to insulate the window box during the winter.

Bucket of life
A bucket of water left outside the back door will soon be teeming with larval insect life. Mosquitoes lay their eggs in still water. Once they hatch, the larvae mostly stay at the surface to breathe, but tap the bucket and they will wiggle underwater. You may also see small red organisms called bloodworms, which are the larvae of nonbiting midges.

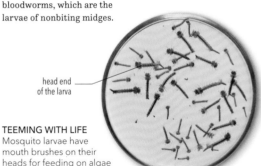

head end of the larva

TEEMING WITH LIFE
Mosquito larvae have mouth brushes on their heads for feeding on algae and bacteria in the water.

Bird bath
Birds require water to drink and wash in all year round. Place a bird bath close to bushes, but where the birds have good visibility. Clean and refill the bath regularly with fresh water, and break any ice. Water between 1 and 3 inches (2.5–7.5 cm) deep will suit a variety of species.

BATH IN THE AIR
Commercially produced bird baths include those that can be suspended from a tree.

SPLASHING AROUND
An up-turned trash can lid, supported by discarded bricks, makes an effective and affordable bird bath.

Helping the bees

Bees are vital for the pollination of many plants and food crops. They are in decline and need our help. Solitary bees nest in holes in the ground or in hollow plant stems. They seal an egg in a cell within the nest with some food for the larva to eat once it hatches. Provide tiny nooks for the bee larvae to mature with a bought or homemade bee house. Locate it in a sunny place where rain will not flood the house.

BEE HOTEL

Make your own bee house from a bamboo cane, modeling clay, and a clay pot. Cut the cane into 20 equal lengths, according to the size of your pot. Bind the canes with tape and press the end of the bundle into the modeling clay. Wedge it into the pot with the open ends facing out.

Brush pile

Replicate the valuable habitat of fallen trees with a pile of logs and branches in a shady part of your garden. This creates a damp, dark refuge and source of food for numerous animals, including beetles, centipedes, toads, frogs, and newts. Leave the wood to decay and you may see some intriguing fungi as it rots, especially if the logs are from different tree species. Add new logs periodically.

ROTTEN MEAL

Giant stag beetle larvae eat decomposing wood. Rotting wood is in short supply in well-groomed forests.

Leaf piles and nesting boxes

Rather than burning leaves or raking them into bags to be taken from your property, rake them into piles under shrubs where they will rot, creating habitat for insects, spiders, and other invertebrates—all important to birds. Nest boxes designed for specific species of birds are widely available and a great winter project for wood workers.

SOUTHERN FLYING SQUIRREL

Flying squirrels require tree cavities in which to raise their families. Where dead trees with woodpecker holes are scarce, they will also use bird houses attached to forest trees.

Look for invertebrates, such as snails, in leaf piles.

COSY NEST

In addition to small mammals, hibernating toads may also use your leaf pile.

Bird and bat boxes

There are numerous types of bird and bat boxes designed for nesting and roosting. Consider the species you are hoping to attract when choosing which one to buy or build. Attach the box to a tree, post, or wall in a sheltered, quiet part of your garden. Clean it out in the late winter or early spring to remove abandoned nests and make room for new ones.

1 Position several bat boxes around the tree so they offer different temperatures during the day. Bats enter through a narrow slit in the base.

2 A front- or side-opening box design is a key requirement for a successful nest box. This allows it to be cleaned annually to attract new or returning residents.

3 Purple Martins require a special nest box with multiple compartments. Position the house on a tall pole in an open field, preferably near some water.

Compost dwellers

ANT
Ants often nest inside compost piles. They also feed on some composting materials.

CENTIPEDE
Centipedes patrol the top layers of compost piles, feeding on other insects and spiders.

EARWIG
Earwigs eat plant matter in compost. They use the pincers at their back ends to deter predators.

OPOSSUM
Opossums and other small mammals might scavenge food from your compost pile.

Composting

Compost is a mixture of decaying organic substances. Making a compost pile is a fantastic way of recycling your garden weeds, lawn clippings, and household waste. You will also reduce the amount of garbage going into landfills, while producing an organic soil enhancer for your garden. The warm, moist environment attracts various animals to live and feed there. Add some old compost or soil to a new pile to introduce beneficial soil microbes and earthworms. Turn the pile regularly to add oxygen to it, but take care not to injure any animals.

RAW MATERIALS
Add fallen leaves, clippings, or food waste to the top of the pile. This provides a home for numerous insects, and will attract creatures that prey on them. You may even see birds picking over the top of your pile.

MATURING COMPOST
Bacteria cause most of the decay in a good compost pile. The heat they produce through digestion warms the pile and speeds up the composting process. Fungi, earthworms, and other invertebrates help too.

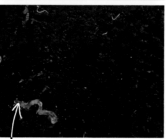

FINISHED COMPOST
The compost should be ready after four to eight months, depending on the pile's temperature. Add finished compost to flower beds and vegetable patches to improve the structure of the soil and help your plants grow.

Worms can burrow down as deep as 6 ft (1.8 m), but they surface after a rain.

RECYCLING NUTRIENTS
Add your kitchen and garden waste to your home composting bin, and it will turn into valuable nutrients to put back into your garden.

Ingredients of good compost

To make good compost pile, you will need a mix of nitrogen-rich "green" ingredients such as fruit and vegetable peelings and grass clippings, and dry, carbon-rich "brown" matter such as leaves, straw, and wood shavings. Keep the pile moist and well aerated, and avoid adding meat or fat to the compost—these items attract rodents.

BROWN RAT

The different layers allow you to see how worms tunnel and process soil.

WORMERY

Earthworms add oxygen and nutrients to the soil. You can build a wormery in a clear container to watch them at work. Make drainage holes in the bottom, then add alternating layers of sand, soil, compost, and leaf litter. Finally, put in some earthworms. Keep the wormery in a dark place. The different layers allow you to see how worms tunnel and process soil. However, some invasive jumping worms can damage forests by breaking down the thick organic layer required by some trees and animals.

Making a pond in your garden

A pond is a valuable asset to any wildlife garden. It can attract aquatic insects including water striders, whirligig beetles, dragonflies, and damselflies, and amphibians such as frogs and newts. It also provides drinking water for birds and mammals. Stock your pond with native plants; be careful not to introduce alien species that could cause damage. Avoid goldfish, too, because they eat freshwater snails and tadpoles. Position your pond in a semishaded, sheltered location away from trees, and wait for the wildlife to arrive.

1 Dig a shallow hole with a sloping edge and shelved sections for easier access. Line the hole with a pond liner and temporarily weigh it down.

2 Cover the liner with sand, soil, and gravel. Ideally, fill the pond with rainwater from rain barrels, or allow it to fill naturally with rain.

3 Add plants, using bricks or stones if necessary to raise them to the required level in the water. A variety of submerged, floating, and emergent plants is recommended in order to attract as much wildlife as possible to your pond.

POND IN A BARREL
Even if you have no garden, you can turn a container into a small pond. Steep sides cause problems for small creatures, so be sure to create access points.

pond plants provide cover

BATHTUB POND
Old bathtubs make great ponds, especially if you sink them into the ground. Be sure to clear out any leaves that have fallen in.

Water plants

OXYGENATING
Hornwort helps keep the pond water clear, and also adds oxygen during photosynthesis.

DEEP WATER
Water lilies are a good choice for ponds as they provide habitat for frogs and other wildlife and are hardy through the winter.

MARGINALS
Blue irises grow at the pond margin, providing resting places for insects and protection for wildlife.

FLOATING
Frog's-bit plants float without putting down roots. They provide valuable cover on the pond's surface but are invasive.

63

Butterflies and moths

You can make your garden more attractive to butterflies and moths by planting native plants with abundant nectar and leaves.

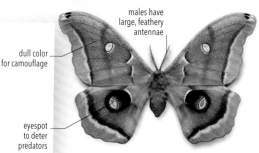

POLYPHEMUS MOTH
These North American moths live for only one week as adults—just long enough to breed.

males have large, feathery antennae

dull color for camouflage

eyespot to deter predators

Butterfly or moth?

Butterflies and moths both belong to the insect order Lepidoptera, meaning "scale wings," which has over 170,000 species. Most butterflies are diurnal, while many, though not all, moths are nocturnal. Many moths appear drab in comparison to more brightly-colored butterflies—their colors camouflage them while they are resting. Moths usually rest with their wings outstretched, while butterflies fold their wings vertically over their backs, unless they are basking in the Sun.

forewing

hind wing

METAMORPHOSIS

Butterflies and moths undergo a spectacular transformation, or metamorphosis, from leaf-munching caterpillars to winged adults. During a process called pupation, the juvenile cells in the caterpillar's body are destroyed, while the undifferentiated cells, known as imaginal disks, divide, elongate, and become specialized. The nervous system is restructured too. Butterfly pupae are encased in a hardened shell, called a chrysalis, while some moths spin a protective silk cocoon.

1 Butterflies and moths usually lay their eggs on plants. Look for clusters of tiny, hard-shelled eggs that are "glued" to the upper or lower surface of a leaf.

2 The eggs hatch into caterpillars that devour the plant. This is the growth stage. If you see a plant with ragged, eaten leaves, look for the caterpillar responsible.

pupa has a protective, hard case

3 When the caterpillar is fully grown, it looks for a safe place to pupate. Its skin splits to reveal the pupa, inside which it transforms into an adult.

wings expand as they fill with blood

4 When metamorphosis is complete, the adult breaks out of its chrysalis. It hangs while its moist wings unfold and gradually harden. It is now ready to disperse and breed.

MONARCH BUTTERFLY
Monarch butterflies are famous for their long migrations. Eastern monarchs winter in mountain forests of Mexico. Western monarchs winter in forests of coastal central and southern California. They are safe from bird predators because their caterpillars feed on milkweed, which makes them taste bad.

MOTH AND BUTTERFLY BEAUTIES

Butterflies and moths come in an astonishing variety of sizes, colors, shapes, and patterns. Keep a record of those that you spot, noting distinctive markings.

GREAT SPANGLED FRITILLARY

CABBAGE BUTTERFLY

jointed antenna acts as a sensory organ

thorax

eye is large and compound

small head

distinctive, dark wing vein

Individuals within a species have generally the same wing pattern because the pigments are genetically predetermined.

scalloped wing marking

WHITE-LINED SPHINX MOTH

ATTRACTING BUTTERFLIES

Gardens can be made butterfly-friendly. Plant flowering plants, such as goldenrod (pictured with buckeye butterfly, below), in dense clusters in sunny positions, and grow the right food for their caterpillars. Avoid using pesticides and provide sunny resting spots and patches of wet soil, where they can get essential minerals.

tiny, colored scales cover the wing

abdomen contains the digestive system and reproductive organs

MONARCH WING DETAIL
Butterfly and moth wings are covered with rows of minute, overlapping scales that give the creature its distinctive color and pattern. The color comes from pigments or from reflected light.

Farm and field

Farmland may be a modified aspect of our landscape, but it is often the most accessible type of countryside for people to explore. And while it's true that modern farmland and planted forests often support very few native species, in some places less intensive agriculture has actually created new habitats that are far richer than some natural environments, sometimes allowing small groups of species to prosper artificially. In the US, for example, meadowlarks and Bobolinks are now largely limited to the hayfields so typical of farmland—and who would not be excited by a walk across a planted flower-filled "unimproved" meadow? Indeed, these are all national—and natural—treasures.

ORCHID

Pasture

Grazing helps maintain grassland habitats for wildlife. Without livestock to crop vegetation, shrubs would take over, and many wildflowers would be lost. Grasslands are vital to butterflies and birds such as meadowlarks, the Bobolink, and the Vesper Sparrow. Flooded water meadows provide a seasonal refuge for water birds, and many insects depend on livestock dung for reproduction and food.

MUSHROOMS

EASTERN COTTONTAIL

Farm and field

Farmland is an artificially created landscape in which wildlife has to adapt to constant changes. It is a mosaic of many habitats: pasture, crop fields, and meadows interspersed with hedges, woodland, ditches, and settlements.

Arable land

Arable fields, where crops are grown, are home to birds that prefer to nest on open ground. You might also see small rodents such as harvest mice and voles. The value of arable land for wildlife can be improved by leaving crop remnants in the fields during the winter after harvesting, rotating the crops, reinstating lost hedgerows, and leaving wide field margins.

CORNFLOWER   POPPY   EASTERN MEADOWLARK

Field boundary

Much of the value of farmland to wildlife is found at field edges, where machines and chemicals are kept at bay. Hedgerows, ditches, and stone walls are all types of field boundary. They can provide wildlife, such as songbirds and reptiles, with food, shelter, and corridors through which they can safely travel.

LEAST SHREW

WHITE-CROWNED
SPARROW

Hayfields

Wildflower-rich hayfields aren't just beautiful—they support a myriad of insects that feed on nectar, including bumblebees, honeybees, and butterflies. Sadly, traditional hayfields are now few and far between because of changes to cutting regimes and the use of herbicides. This has resulted in a reduction in insect numbers.

BUTTERCUP

Barns and outbuildings

Farm buildings provide homes for Barn Owls, swallows, bats, and rodents such as mice. When a little rundown and seldom disturbed, barns and outbuildings are excellent places to watch wildlife. An open window or gap in a door allows animals to enter and find shelter. Old farm buildings can be appropriately restored to ensure they continue to welcome wildlife in the future.

BARN OWL

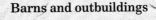

WESTERN
HARVEST
MOUSE

Farm and field

Nature's highways

Despite being cultivated, farmland can play host to an abundance of wildlife. Field boundaries provide animals with safe passage.

Field boundaries
Different farming systems have used different ways of defining fields according to their requirements, available materials, and the climate. Traditional methods include hedges, ditches, and stone walls, all of which provide opportunities for wildlife to inhabit and travel through the agricultural landscape. The loss of field boundaries from the environment, whether by removing hedgerows to create larger fields, or replacing stone walls with fences, is detrimental to the wildlife that depends on them.

VIEW FROM ABOVE
Look down from an airplane and you can see how fields are separated by hedges, tree lines, ditches, or walls. A mixture of boundary types creates the most wildlife-rich farmland.

Hedges
Hedges are rows of shrubby plants grown to demarcate fields, the edges of lanes, or settlements. You can estimate a hedge's age by counting its plant species—some hedges can be hundreds of years old. Many different types of animals and plants thrive in the shelter created by hedgerows, including birds, insects, mammals, wildflowers, mosses, and fungi.

MEADOW VOLE
Meadow voles are tiny rodents native to North America that require grassy habitats. They may hide in hedges to escape being noticed by passing birds of prey—or run to them for protection.

Ditches
Ditches drain low-lying land for agriculture, but they may also be home to insects, such as water beetles and dragonflies; water birds; newts and other amphibians; and mammals, including otters and water voles. Ditches must be managed to prevent silt blockage or clogging with vegetation. They may also be adversely affected by fertilizer and pesticide run-off from adjacent agricultural land.

AMERICAN MINK
The American mink is native to North America but has been introduced to Europe. You may see it using agricultural ditches for hunting and hiding.

GARTER SNAKE
Various reptiles find food and shelter in hedges, including snakes such as the garter snake.

WOOD DUCK
Wood Ducks are just one species of waterfowl you might find in farmland ditches.

GERMINATION IN ACTION

Germination is the process by which a plant seed begins to grow into a plant. It can be monitored at home by placing bean seeds on moist paper towels in a clear sealed plastic bag, and then leaving it for a week or so at room temperature. Seeds are contained within a fruit—or, in the case of beans, a pod, which splits open. Each bean is a seed that will become a new plant, provided that conditions such as temperature, water availability, and light intensity are suitable. Cactus hedges may be ideal for black-bean germination.

1 The black bean seed contains the plant embryo and a store of protein surrounded by a seed coat.

hilum scar where seed was attached to parent plant

radicle simple first root of plant

2 Germination begins, and an embryonic root called the radicle emerges from the seed and grows downward.

cotyledons first plant leaves, which begin process of photosynthesis

3 The seed leaves, or cotyledons, are pushed toward the surface by growth in the embryonic shoot, or hypocotyl.

secondary roots begin to anchor plant, and take in water and nutrients

Cactus hedges

Cactus hedgerows are found in arid areas where it is too dry for other hedging plants to survive. They are found in Central and South America, where people used cacti such as prickly pear to mark out their agricultural plots. Just as in European hedgerows, birds and other animals nest and find food in them, and the base of the hedge makes a good environment for wild plant seeds to germinate.

CACTUS POLLINATOR
Bats can pollinate cacti by drinking nectar from their flowers, and some disperse cacti seeds by eating the fruit and depositing the seeds.

JAVELINA
The javelina or peccary feeds on the prickly pear cactus. It can be found in South, Central, and parts of North America.

Stone walls

Stone walls have long been used to enclose fields such as New England fields and forest edges. If built without mortar or cement, they provide plenty of nooks and crannies for plants and animals. Look for insects, reptiles, and amphibians that make their homes in stone walls, and study the surface of the stone closely to see lichens growing.

SUN LOUNGER
Reptiles, such as this Great Plains skink, bask on and hide between the warm rocks of stone walls.

BROADLEAF LEWISIA
This plant thrives in dry, rocky soil in western North America. Wildflowers like this may seed in wall crevices.

Beetles

Beetles can be found in almost all habitats, from deserts, ponds, and mountain tops. They are thought to represent one third of all insects.

Beetle diversity and distribution

Beetles (order Coleoptera) are arthropods, a major group of invertebrates that also includes arachnids and crustaceans. They have jointed legs and front wing covers (elytra) that protect the more delicate hind wings. There are believed to be well over 350,000 species of beetle worldwide, with many more species yet to be discovered. Beetles play an important role in the natural world—they recycle nutrients by helping to break down animal and plant waste. Most beetles are herbivorous.

POTATO-EATER
Native to North America, the Colorado potato beetle (family Chrysomelidae) has spread widely. It can cause damage to potato crops.

Beetle varieties

There are currently around 188 different families of beetles, but their classification is constantly being reviewed. They range in size from tiny species smaller than 1 mm, to giants, such as the titan beetle of the Amazon rainforest, that are nearly 8 in (20 cm) long. Here are some common families.

LADYBUG (COCCINELLIDAE)
Ladybugs are small, domed beetles. The most familiar pattern is red with black spots, but other patterns also exist.

ROVE BEETLE (STAPHYLINIDAE)
The carnivorous rove beetles have long, flexible abdomens visible beneath short wing covers.

WEEVIL (CURCULIONIDAE)
Weevils, or snout beetles, are small plant eaters with bent, clubbed antennae. Over 60,000 species are known.

SCARAB BEETLE (SCARABAEIDAE)
Scarab beetles vary enormously in color, shape, and size. All have a distinctive club at the ends of their antennae.

LONGHORN BEETLE (CERAMBYCIDAE)
These beetles are well-named for their antennae, which may be as long as, or longer than, their bodies.

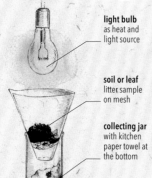

light bulb
as heat and light source

soil or leaf litter sample on mesh

collecting jar with kitchen paper towel at the bottom

MAKING A BERLESE FUNNEL

A Berlese funnel lets you see the variety of insects that hide in soil and leaf litter. Put some soil on a piece of mesh in a funnel, paper cone, or half an empty plastic bottle and suspend it over a jar lined with a paper towel. Shine a lamp onto the sample from at least 4 in (10 cm) above. The heat and light will coax any insects to move through the mesh into the jar. After observing, let them go.

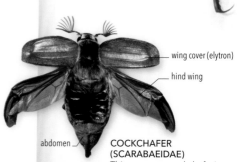

wing cover (elytron)

hind wing

abdomen

COCKCHAFER (SCARABAEIDAE)
This common cockchafer's wings are outstretched for flying. Their antennae fan out to sense air currents.

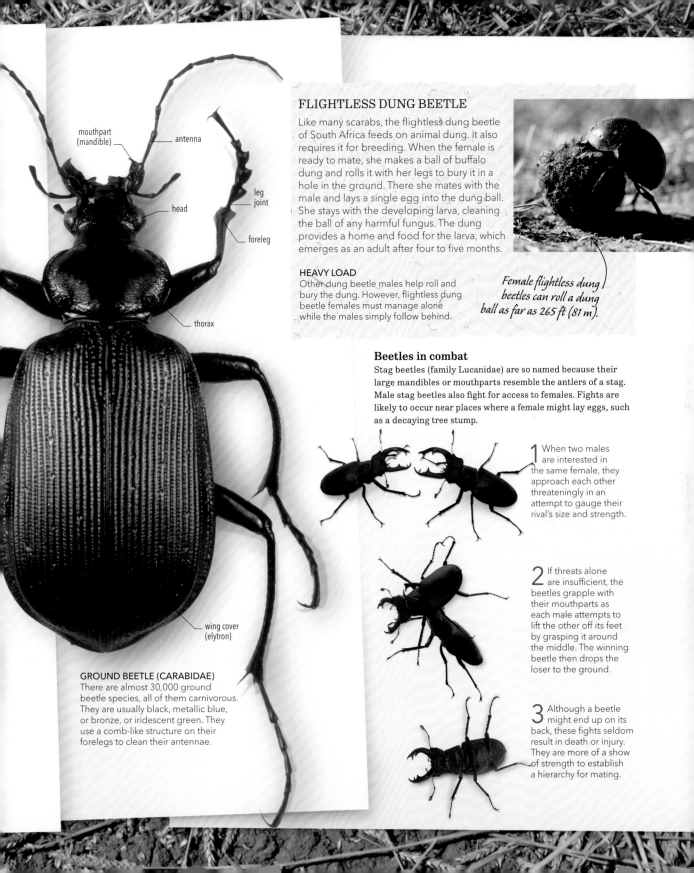

mouthpart
(mandible)

antenna

head

leg
joint

foreleg

thorax

wing cover
(elytron)

FLIGHTLESS DUNG BEETLE

Like many scarabs, the flightless dung beetle of South Africa feeds on animal dung. It also requires it for breeding. When the female is ready to mate, she makes a ball of buffalo dung and rolls it with her legs to bury it in a hole in the ground. There she mates with the male and lays a single egg into the dung ball. She stays with the developing larva, cleaning the ball of any harmful fungus. The dung provides a home and food for the larva, which emerges as an adult after four to five months.

HEAVY LOAD
Other dung beetle males help roll and bury the dung. However, flightless dung beetle females must manage alone while the males simply follow behind.

Female flightless dung beetles can roll a dung ball as far as 265 ft (81 m).

Beetles in combat
Stag beetles (family Lucanidae) are so named because their large mandibles or mouthparts resemble the antlers of a stag. Male stag beetles also fight for access to females. Fights are likely to occur near places where a female might lay eggs, such as a decaying tree stump.

1 When two males are interested in the same female, they approach each other threateningly in an attempt to gauge their rival's size and strength.

2 If threats alone are insufficient, the beetles grapple with their mouthparts as each male attempts to lift the other off its feet by grasping it around the middle. The winning beetle then drops the loser to the ground.

3 Although a beetle might end up on its back, these fights seldom result in death or injury. They are more of a show of strength to establish a hierarchy for mating.

GROUND BEETLE (CARABIDAE)
There are almost 30,000 ground beetle species, all of them carnivorous. They are usually black, metallic blue, or bronze, or iridescent green. They use a comb-like structure on their forelegs to clean their antennae.

Open farmland

Farming need not replace nature. If farmland is thoughtfully managed, wild flowers and animals can thrive at its edges, or within the fields themselves.

Exploring farmland

Farmland can be a great place for wildlife watching, but take care before exploring it. If there are no public rights of way (see p.40), you must get permission from the landowner before going on private land. Always keep to footpaths or field edges to avoid damaging crops. Don't startle livestock, always leave gates as you find them, and avoid any fields that have been recently sprayed with herbicide or fertilizer.

GROUND SQUIRRELS
These small mammals live underground in open fields. When they come to the surface they are always alert to the danger of attack from predators such as foxes.

HARVEST TIME
The mechanization of farming during the last century has meant more arable land—but loss of wildlife habitat.

MOLE HILLS
Little heaps of earth in pastures are a sure sign that moles are tunneling beneath, looking for earthworms.

Wildlife

Environmentally friendly farming can benefit insects such as bees and butterflies and birds and mammals including deer, rabbits, foxes, and bats. A good way to observe farmland wildlife is to choose a position downwind on a footpath where you can watch from behind a tree or hedge without giving away your presence or disturbing any animals. Use binoculars to help you spot and identify species. Wildflowers, such as wild lupines, coneflowers, and Queen Anne's lace can be found in arable fields, but only at the edges if herbicides have been used on the crops.

MEADOW VOLE
These tiny rodents feed on grasses in open North American farmland. They are prey for larger animals, including birds and mammals.

FARMLAND FOR BIRDS

Audubon advises landowners on ways to improve habitat quality on ranches and cropland—habitats that cover 1 billion acres of the US. The Working Lands initiative aims to help 20 flagship bird species, including prairie-chickens (right), Long-billed Curlews, meadowlarks, sparrows, and longspurs.

Farmland birds

Many birds that inhabit farmland nest on the ground, including meadowlarks, Dickcissels, Vesper and Savannah sparrows, and Sharp-tailed Grouse. They are difficult to see on their nests, but you may catch sight of them in flight or when feeding. Also look for birds of prey, such as American Kestrels or Barn Owls, hunting for small rodents. Grassland birds are declining in North America, largely due to changing agricultural practices. However, a number of major conservation efforts are under way to help reverse the decline, such as providing uncultivated areas within fields where birds can nest and forage, and growing flower-rich margins at field edges to attract insects.

UPLAND SANDPIPER
Upland Sandpipers forage and nest on short grassland. They eat a variety of insects.

SHARP-TAILED GROUSE
These birds of prairie and grassland fly between feeding and roosting areas.

RING-NECKED PHEASANT
Pheasants, originally from Asia, are reared and released by the millions for people to shoot. Such numbers greatly impact native wildlife.

Cow patties

Untreated cattle dung supports over 200 species, mainly because cow patties are a great source of food for worms, flies, beetles, and springtails. In return, these tiny creatures do a great job of removing cow patties and recycling their nutrients back into the soil. Dung beetles also help keep the number of harmful flies, such as horn flies and face flies, low in farmland by outcompeting them in the dung. Sadly, drugs and other chemicals fed to cows can destroy these communities.

SPRINGTAIL

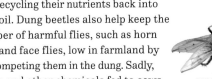

DUNG FLY

DUNG BEETLE

COW PATTY SOCIETY
On farms that use fewer pesticides, you can see male yellow dung flies establish territories on fresh dung and wait for females. After mating, the females lay their eggs on the dung's surface.

A healthy dung insect community will remove a cow patty from the soil's surface within 24 hours.

Farmland close-up

Farmland varies widely around the world and the wildlife inhabiting it depends upon the type and method of agriculture being practiced. Wherever you are, look along field margins for signs of life.

SHAGBARK HICKORY

THISTLE

CULTIVATED NUTS

HICKORY NUTS

Fall brings a rich harvest of fruits, nuts, and grains.

Look for blossoms adding color to fields in spring and seedheads in late summer.

TRAVELER'S JOY

WOOD BETONY

QUEEN ANNE'S LACE

CORN

CRAB APPLE BLOSSOM

WHEAT EARS

MONARCH
BUTTERFLY

*Look for
butterflies in
meadows and
hedgerows.*

BLACK SWALLOWTAIL
BUTTERFLY

TWO-SPOT
LADYBUG

SOLDIER
BEETLES

*Beetles may be
found feeding on
flower heads.*

BIRD
FEATHERS

ABANDONED BIRD'S
NEST

*Only collect feathers
of landfowl (game
birds) but never
disturb nests.*

BLACKBERRIES

DRIED DUNG

*Animal remains give
valuable clues to the
lives, and deaths, of
farmland wildlife.*

OWL
PELLETS

HACKBERRY

MOLE SKELETON

DISCARDED SNAKE SKIN

Forest

You walk through a grassland or bog, but you walk in a forest. It envelops you, and this points to a significant difference: there are many more opportunities here for life to exploit distinct niches. Thus, forests support our richest biodiversities, especially those seasonally stable and ancient swathes that ring the Equator. These are complex places, where the connections between the species that form communities are still revealing surprises. Yet forests can also be difficult habitats to explore—you can't see much of the life for the trees. You will need a lifetime of patience to uncover their secrets.

Ancient forest

Ancient forests are woodlands that have never been cleared by humans. Surprisingly, only about 0.5 percent of North America's original forest remains; all other forests are regrown secondary forests. Ancient forest is valuable because it provides a baseline for what forests can look like without human disturbance. The massive trunks and long-reaching limbs of ancient trees provide homes to many plants and animals.

BARRED OWL

PANDORA SPHINX MOTH

Deciduous woodlands

From the tropics to temperate zones, broadleaved woods are beautiful habitats. Deciduous forests that are leafless in winter are found mainly in moist, relatively cool habitats, and at higher elevations closer to the tropics.

Appalachian deciduous forest

The lower-elevation forests of the Appalachian Mountains support one of the world's richest temperate deciduous forests. Originally, it was mainly oak and chestnut; today maple and beech are common. More than 1,400 plants, including 158 tree species, and 225 land vertebrates exist in these glorious woodlands. However, centuries of logging have altered 83 percent of the forest.

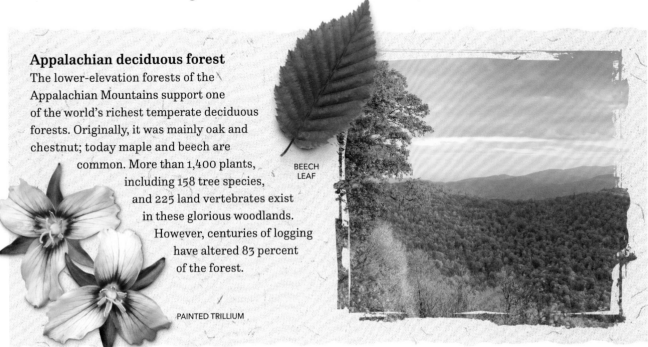

BEECH LEAF

PAINTED TRILLIUM

Parkland

Parkland is largely artificial in North America and Europe, often associated with estates around large houses. The shrub layer is often weak or absent, so you won't see as many butterflies and forest flowers as on a shrubland or grassland area; however, old, rotting trees still attract birds such as nuthatches and woodpeckers, as well as insects, and you may encounter mammals such as deer or squirrels.

FOXGLOVE

HORSE FLY

Bottomland hardwoods

Bottomland hardwood forests occur along rivers and streams in the southeast and south central US, usually in broad floodplains. These deciduous forest wetlands are usually flooded part or all year and include many kinds of gum, oaks, and bald cypress. The branches are often festooned with draping Spanish moss, an epiphyte related to pineapple used by the parula warbler for nests. Prothonotary Warblers often nest in tree cavities.

MAGNOLIA

PROTHONOTARY
WARBLER

OAK LEAVES
AND ACORNS

BLACKBERRIES

RED-SPOTTED
PURPLE BUTTERFLY

Remember to look up for birds and squirrels in the trees.

A walk in the woods

A deciduous forest is packed with a myriad of sights, smells, and sounds. Tall trees envelop you, shielding you from the interference of the human-made world.

The character of the wood changes dramatically with each season, so visit throughout the year to see how the forest develops. In spring, the wood comes alive with colorful flowers, insects, and birds. Trees are in full leaf during summer, providing food and shelter for insects in the canopy and covering the forest floor in shade. Look for fungi in autumn and for leaves of deciduous trees, which turn beautiful shades of yellow, orange, and red. In winter, the leaf litter is still a place of abundant activity.

BEECH
NUT

Look at fallen branches, which create food and homes for insects—the gaps they leave behind let sunlight shine in.

Sift through rotting leaves to find a thriving habitat of tiny plants and animals.

SOLOMON'S
SEAL

WHITE TRILLIUM

SUGAR MAPLE
LEAF IN
AUTUMN

*Look for holes
in trees—
many birds
nest in them.*

NURSERY WEB
SPIDER

*Summer leaves
hide squirrels
and birds—listen
for their calls.*

TULIP TREE
BLOSSOM

*See how bracken thrives
where sunlight reaches
through to the ground.*

SPHAGNUM
MOSS

GREAT PURPLE
HAIRSTREAK BUTTERFLY

5 CANOPY

Treetops create a canopy, with each tree letting through a different level of light. Some animals, such as birds and butterflies, are canopy specialists and may choose different "stories" within the forest for different needs. Birds such as thrushes feed and sing in the canopy but nest at lower levels. Caterpillars may feed in the canopy, while adult butterflies feed from flowers far below.

WOOD THRUSH

GRAY SQUIRREL

Living space

From the roots to the canopy, trees provide living space for a wide variety of wildlife, vertically increasing the habitable area of a forest.

Forest builders

Just a moment spent looking at a large tree reveals that it abounds with life. They provide food and shelter for animals both large and small, from the microscopic organisms in rotting leaves to the birds in the highest branches. Each tree creates a host of niches at every level—the larger a natural forest, the more diversity it contains. Because the forest is so interdependent, it functions much like a single living entity, with each species being reliant on another species for its survival. At the bottom of this chain is the soil.

FOREST WEB

Plant growth in a forest produces enough food to support three levels of consumers: herbivores, predators, and top predators.

tree

beetle, worm, finch, mouse, vole, deer

fox, American marten, owl

gray wolf

MEASURING UP

Trees are the Earth's largest living organisms. Measuring a tree and counting its annual growth rings can provide more than dimensions and age—it can also reveal how environmental conditions have affected it over the years. The growth rings on this tree are off-center, suggesting that one side of the tree may have been exposed to harsh, windy conditions.

rapid growth on sheltered side

CROSS-SECTION FROM FELLED TREE

GIRTH GROWTH

The girth (circumference) of a tree increases each year. Measure it with a tape measure at least 5 ft (1.5 m) above the ground. Keep a record of your measurements and compare your readings over a number of years to see how the tree is growing.

4 SHRUB
Shrubs and saplings grow beneath some trees. For example, viburnum grows under large trees to create a shrub layer.

VIBURNUM

3 FIELD
Herbs and low-growing flowers, ferns, and mosses create a field layer close to the ground.

COLUMBINE

2 LEAF LITTER
Rotting leaves from past seasons create leaf litter, which has a thriving wildlife system of its own. Oak and sycamore leaf litter is especially rich.

1 SOIL
Humus from rotting foliage and dead wood mixes with underlying minerals to create the soil upon which all life depends.

EARTHWORM

Tree shapes

Individual trees can develop unusual shapes, especially if they are growing in harsh conditions. Look for short, gnarled, and stunted trees at high altitudes, cold and windy areas, or poor soils. In dense forests you might find very tall and straight trees, while coastal trees tend to bend away from prevailing winds because twigs and branches on the exposed side die or fail to develop. Trees with bark, leaves, and branches stripped to a specific level may be showing damage from browsing animals, such as deer.

SPECIES SHAPES
The outline of a mature tree can help you identify it. With or without leaves, each species has its own characteristic shape, based largely on the number and thickness of the smaller twigs and the angle at which they grow from the main branches.

BROAD
(WHITE OAK)

BROAD COLUMNAR
(SUGAR MAPLE)

CONICAL
(BASSWOOD)

COLUMNAR
(INCENSE CEDAR)

NARROW AND WEEPING
(GRAY BIRCH)

SLENDER AND GNARLED
(WILD BLACK CHERRY)

SPREADING
(HORNBEAM)

COLUMNAR TO SPREADING
(CULTIVATED CHERRY)

85

Leaves

Leaves are the crowning glory of most plants. They convert energy from the Sun—the basis of all life on Earth.

How leaves work

Plants collect nutrients by photosynthesis. Chlorophyll in leaves uses sunlight to convert carbon dioxide from the air into starches and sugars. As leaf cells (stomata) take in carbon dioxide, water is lost, or transpired. Nutrient-rich sap rises, pulling water in from the soil via the roots in a process called transpiration.

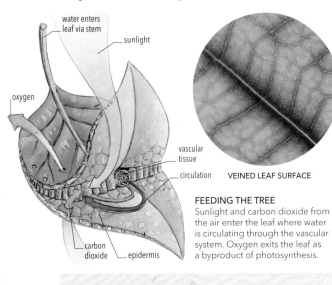

water enters leaf via stem

sunlight

oxygen

vascular tissue

circulation

VEINED LEAF SURFACE

carbon dioxide

epidermis

FEEDING THE TREE
Sunlight and carbon dioxide from the air enter the leaf where water is circulating through the vascular system. Oxygen exits the leaf as a byproduct of photosynthesis.

CHLOROPHYLL

Chlorophyll is an essential pigment contained in plants. It is responsible for the great variety of greens you can see in different kinds of plants; it achieves this by mostly absorbing blue and red light and reflecting green light. Known as a "photoreceptor," chlorophyll is essential for photosynthesis. In winter, when days are shorter, photosynthesis is not as efficient and chlorophyll is withdrawn from the leaf cells, unmasking a variety of other colors. Leafless trees shut down and survive on stored starches until spring.

young leaf

old leaf

LEAF SURFACE
A waxy cuticle reduces water loss and tiny hairs control evaporation. When old leaves become pitted and mottled, they lose this function.

Leaf structure

You will notice most conifers have needlelike leaves, but deciduous trees have broader leaves with a stiff midrib and supporting side ribs. The leaf stalk (petiole) provides mobility, reducing wind damage.

Leaf shape

Leaves come in a great variety of shapes and sizes. They may be simple single leaves or compound leaves, which contain a number of leaflets in a "palmate" (hand-shaped) or "pinnate" (feather-shaped) formation. Teeth, notches, points, and lobes direct water droplets to drip off the leaf.

OVAL (ELLIPTIC)

TEARDROP (ARISTATE)

ROUND (ORBICULAR)

COMPOUND (PEDATE)

HEART-SHAPED (CORDATE)

ELONGATED (LINEAR)

Arrangement

Look for leaves with different arrangements. They can be opposite each other or alternate. Some leaves are solitary, while others are clustered.

branch from same point

OPPOSITE

branch alternately on each side

CLUSTERED

branch from central point

ALTERNATE

Color varieties

Leaves come in a variety of colors. Yellow-orange pigments called carotenoids are present in leaves throughout the year, but their colors are usually masked by green chlorophyll. In the fall, as chlorophyll fades, carotenoids become visible and anthocyanins are created. This red pigment also creates "copper" plant varieties.

green upper side

AUTUMN RED
(RED MAPLE)

newer leaf

older leaf

silver underside

**CONTRAST
(SILVER MAPLE)**

**NEW GROWTH
(CHERRY)**

prominent, light veins

paler outside

hairy surface

**PROMINENT VEINS
(RAULI)**

**WHITE UNDERSIDE
(POPLAR)**

**VARIEGATED
(NORWAY MAPLE)**

Margin and texture

Smooth, waxy leaves better tolerate dry or harsh conditions, while other leaves are coarse with rough surfaces. The great variety of leaves are adapted to different habitats.

**SMOOTH
WAVES (BEECH)**

**LOBED
(OAK)**

**COARSELY
TOOTHED
(HORNBEAM)**

**SPINY
(HOLLY)**

SMALL TEETH (BIRCH)

**CRINKLED
(ELM)**

NEW ENGLAND FALL

New England is one of the best places to visit to see spectacular autumn colors. Most leaves live for about six months, before dropping in a process called abscission; they are replaced every year. A large, mature tree may have around 250,000 leaves. Cold nights reduce the flow of sugars around the tree. Sugar becomes trapped in the leaves by the abscission layer, resulting in the formation of anthocyanin, a red pigment. Along with the lack of chlorophyll, this creates the reds and yellows of a glorious fall.

Look for maple trees: they turn the most vivid colors.

Seasonal change

A new leaf is usually a vivid, light green. Weeks of hard work, plus the effects of wind, rain, and temperature fluctuations gradually hardens the leaf and makes it duller and darker with age, until it finally begins to "turn" and decompose.

Try photographing leaves from one plant throughout the year, to compare the colors as the year progresses.

LIFE CYCLE
Most leaves start out bright green, but change color as they age and begin to degrade.

as chlorophyll fades away, it reveals the colors of other pigments in the leaf

the leaf over time becomes a distinctive red color

Forest floor

The forest floor in spring can be stunning, with swathes of flowers, while in fall, it is a scene of decay—yet still full of life.

Exploring leaf litter

Leaf litter is full to the brim with tiny animals such as insects, spiders, and salamanders. These are exploited by bigger ones, such as badgers, thrushes, and woodcocks. A careful look at the leaf litter will reveal a wealth of wildlife. Identifying leaf litter flora and fauna is a specialist's job, but you can get an idea of what is around in your local wood.

FINDING CLUES
Distinctive droppings or tooth marks on nibbled seeds offer clues to a woodland's inhabitants.

SNAIL TRAIL
Snails move on a muscular foot, coated with mucus to reduce friction and protect against sharp surfaces, leaving a slimy trail.

INSECT HUNTER
All kinds of insectivores, including shrews such as this pygmy shrew, can be found in leaf litter rich with insects, worms, and spiders.

MOISTURE LOVER
Small, slender, and moist-skinned, salamanders, such as this spotted salamander found in North America, need a damp environment to survive.

Take a clear plastic box and a hand lens to examine small insects.

leaf-litter spiders ambush prey, rather than relying on webs in this mobile environment

fallen leaves provide food, shelter, and a vital moist environment

beetles and their larvae feed in dead leaves

sow bugs have tough, hard skins to retain moisture

earthworms process vast amounts of soil and leaf matter

USING AN ASPIRATOR

The aspirator has a short tube with gauze at one end, and a long open tube. Put the long tube over an insect, then suck sharply through the short tube. The insect should shoot into the cylinder. The membrane keeps you from sucking it into your mouth so you won't swallow it, but always make sure you're sucking the right tube.

BUG COLLECTOR
Aspirators are devices for catching insects that let you identify them, then release them unharmed.

Forest flowers

Flowering plants face many challenges in woodland—trees demand a huge amount of water from the soil, and, when in full leaf, cast a deep shade on the forest floor. Flowers have evolved many ways to deal with such problems. Some, such as trillium, hepatica, and bloodroot, flower very early, before the trees are in full leaf. Others, such as toothwort and several kinds of orchids, parasitize other plants. Many simply grow on the sunny edges of woodland or forest glades.

FLOWER CARPET
Flowers such as Virginia bluebells carpet forest floors. Like the trout lily, they bloom in early spring.

slugs feed on forest floor debris and fungi, which helps disperse seeds and spores

saddle-shaped mantle has a respiratory opening

A small garden trowel will help lift a soil sample as well as leaf litter.

earthworms leave curly "casts" of decomposed matter

larvae developing underground are sheltered from cold winters

TROUT LILY

CREATING TOPSOIL
A cross-section of the leaf litter and upper soil layer on the forest floor reveals a host of animals and plants that help digest the fallen leaves.

Nature's recyclers

The world of rotting logs and fallen leaves appears to be dead but is actually alive with miniscule animals, not all of them visible to the naked eye.

A forest is a celebration of life's abundance, and even so-called "dead wood," such as this rotting log, is actually alive and important. The nutrients that fuel life in the forest are broken down by decomposers, recycled, and made available for further use. Take time to examine fallen wood and you will see a host of creatures—insects, mosses, lichens, fungi, and ferns—that take advantage of this decay and in turn make a vital contribution by enriching the soil from which forests grow.

LICHENS AND BACTERIA
Both bacteria and some lichens—tangles of algae and fungi—thrive in areas of dappled shade.

CENTIPEDE
A centipede's soft, permeable skin loses moisture, so this tiny predator inhabits damp, sheltered places.

cavity in log becomes home for bees and wasps, even if made by other insects

loose bark offers shelter, food, and moisture

ivy growing over log provides shelter, and its berries are a vital food source in winter

INSECT LARVAE
Some fly and beetle larvae inhabit decaying wood; others feed on the fungi associated with it.

holly grows in shelter of oak trees—look for young plants on fallen oak

LONGHORN BEETLE
The larvae of some woodland beetles, such as this longhorn, develop in dead wood, where they are sheltered and can break down the rotting log into digestible materials.

MONITORING A LOG

A newly fallen log offers a habitat for wildlife for many years, but the creatures that use it change as time goes by. This is a perfect chance for you to watch and record what happens as a fascinating ecosystem develops. Keep a "log file" with notes, lists of the wildlife inhabiting it, and photos—especially from a fixed position nearby—over several years.

firm, complete bark

shelf fungi

flexible twigs

NEWLY FALLEN
A fresh log with firmly attached bark is a challenge for recyclers. Weak points allow beetle larvae and fungal spores to enter and begin their work.

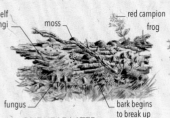

moss

red campion

frog

fungus

bark begins to break up

ONE YEAR LATER
The bark begins to break up, and twigs become brittle. Mosses, lichens, fungi, and plants appear. Larvae, centipedes, and ants thrive in and around the decaying log.

wood sorrel

woodpecker

beetle hole

fungus

ABUNDANT LIFE
The log breaks up, while plants, mats of mosses, lichens, insects, spiders, sow bugs, and feeding birds thrive in and around it.

beech leaves cover fallen wood providing extra shelter and food for insects and their larvae

grasses set seed on patches of damp detritus and decaying leaves in open cavities

bore holes show beetle larva activity

ferns are common in woodlands; many grow on fallen wood

fungi are often found on rotting wood, from which they take nutrients

SPIDER WEB
Some spiders drape tangled web sheets over stumps and logs, rather than creating the usual "cobwebs" across open spaces.

MOSS
The moist, sheltered habitat of a rotting log in a woodland allows many moss species to thrive.

Bark life

Bark does far more than just protect a tree—it is a vital lifeline providing shelter and food for many insects, birds, and other creatures.

BARK BEETLE
Lift a flake of loose bark and you may find a host of patterned lines. What looks like an abstract artist's design is in fact the work of beetle larvae, which burrow through the tree's wood.

Examining bark

If you look closely at bark you will be able to spot the tell-tale signs of life—from insect trails and bore holes to cavities that provide homes for birds and spiders. Some insects lay their eggs in bark because it provides an insulating layer for their larvae over the winter, as well as a good hiding place from predators. Birds, such as treecreepers or woodpeckers, feed on insects in and on bark, or store food caches within it. You may also see a

TELL-TALE HOLES
Look for small holes on a tree trunk—this means a woodpecker has been active. In this case, it is an Acorn Woodpecker storing nuts.

MOTHS
Many moths rest on trees. Some stand out, while some resemble pieces of bark.

well-camouflaged moth blending in on a tree trunk. Whether brightly colored, flaking or polished, scaly, smooth, or woody, bark is an ecosystem in itself.

SHELF FUNGUS
This fungus grows on tree bark as a parasite, taking nutrients from the wood underneath.

3

1

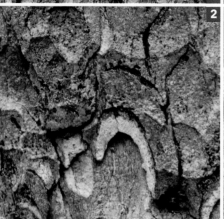

2

4

6

Bark types

Bark differs from tree to tree; on birches it is merely a thin skin, while on conifers it may be up to 12 in (30 cm) thick (see p.109). As the tree grows, a thin inner layer, called the cambium, continually produces new bark. The cambium grows either in large sheets, creating peeling or sheathlike bark, or in overlapping arcs, producing a cracked effect. Examine the colors, structures, and patterns and you will find that each tree species has its own distinctive type of bark.

1 A sugar maple's bark becomes increasingly furrowed with age.

2 Sycamore bark can become gray brown and flaky with age.

3 Striped maple bark has green, brown, and white vertical stripes.

4 White ash bark has deep diamond-shaped patterns.

5 Black cherry bark is sometimes said to resemble burnt corn flakes.

6 Coast redwood trees have thick, fire-resistant red bark.

7 The smooth bark of silver birch is marked by raised pores (lenticels).

8 Shagbark hickories become increasingly shaggy with age.

9 Distinctive "ski tracks" run up the bark of the northern red oak.

10 Yellow birch has a golden sheen and peeling bark.

11 River birch has large flaking patches of bark.

12 Beech bark becomes mottled and fissured as it matures.

BARK RUBBING

You can study different types of bark by taking rubbings with sheets of thick, strong paper and a stick of wax crayon or charcoal. Bark rubbings reveal different patterns without the distractions of surface colors or moss. Make your own carefully labeled collection of bark rubbings to highlight the variety of trees you have discovered in a woodland in your local area.

BARK RUBBING

Looking up

Most of us forget to look up, but glance skyward in a forest and you will discover another layer of woodland activity to explore.

Pollination

Many trees can produce an identical version of themselves by sending out suckers. Flowers, on the other hand, exchange genes through pollination with another plant of the same species, creating genetically different offspring. Pollination is carried out by insects, such as bees or mosquitoes, by birds carrying pollen from flower to flower, or by wind. Look up in any woodland and you will often be able to see pollination in action.

MOSQUITO

MIXED BLOOMS
Both male and female flowers are found on each alder buckthorn plant, which are pollinated by mosquitoes.

RED MULBERRY
Only female mulberry trees bear fruit, which appears from spring through late summer.

Fruits of the forest

Trees are static and rely on external factors to help disperse their seeds. Forests are filled with all kinds of seeds, nuts, berries, and fruits that are eaten by all sorts of animals, from the smallest birds to the largest bears. These animals aid the plants by transporting seeds in their digestive tract and depositing them at a different location. Jays and squirrels bury acorns for later use, thus helping to spread oak woodland.

Never eat wild nuts or berries because they may be toxic.

SWEET TREAT
Juicy berries are packed with high energy and sugary nutrients that make them irresistible to bears.

SERVICEBERRY

WALNUT

ACORNS

LOOK AND LISTEN
Life in the canopy is best
observed by lying down. Take
time to relax, watch the action,
and listen to birdsong and the
hum of insects.

Galls and miners

Close inspection of some woodland plants
may reveal some odd-shaped growths.
These galls are produced in response to
parasites, such as fungi, bacteria, insects,
and mites. Some insects use galls to provide
food and protection for their larvae.
The larvae of leaf miners create tunnels by
feeding on the cells between the upper
and lower surfaces of leaves.

GALL WASPS
Some wasps,
such as this
marble gall
wasp, produce
galls on oak trees.
Gall wasps are
tiny, and most
have shiny
red-brown or
black bodies.

oak spangle gall
eggs laid by wasps

SPANGLE AND CHERRY GALLS
Most galls are produced by
wasps—in this case creating red
galls on the underside of a leaf.

"mines" show
where leaf miners
have tunneled

LEAF MINERS
Some caterpillars, such as the
horse chestnut leaf miner,
injure leaves, but cause no
lasting damage to trees.

FALLEN WONDERS

If you want to find out more about the variety of
invertebrates that live in a healthy tree or shrub, carefully
place a white sheet on the ground or hold out a rigid white
board beneath it. Then, gently shake the branches above it
to encourage insects, spiders, mites, and any other tiny
animals to let go and fall onto the sheet or board. Beware
of any fallen branches that may be dislodged by your
movements. Identify what you can, record everything you
find, and then leave the animals to return to their habitat.

Forest birds

Birds are some of the most lively, colorful, and noisy forest inhabitants, yet they are apt to fly away at the least disturbance.

Woodland chorus

Getting to grips with woodland birds is difficult because many hide in the foliage, and some become very quiet in the summer. To get a better idea of what lives in a wood, and for the sheer enjoyment of hearing the birds at their best, try to hear a spring dawn chorus (see panel, below). Birds sing or call for a variety of reasons—to defend territory, ward off rivals, find a mate, warn of a predator, or locate their chicks. Over time you can learn to distinguish not only the calls of different species but also the types of calls.

RECORDING BIRDSONG

Distinguishing birdsong can be difficult but rewarding. Listen to birdsong CDs or bird apps to prepare for when you are out in the field. Many field guides transcribe bird sounds into words such as *tiks*, *chaks*, and *tchuks*, which are very useful for identification. Try making your own notes when you're out—be creative with your descriptions.

Chshree-ip
Schrree-eew
Shrr-ooo

SOUND GUIDE
When transcribing bird sounds, the lines above the word are used to show variation in pitch.

SWEET SONG
American Robins have several "call notes," but, like many other birds, its "song" is a declaration of territory.

THE DAWN CHORUS

This avian choir is at its best in spring, when males attract females and warn off rivals, but you will need to get up early to catch it—as early as 4am in some areas. Try to choose your location the evening before, because birds such as blackbirds often sing from the same song-post they settle on at dusk. Sit quietly, don't wear bright colors, and enjoy the performance.

Woodland birds

RED-EYED VIREO
More often heard than seen, North American vireos sing from forest canopies.

BLUE JAY
Blue Jays have a close relationship with oak trees and may cache (bury) thousands of acorns each year, some of which mature into grand forest oaks.

NORTHERN PARULA
This is a migratory wood warbler that spends most of its year in the tropics and arrives in spring to nest in northern forests.

Nesting

Birds' nests are not long-term "homes"—they are solely for hatching eggs and rearing chicks. We can learn much about birds from their nests, but take care to never disturb an active one. Over time, the average number of eggs, number of clutches, and chick survival rates give us vital data on the health of bird populations.

AMERICAN CROW NEST

SCRUB-JAY NEST

BUILDING MATERIAL
Materials chosen for the outside of the nest offer camouflage and structure, while birds choose soft plant down, moss, fur, and feathers for lining the interior of the nest to cradle their eggs.

Migrants

Migration is one of nature's extraordinary events. In the Northern Hemisphere, birds head north in spring, to exploit a temporary glut of food, and return south in fall, often sharing winter quarters with species that stay there all year. Some, such as geese, fly in families and learn routes; many others migrate alone, like hummingbirds, navigating by instinct (see p.15).

SHORT-DISTANCE MIGRANT
Brown Creepers are short-distance migrants. They have a downward-curved beak that permits them to extract small insects from tree bark.

BEAUTIFUL SONG
The Wood Thrush's flute-like song echoes through eastern forests, especially in the early evening.

PILEATED WOODPECKER
Pileated Woodpeckers require large trees for nesting. They also use them for loud drumming to attract mates and defend their forest homes.

TOWNSEND'S WARBLER
Townsend's Warblers sing from tree tops in west-coast fir forests. They nest from May through July, before flying to tropical forests for the winter.

CHESTNUT-SIDED WARBLER
Chestnut-sided Warblers are forest-edge birds that migrate to northern forests in the summer.

Deciduous close-up

Deciduous woodlands harbor an enormous diversity of life—including many flowering plants, mammals, insects, and birds—that varies according to its range and with the seasons. Get to know your local forest well, month by month.

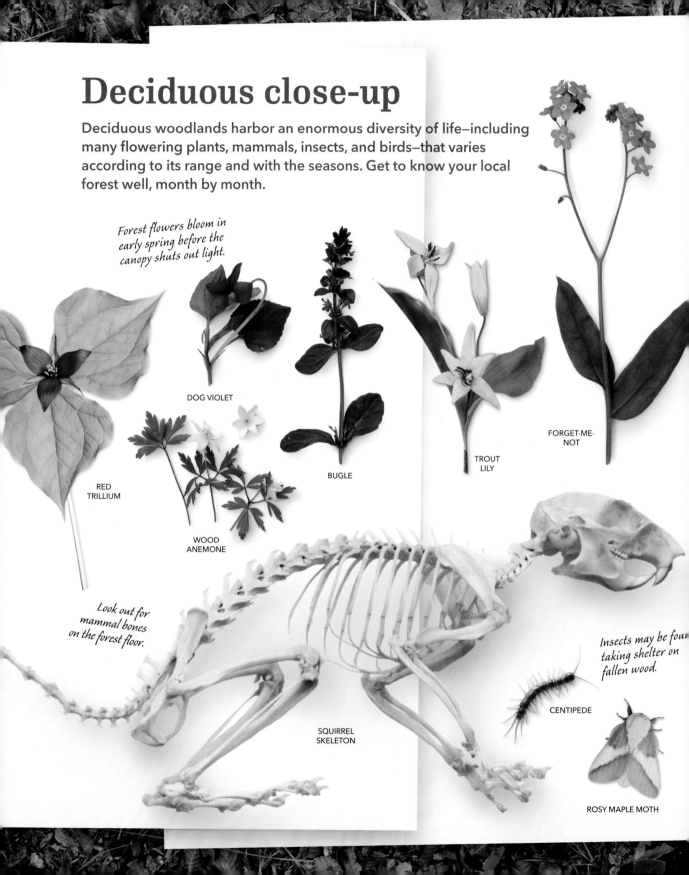

Forest flowers bloom in early spring before the canopy shuts out light.

DOG VIOLET

RED TRILLIUM

WOOD ANEMONE

BUGLE

TROUT LILY

FORGET-ME-NOT

Look out for mammal bones on the forest floor.

SQUIRREL SKELETON

Insects may be found taking shelter on fallen wood.

CENTIPEDE

ROSY MAPLE MOTH

Nuts and seeds ripen and fall in autumn.

Leaves of trees and shrubs provide shade in summer and carpet the floor in fall.

RED MAPLE WINGS

NORWAY MAPLE SEEDS

CHESTNUT

BIRCH LEAVES

PAPER BIRCH LEAVES AND CATKIN

HORSE CHESTNUT

BLACK BRYONY

OAK LEAVES

ORANGE PEEL FUNGUS

MOREL FUNGUS

HAZELNUTS

ACORNS

Many fungi live in close association with trees and are found at their roots.

FLY AGARIC

WOOD FROG

SPOTTED SALAMANDER

HONEY FUNGUS

Look for amphibians near forest pools or decaying wood.

The forest year

Few places reflect the changing seasons as well as a deciduous forest—its colors, sounds, and scents reveal the natural cycle of life.

Observing the changes

Appreciate the uniqueness of each season in a wood by keeping all your senses alert. Spring is the best time for listening to the birds, and the lush growth of summer provides great opportunities for plant hunting. Autumn brings with it the scent of rotting leaves and fungi, while the peacefulness of a winter wood should never be underestimated.

spring flowers provide autumn fruit

CHERRY BLOSSOM

BRINGING UP BABY
Summer is the time when mammals are busy rearing young. Fox cubs may be seen playing outside dens.

1 Spring stimulates new life. Longer days allow the increasing energy from a higher Sun to pour through the trees. Woodland flowers thrive in the light, before the growing canopy casts deep shade.

2 Summer is a quieter time as animals and birds move on from the frenzy of courtship and defining territories to the hard grind of raising families. At this time of year, ferns and lichens become more obvious than flowers.

Examine plants to see insects feeding on them—many are camouflaged.

SPHINX MOTH

EATING GREENS
Caterpillars gorge themselves on lush, summer foliage.

ROOTING FOR FOOD
Wild boars turn over soil in their search for roots and invertebrates.

NEW SHOOTS
Conditions in spring—longer, warmer days with more sunlight—give plants, such as this hazel, the energy to sprout new growth.

SPRING TOADS

American toads spend the winter buried in soft ground and emerge early in the year. They gather in shallow water in March, where females lay long strings of jelly containing three or four rows of black eggs—unlike the shapeless mass produced by frogs so they are easy to tell apart. Toad tadpoles often form dense schools, have flatter bodies, and are blacker than frog tadpoles.

TRACK A FOREST YEAR

Really get to know a particular wooded area, or even a single large tree, by visiting and recording it throughout the year. Choose somewhere close by and easy to get to so that you can visit every week. Note down anything that is new or has changed, and take photographs to compare at the end of the year. Identify and count all the trees in your chosen area, and as other plants begin to appear identify them and note their flowering dates. Listen for birdsong, try to identify it, and record it on a sound recorder if you can. Look closely for insects, fungi, and other forest wildlife.

SPRING

SUMMER

FALL

WINTER

earwigs burrow into the ground to survive winter

EARWIG

OUT IN THE COLD Some mammals, including cottontails, stay active all winter.

3 Autumn sees a lowering Sun, and with it, reduced light penetrating the forest. Insects decline and migrant birds leave, but the immense bounty of nuts, seeds, and berries that remains tempts some species to stay and begin storing food for the winter.

FALL FEAST
Rodents such as this eastern chipmunk bulk up on autumn berries, seeds, and nuts before hibernating.

The mourning cloak is the first butterfly seen in the spring because it hibernates during winter in tree cavities.

FATAL FREEZE
As the weather turns cold some moths and butterflies hibernate while others die.

4 To survive winter, some animals hibernate, while birds roam in mixed, nomadic flocks for safety. A lack of foliage can make birds and animals easier to see at this time of year, and look for their tracks in mud and snow.

WINTER GREEN
Look up to see mistletoe clinging to bare winter trees.

Signs of life

Mammals are sometimes difficult to see in a forest, but finding evidence of their activities—such as dens, nests, and tracks—is often much easier.

Making tracks

Most tracks are left in mud, which can last a few days, or snow, which can be very short-lived. The best prints are those found in mud, which preserves details of the structure of the foot or paw. Snow tracks are far often less well-shaped, unless they have been made in a thin layer of snow on soft ground, especially after a new snowfall. Look for prints and tracks around muddy puddles, on wet trails in the woods, or near rivers and streams.

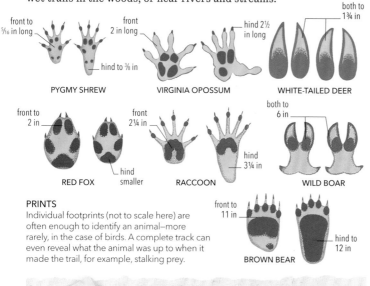

front to ⁵⁄₁₆ in long — hind to ³⁄₈ in
PYGMY SHREW

front 2 in long
VIRGINIA OPOSSUM

hind 2½ in long — both to 1¾ in
WHITE-TAILED DEER

front to 2 in — hind smaller
RED FOX

front 2¼ in — hind 3¼ in
both to 6 in
RACCOON

WILD BOAR

front to 11 in — hind to 12 in
BROWN BEAR

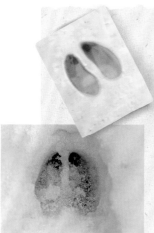

PRINTS
Individual footprints (not to scale here) are often enough to identify an animal—more rarely, in the case of birds. A complete track can even reveal what the animal was up to when it made the trail, for example, stalking prey.

MAKING A PLASTER CAST

Good tracks are worth preserving. Photographs are valuable, but it's rewarding—and sometimes more informative—to make a plaster cast. If the track is in mud, first spray with a very light oil, such as cooking oil, then surround it with a "wall" made up of thin strips of wood, plastic, or cardboard, so that the plaster has a barrier and won't seep away. Carefully pour a runny plaster mix over the print. When it is set hard, lift it to reveal a "negative" cast. You can then make a second cast of the first to get back to the original imprint.

WHITE-TAILED DEER TRACK AND CAST
White-tailed deer are active throughout the year. The best place to track them is in the snow.

Resting places

Most birds build nests solely for incubating eggs and raising their young, but mammals use their resting places as shelter for much longer. Some, such as a badger's den, are daily retreats; others, like a bear's den, are seasonal. Shelters can be found in all sorts of places: some are dug into the ground, while others might be nestled in a tree hollow.

1 Look out for a loosely structured, roofed nest—this will be a squirrel's drey. A summer drey is used for resting, while a winter, or family, drey is stronger to provide better shelter.

2 This brown bear is hauling itself from its den under some rocks at the end of the winter. Brown bears put on fat, then hibernate during winter, eating little or nothing.

3 Look out for mouse droppings beneath a woodpecker hole. They could be a sign of a deer mouse, pictured, or white-footed mouse nesting inside.

4 Foxes dig burrows called earths. Simple ones are daytime or emergency retreats; larger ones are for raising young.

5 Raccoons usually raise young in tree cavities, but sometimes nest in rock crevices or underground in burrows dug by other animals such as groundhogs.

6 Short-tailed shrews build nests of leaves, grass, and hair under leaves or underground.

Watching at night

Many animals are active at night, so an evening watch can yield amazing sights. You may be in for a long wait, so dress warmly and get comfortable. Nocturnal animals have poor vision but excellent hearing and smelling abilities, so sit still on a bank or log above their level and downwind from them. Keep quiet, and don't smoke or wear perfume. Use a flashlight with a red filter—red light is at a wavelength that animals can't easily see.

Tips for your blind
1. Prepare a comfortable perch in advance.
2. Wear dull, dark clothes.
3. Turn off cell phones.
4. Cover your flashlight with red cellophane.
5. Always tell someone where you are going.

BADGER TRACK
Wait quietly and don't make a sound at a den (sett) and you may get a close view.

Conifer plantation

Demand for lumber has led to extensive planting of conifers in stands of single species, such as sitka spruce. Young plantations are dense and dark, but thinning as the trees age creates more light in the understory. Before they are harvested, trees may lose branches or be blown over by gales. This creates space for wildlife, where fungi such as morels may grow.

SITKA SPRUCE

MOREL FUNGUS

Coniferous forests

Conifer forests are not all dark swathes of "Christmas trees." While many plantations are poor habitats for wildlife, natural forests are home to a diverse range of plants and animals, some of them found nowhere else.

Redwood forest

Giant sequoias grow naturally only in a 260-mile (418-km) belt of forest on the western slopes of California's Sierra Nevada mountains; redwoods grow in the coastal fog belt. Coastal forests are often too dense for visitors to appreciate the trees' vast size. These giants act as multistory dwellings for countless creatures such as salamanders, birds, insects, and bats that call the trees home—even small mammals such as chipmunks living on branches.

CHIPMUNK

BROOM

Pacific rainforest

The Pacific temperate rainforest occurs on the west coast from southern Alaska to the northern tip of California. It is the largest temperate rainforest in the world and receives 60–120 in (152–305 cm) of rain every year. It is dominated by huge trees including Sitka spruce, Douglas fir, and Western hemlock. Due to logging, it is the most endangered forest in the world.

NORTHERN GOSHAWK

SPOTTED OWL

PACIFIC GIANT SALAMANDER

Taiga

Taiga is the cold forest zone south of the Arctic tundra. Trees such as the black spruce have shallow roots adapted to grow in thin soil, downward-pointing branches to help shed snow, and dark needles to absorb weak sunlight efficiently. Ground beetles shelter in needle litter while wolverines have thick fur coats for insulation.

GROUND BEETLE

WOLVERINE

BLACK SPRUCE

HUCKLEBERRY

Keep quiet and scan the canopy for shy animals such as squirrels and martens— watch for any movement against the bright sky.

Conifer forest walk

With their year-round greenery, coniferous woods have a characteristic beauty. There is a wealth of wildlife to discover once you know where to look.

A walk through a conifer forest can be a satisfying experience that engages all your senses. Experiencing the fresh scent of the evergreen trees is a distinctive part of any visit to this habitat, and like all forests, it can be a quiet, undisturbed place for a budding naturalist to explore. From insects scurrying on the forest floor to birds calling in the canopy, coniferous woodlands harbor a wide range of animals, as well as plants and fungi.

Search the undergrowth of northwestern coniferous forests for colorful herbaceous plants, such as bunchberry and wintergreen.

MOSS

LADY'S-TRESSES ORCHID

Listen for bird calls and other tell-tale noises. The sound of pine cones falling may indicate squirrels or birds, such as crossbills, feeding above.

AMERICAN BEAUTYBERRY

LADYBUG

VIOLET-TOOTHED POLYPORE

Remember to keep one eye on the ground: here you might find ant nests, flowers, or fungi, or the entrances to badger setts and fox earths.

WOOD ANTS

Coniferous trees

Conifers are handsome trees—deeply colored and clothed in needlelike leaves. They vary in shape and adapt to different conditions.

Recognizing conifers

Conifers are fairly easy to identify. Most are evergreen, which means they keep their leaves, or "needles," year round and shed them continually, rather than each autumn, as do deciduous trees. The most distinctive feature of most conifers is their "cone," which is usually woody, but in some species, such as yew, it is more like a soft berry. The cones, leaf structure, and bark can help you identify different conifer types.

FIRS
Fir trees, such as the balsam fir, have soft, flattened needles, a pungent aroma, and distinctive cones that grow upward rather than droop.

CONE AND NEEDLES

SPRUCES
The Norway spruce is one of the classic "Christmas trees." Spruce twigs are spiky and covered in pointy needles in opposite bands.

CONE AND NEEDLES

PINES
Pines, such as the Scotch pine, usually have thick, scaly bark, and clustered needles. Cones vary widely between families.

CONE AND NEEDLES

CYPRESSES
Cypress trees, such as the Monterey cypress, have dark green scalelike leaves and small cones that remain on the tree for years.

CONE AND SCALES

Redwood inhabitants

CHIPMUNK
Rodents, such as the eastern chipmunk, nest in underground burrows or logs.

FERN
Licorice ferns grow on soil mats on branches of mature trees.

BAT
The red bat scans its surroundings with a series of echolocation calls before taking flight on a nocturnal hunting trip.

SPOTTED OWL
This endangered Spotted Owl perches on branches to watch and listen for prey.

SORREL AND TRILLIUM
Both of these plants thrive in low light levels on the forest floor.

ORANGE WITCH'S BUTTER
Also known as orange jelly fungus, look for this edible fungus on dead conifer wood.

ROOM FOR LIFE
A mature conifer tree provides many levels for wildlife to inhabit—from rodents, such as squirrels in the canopy to fungus at its roots. A team of scientists climbed this 295-ft (90-m) giant redwood in the coastal forest of California, to map the complex structure of its crown.

WORLD'S OLDEST ORGANISMS

At 12,000 years old, Antarctic beech, growing as a clone, holds the record for the oldest tree on Earth. Other ancient trees include the gnarled bristlecone pines (left) found high in western US mountains, where they are able to survive even the most severe droughts. The oldest bristlecone is nearing its 5,000th birthday. Coastal redwoods (see main image, right) can reach 3,000 years old, and ancient yews can live up to 2,000 years.

How typical conifers survive extremes

Unlike deciduous trees, typical conifers keep their leaves all year. The waxy, needlelike or scalelike leaves minimize water loss to help the tree survive both drought and severe cold. Sap within the tree moves through much smaller cells than those in deciduous trees, which limits damage if the sap freezes in extreme cold. Where soils permit, pines typically have a deep taproot that anchors them in place.

THICK BARK
Most evergreens have thick, scaly, sometimes spongy bark, which offers protection for the sensitive growth layers lying just beneath.

TREE CIRCULATION
Sap draws minerals up from the ground, through the roots, and draws nutrients down from the leaves. Tree trunks act as pathways for this food, with sap flowing up in the sapwood and down in the inner bark layer.

heartwood consists mostly of dead cells

sapwood in which sap flows upward

inner bark in which sap descends

cambium layer widens trunk by adding new bark

outer bark is hard protective outer layer

Forest fungi

Looking for fungi adds to any walk. You can find mushrooms in a variety of shapes and sizes—but that's only one part of the story.

STRANGE FRUIT
Many fungi are poisonous, and it is important to never pick or eat any unfamiliar mushrooms you find in the wild.

What are fungi?

Fungi are neither plants nor animals, but organisms that feed on rotting organic material, breaking it down to enrich the soil. The parts we see—from delicate mushrooms to thick shelf fungi—are only the parts involved in reproduction, known as fruiting bodies. Underground, threadlike filaments known as *hyphae* spread out to form a colonylike *mycelium*: a mass often many acres in size and sometimes thousands of years old.

MOLDY WOOD
Slime mold, which closely resembles fungi, can be found growing on rotting wood on the forest floor.

Fruiting body shapes

Most fungi have a stem topped by a cap. With puffballs, though, the stems are almost invisible, while with stinkhorns, the stems are more striking than the caps.

PHALLIC

TRUMPET

CUP

CAP AND STEM

SHELF

BRAINLIKE

BALL

Cap shape and texture

Mushroom caps may be conical, domed, flattened, or dish-shaped and may develop from round "buttons" into broad "dishes." They can be dry, flaky, silky, or greasy.

CONVEX

FUNNEL

GROOVED

DEPRESSED

CONICAL

LOOSE SCALES

A BENEFICIAL RELATIONSHIP

Many fungi live in close association with plants and algae, usually to the benefit of both; scientists estimate that more than 90 percent of plants need fungi to survive. Fungi help plants take up nutrients, such as nitrates and phosphates, from poor soils. This system is known as "mycorrhizal symbiosis"—a partnership that benefits both parties. Fungi living in close association with algae form lichens, which are abundant in unpolluted forests, as well as on rocks, roofs, and walls. Some fungi parasitize animals, such as bees, while some ants and beetles cultivate fungi for food.

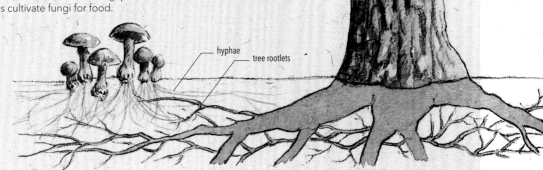

hyphae

tree rootlets

FUNGUS ROOTS
The word mycorrhizae means "fungus roots." Mycorrhizae colonize plant roots, helping the fungi access carbohydrates, and helping the plant absorb water and mineral nutrients.

Stem
The mushroom stem, called a stipe, raises the cap to allow a fungus to release spores to reproduce. In some species, the cap bursts open from a spherical shape, leaving a ring on the stipe.

SOLID FLESH

VOLVA AT BASE

SLENDER

HOLLOW

RINGED

BULBOUS

Color
Color is important in mushroom identification but subtle shades of brown, pink, yellow, and orange can be difficult to describe. Find a color chart, or use your own terms for comparison.

RINGS OF COLOR

DARK CENTER

SPORE PRINTS
Spores are ejected from a fungus by a buildup of internal pressure or by the force of a raindrop. You can easily take a spore print to help identify a fungus. Put the cap on paper, place a glass over it, and leave it overnight. Then carefully remove the glass and fungus. You can spray the image lightly with hairspray to "fix" the spore print.

Gills
Some fungi have caps with "gills" underneath—this is where the spores are produced. Observing the structure of the gills and the color of the spores will help you identify the mushroom.

UNEQUAL LENGTH

BROADLY SPACED

CROWDED

111

Coniferous close-up

Coniferous forests are widespread in the Northern Hemisphere and support an array of specialized flora and fauna throughout their range. The exact species of fungi, insects, and plants depends upon location, but all are home to a rich variety of wildlife.

PUFFBALL FUNGI

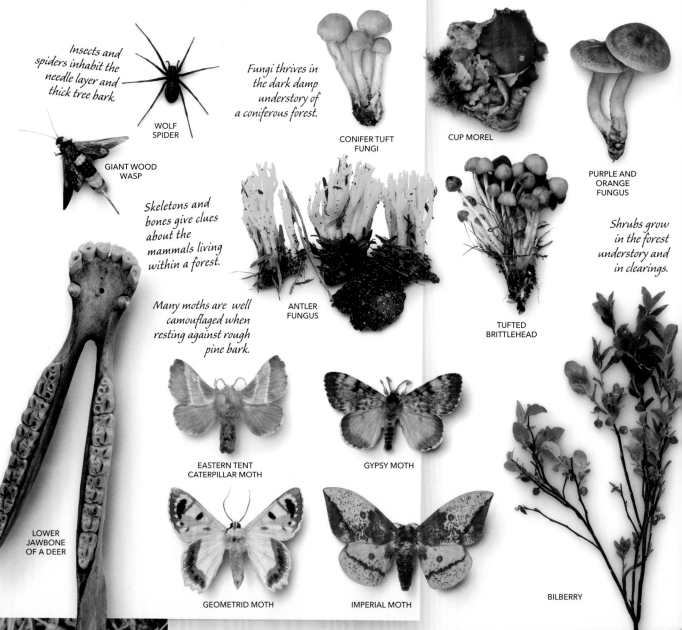

Insects and spiders inhabit the needle layer and thick tree bark.

WOLF SPIDER

GIANT WOOD WASP

Fungi thrives in the dark damp understory of a coniferous forest.

CONIFER TUFT FUNGI

CUP MOREL

PURPLE AND ORANGE FUNGUS

Skeletons and bones give clues about the mammals living within a forest.

ANTLER FUNGUS

TUFTED BRITTLEHEAD

Shrubs grow in the forest understory and in clearings.

Many moths are well camouflaged when resting against rough pine bark.

EASTERN TENT CATERPILLAR MOTH

GYPSY MOTH

LOWER JAWBONE OF A DEER

GEOMETRID MOTH

IMPERIAL MOTH

BILBERRY

WINTERGREEN

SITKA SPRUCE
NEEDLES AND CONE

JUNIPER

*Lichens hang
from low
branches and
spread over
dead wood
and rocks.*

WILD
RASPBERRIES

FOLIOSE
LICHEN

TWINFLOWER

NORWAY
SPRUCE
CONES

SCOTCH PINE CONES

*Cones litter
the forest
floor.*

Coniferous specialists

Cones provide excellent seed protection for trees, but can prove tricky for animals bent on eating these seeds.

The pine cone

Most pine trees bear both male and female cones. Male cones are small, with modified scales covering pollen sacs. Female cones are the more familiar larger woody cones containing ovules that, once fertilized by pollen, develop into seeds beneath tough scales. While cone structure is similar, the size, shape, and woodiness of cones vary from species to species.

TOP OF CONE

tightly packed scales at base

BOTTOM OF CONE

cone tip

You can tell if humidity is high or low by whether a cone is open or not.

closed scale

algae

open scales release seeds

SCOTCH PINE CONES
Rosy-pink Scotch pine flowers turn purple in summer, with small scales that become bright green but woody the following year. The year after that, the cones are mature, and turn a dull gray.

branch

immature cones

clustered pine needles

attachment

CLOSED CONE
Female cones have seed scales, which open initially to receive pollen, then close tightly while the seeds mature. Later, they will also close in wet weather to protect and retain the growing seeds.

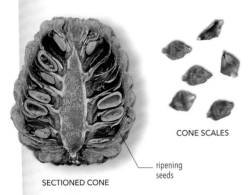

CONE SCALES

SECTIONED CONE

ripening
seeds

Cone crackers

Seeds within pine cones lie deep between the scales, at the base of these woody, winglike structures. The seeds are nutritious but difficult to reach, and eating the cone, with its hard, rough, sharp-edged, woody scales, would be impossible or inefficient, so many animals have developed ways to get inside the cone. In damp weather, scales close up tight—dry conditions open them—but this happens many times, even long after the seeds have been dispersed and long after the cone has fallen to the ground. Seed-eaters must first decide which cones are worth their attention.

Start a cone collection and look for clues to find out which animals opened them.

protrusion on scale

1 Crossbills have evolved into several bird species, often in response to the size and shape of their local cones. They push their mandibles between scales, then close or twist their bills to part them. Seeds are then extracted with the tip of the tongue.

2 Squirrels simply bite the scales and gnaw their way into the seeds. You can easily tell cones bitten down by a squirrel from those worked on by a crossbill.

3 Clark's Nutcrackers use their long pointed beak to probe for seeds at the base of scales.

WOODPECKING

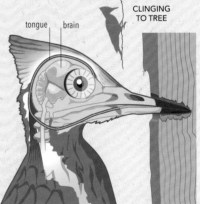

Woodpeckers chisel into living or dead wood. The bird's long, sticky, spiny tongue (which wraps around the skull) probes deeply into tree holes in order to extract larvae. A woodpecker steadies itself with its stiff tail by using it as a prop, and grasps the tree firmly with its specially adapted feet: two toes point forward, and two point back. It also has sinewy attachments at the base of its bill and around its brain to cushion the shock of the fierce bombardment of bill on wood.

tongue   brain

CLINGING TO TREE

OPEN CONE
Mature cones open in dry weather, ensuring that the seeds are released under ideal conditions for wind dispersal.

Bear country

Bears are very powerful animals, and although negative encounters are rare, it's best to be aware within their habitats.

The most common American bear is the black bear: around 800,000 live in forests from Alaska to Mexico and they sometimes stray into suburbs. These omnivores eat fruit, seeds, and bark; however they also raid beehives for honey and grubs and sometimes pull down bird feeders. Smaller than brown bears, at 7 ft (2 m) when standing, black bears are still powerful beasts. The largest brown bears of North America, Europe, and Asia, at 220–1,500 lb (100–680 kg), match the polar bear as the world's largest land predator. American brown bears inhabit open, mountainous country, while Eurasian bears prefer dense forests. Standing upright at over 9 ft (2¾ m), adult brown bears are largely nocturnal, either by natural preference or through increasing fear of human predators. They pile on 400 lb (181 kg) of fat in summer, then retreat to a den where they are dormant during the winter.

WILD BERRIES
To prepare for hibernation, bears fatten up on berries and acorns, among other high-fat foods, consuming 20–30 lb (9–14 kg) daily, for their hibernation between October and April.

CLOSE ENCOUNTERS

Black bears are forest animals. They seldom attack people unless they are threatened, wounded, or protecting their cubs. Yet the logging of forests and the growth of cities means that bears are increasingly encountering humans. Bear attacks are relatively rare—they are more likely to seek cover if they see you coming—but the best way to stay safe is to follow some simple rules. Always explore bear territory with other people, and avoid areas where bears have been recently spotted. Make noise, such as talking or whistling, as you walk, so you don't startle any nearby bears.

LOGGED OUT
The clear-cutting of forests forces bears to survive in less productive habitats.

SUPERIOR SMELL
Bears have a great sense of smell, which can lead them to human food. When in bear territory, always keep food in air-tight containers.

Desert and chaparral

Most deserts remain sparsely populated by people, but other animals and plants prosper in the searing heat, bitter cold, and scarce moisture. These desert specialists never flourish in massive numbers, yet their adaptations of form and behavior are a reminder that even in these daunting conditions, life finds a way to thrive. Deserts typically have less than 20 in (50cm) of annual precipitation, which excludes most woody plants. In contrast, in southern California, where hot, dry summers are relieved by mild, rainy winters, the semi-arid climate creates a habitat of short, evergreen shrubs called chaparral.

Chaparral

Chaparral is a type of scrubland found across the western US, its age and extent determined by the periodic fires that sweep the area. The dense undergrowth of chamise and toyon shrubs shelters birdlife such as quails, thrashers, and roadrunners, while predatory mammals include coyotes, bobcats, and mountain lions.

WILD TURKEY

BLAINVILLE'S HORNED LIZARD

Deserts and chaparral

These habitats are usually found on nutrient-poor soils and are shaped by factors such as grazing and fire. Despite their inhospitable appearance, their unique conditions provide a home to many interesting types of wildlife.

Cold deserts

High-altitude cold deserts, such as the Great Basin, have some of the most extreme conditions anywhere. Mammals such as black-tailed jackrabbits and pronghorns must withstand the bitter winter cold and frequent snow, while vegetation is sparse and highly seasonal. Predators such as hawks and eagles soar above, looking for weakened prey.

LOGGERHEAD SHRIKE

BLACK-TAILED JACKRABBIT

Seasonal lakes and salt pans

Water is always scarce in the desert, but heavy rainfall often forms temporary lakes. These can spread over huge areas, providing a lifeline for amphibians, visiting birds, and other animals. Salt pans are more permanent, and are often home to specialized feeders like Eared Grebes, which rely on the brine shrimps that thrive there.

AMERICAN WHITE PELICAN

BRINE SHRIMP

Sandy deserts

Consisting of expanses of gravel, stones, and sand, deserts such as the Mojave are still home to many animals. These animals, such as scorpions, tend to be secretive during the day, burrowing into sand or hiding under rocks, and venturing out only at night. Sometimes spring rains in southwestern deserts can bring seemingly lifeless habitats into a blaze of color when wildflowers bloom.

DESERT SCORPION

Bajada

The bajada consists of fans of river-deposited gravel where open plains abut mountains. Water often gathers here, which allows many cacti and other plants to flourish. This diverse habitat supports a range of wildlife, from reptiles such as rattlesnakes and gila monsters to specialized birds like the Gilded Flicker. Mammals include ground squirrels, which must outwit predators like foxes and bobcats.

GILA MONSTER

BOBCAT

Day and night in the desert

Some creatures have ways of coping with searing daytime desert heat, while a host of others are only active when the temperature drops at night.

Daytime action

Although the heat of the day can be very intense, desert animals and birds are well adapted to cope with it. Many reptile species rely on the morning Sun to raise their body temperature to the required level for them to become active. They then hide in crevices and under stones when they become too hot. Most birds and larger mammals often start looking for food before dawn. They then seek shade and rest when the heat becomes excessive, emerging again to forage toward the end of the day.

POLLINATING AROUND THE CLOCK

Desert plants rely on a variety of pollinating agents, including bees, butterflies, moths, birds, and even small mammals and reptiles. Drawn to the plants' nectar, these creatures unwittingly transfer the pollen to their next destination. Some plants only bloom when certain specialized pollinators are visiting the desert.

DURING THE DAY
Hummingbirds move through deserts, such as the Sonoran Desert, on migration; they can visit up to several hundred flowers in a day.

AT NIGHT
Bats are important pollinators of cacti and other desert plants, some of which bloom at night.

BURROWING OWL
Burrowing Owls are the only North American owls that nest underground, usually using a burrow created by a prairie dog or other burrowing mammal.

EARLY IN THE MORNING
Tortoises and other reptiles emerge and warm up in the Sun, before starting to look for food.

BOILING AT NOON
Gila monsters spend most of their time in their burrows. They move slowly, eating eggs, small mammals, and nestling birds.

COOLER AFTERNOON
As the heat eases, birds of prey like this Harris's Hawk become more active and start scouting for small mammals and reptiles.

SPEEDSTER
Pronghorns can move across open sagebrush habitat at 60 mph (96.5 kph), making them the fastest mammal in North America.

As darkness falls...

Night falls swiftly in the desert and the temperature can drop dramatically. As the last rays of the Sun sink below the horizon there is a changing of the guard for wildlife. Almost all desert birds roost as high up as they can, while most large mammals, such as desert bighorn sheep, also settle down for the night. They are replaced by an army of small rodents that emerge from their burrows to forage for seeds, fruit, and invertebrates. Creatures such as scorpions come out from rock crevices and under stones, and the hours of darkness also provide cover for predators, such as coyotes and foxes.

NIGHT VISION

Watching wildlife at night is not always easy—you should always be careful and, where possible, use a professional guide. A night vision device lets you see wildlife in the dark, but even if you explore just by the light of the moon, you will be amazed at how much there is to see. Look for signs of movement, walk slowly, and keep your attention on the ground. But also remember to stop and look up at trees and tall cacti, which is where birds, such as Great Horned Owls, sit and scan for prey.

NIGHT VISION BINOCULARS

ULTRAVIOLET LIGHT
Special optics, such as ultraviolet light, make it easier to see some nocturnal creatures.

DESERT NIGHT
Many desert animals take advantage of the cooler temperatures, and become active at nightfall.

Look for birds, gathering at dusk to roost on cacti.

See a prowling fox hunting at dusk.

NIGHT BLOOMERS
Many cacti open their large, showy flowers at night when bats and moths provide pollinating services.

NIGHT PATROL
Ringtails are agile, nocturnal raccoon relatives. Capable of climbing trees, they are restless patrollers. They scent trees with urine to mark their territories.

ALL EARS
The huge ears of Townsend's big-eared bats aid hearing and temperature regulation, and may offer lift during flight.

NIGHT CRAWLERS
Tarantulas hunt largely at night and spend the day in burrows lined with their own silk.

Tarantulas eat insects and small lizards.

Living in the desert

Deserts are one of the harshest environments on the planet; yet a surprising diversity of plants and animals live here, all specially equipped for the difficult conditions.

Coping with extremes

Epic temperatures and a scarcity of water are the two main factors affecting wildlife in the desert; they also make it a hostile place to explore. Key requirements are the ability to obtain and retain moisture, as well as to reduce the impacts of the Sun and wind—both are dehydrating factors. Desert animals and birds do this in a variety of ways, including deriving almost all their moisture from their food, thereby reducing the need to drink. Low metabolic rates help them conserve energy, while pale-colored coats and plumage reflect the sun's heat.

UNDER THREAT

Most desert environments are highly vulnerable to human activity. The "greening" of the desert, when irrigation is used to convert arid areas to farmland, can ruin habitats. Even more environmentally destructive are activities such as mining, road building, and overgrazing by domestic livestock.

DUNE BASHING

Pleasure-seekers driving off-road vehicles over sand dunes can cause long-lasting damage and disturbance to wildlife.

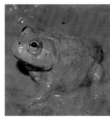

WATER STORERS
Water-holding frogs and toads survive the heat by temporarily burying themselves.

SUPERSIZE EARS
The kit fox has huge ears for its size. They not only help them find prey, but they also help to keep the fox cool by radiating heat. This fox also has a cool burrow to retreat into on hot days.

SHADE DWELLER
Desert tortoises dig burrows to stay cool and usually stay in the shade when they can find shelter from Sun exposure.

The back of bobcat ears have white spots which kittens may follow in dim light.

COOL CAT
Bobcats that live in deserts have lighter colored fur and fainter spots than orange-colored bobcats that live in cool, forested habitat. Lighter colors reflect sunlight, keeping cats cool.

Cat claws retract, keeping them sharp and quiet for night stalking.

RATTLESNAKES IN RESIDENCE
During colder winter weather, reptiles such as rattlesnakes and gila monsters move to communal shelters (hibernacula), usually on south-facing slopes, to hibernate.

— gila monster

— rattlesnake

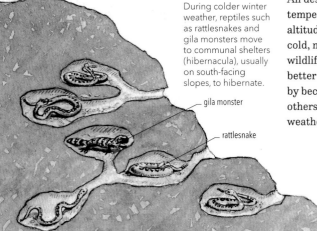

The desert winter

All deserts are dry, but not all are necessarily hot. In some deserts temperatures can drop well below freezing in winter, especially at high altitudes, and they can remain low for months. Biting winds intensify the cold, making winter deserts very inhospitable. During such periods, wildlife is forced to hunker down and wait for better conditions in spring. Some species survive by becoming dormant or hibernating, while others migrate and only return when the weather warms up.

A COLD BLAST
Even in hot deserts, such as the Sonoran Desert in Mexico and the southwestern US, snow can fall in midwinter, but frost is usually more damaging to plants.

Drought busters

Desert plants have evolved various strategies to cope with the lack of moisture. Many become dormant during very dry spells, springing back to life when rain falls. Their life cycle is often very short, enabling them to take advantage of short-lived times of plenty. Desert plant leaves usually have a small surface area, which helps reduce evaporation rates. In the case of cacti, the leaves are reduced to spines.

TOUGH SHRUB
The creosote bush has waxy, resinous leaves to reduce water loss, and long roots that penetrate deep into the soil.

WATERTIGHT
Joshua trees, a type of yucca, are desert tough with thick bark, deep roots, and waxy leaf surfaces that resist water loss.

waxy skin with spines growing from it

water storage tissue

water-conducting tissue

DESERT SCULPTURES
The American saguaro cactus can grow more than 50 ft (15 m) tall. The main trunk expands and contracts according to how much water is available.

INSIDE VIEW
Cacti store water within a spiny body that protects against the effects of the Sun and browsing animals.

shallow roots soak up water from rainfall

Spotting desert dwellers

Though deserts may seem barren, you can find signs of life everywhere—if you know where to look. Be sure to carry plenty of water and wear sunblock in this challenging environment.

Social water holes and saltpans

Water is a scarce resource in the desert. Although most desert animals can cope for long periods without drinking, very few species will turn down an opportunity to do so when water is available. Dawn and dusk are the best times to observe watering holes. If you do so, it is important to select a safe location where you can sit quietly and out of sight. Some animals will visit for just a few minutes, while others may live there all the time. Salt flats attract a less diverse range of wildlife, but are important for birds such as flamingoes, which often breed in these habitats.

THIRST QUENCHER
Rare rains satisfy this Scaled Quail's thirst. Quails and most desert animals obtain most of their water from seeds and other foods.

WHEN IT RAINS...

Rainfall in the desert is a dramatic event. Often an entire year's worth of precipitation falls in seconds and flash floods are common. Some animals, including fairy shrimps, take advantage of temporary rainwater pools in which to hatch and reproduce before the water dries up.

RARE BLOOMS
The seeds of many desert plants lay dormant in the soil and burst into life as soon as rain falls. An accelerated life cycle enables them to germinate, flower, and set seed quickly.

Desert homes

All animals need a place in which to shelter, feed, and reproduce. Identifying their homes and knowing what animal lives where is an essential skill for watching desert wildlife. Crevices and holes in rocks and cactus plants are often used by reptiles and small mammals, and as nesting sites by birds like Cactus Wrens. Cacti and other plants are also excellent places to search for invertebrates, which can also be found under rocks and dead vegetation.

SKINK

SUBSTITUTE TREES
Birds such as Cactus Wrens use tall cacti as prominent songposts, while desert-dwelling Gila Woodpeckers excavate nestholes in cactus trunks.

Look out for crescent-shaped sink burrow entrances.

GOING UNDERGROUND
Skinks make a distinctive burrow that offers respite from the heat and security from potential predators.

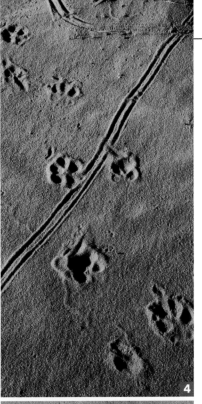

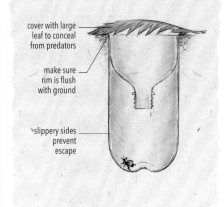

Desert tracks

One of the best ways of finding out what wildlife inhabits a desert is by looking for their tracks in loose sand. Early morning is the best time for this, before wind and other factors have disturbed the evidence. Each animal has a very distinctive trail, so it is worth learning to recognize the tracks they leave.

1 Grasshoppers and crickets (pictured) usually leave neat lines of footprints in two distinct lines. These can become random if the insect jumps.

2 Scorpions leave a tightly grouped trail with four footprints on each side that may appear fused. The forward pincers are carried up off the ground.

3 Darkling beetles make a very recognizable, tirelike track that may run for considerable distances across open dunes.

4 Cats leave characteristic round paw prints with no claws showing. By contrast, fox prints are more narrow and the claws are always visible.

5 Beetle tracks are highly variable, depending on the species. Scarab beetles leave a distinctive, but confusing, trail as they hunt for food.

6 Sidewinders (a type of rattlesnake) leave J-shaped marks—if the tracks stop suddenly the snake may have buried itself in the sand to escape the heat.

MAKE A PITFALL TRAP

Pitfall traps are a great way to catch insects or other small animals in any habitat. Take a clean plastic soda bottle and cut it about two-thirds from the base. Invert the top into the base and sink it into the sand or soil. Check the trap daily and release your catch, taking care not to get stung or bitten.

cover with large leaf to conceal from predators

make sure rim is flush with ground

slippery sides prevent escape

Chaparral cycle

Natural wildfires are an essential part of the chaparral, heath, and grassland ecosystems, bringing about periods of regrowth.

Tinder dry

High summer temperatures and prolonged periods of drought are normal in the California and Mexico chaparral. With the vegetation so dry you can hear it cracking, late summer and early autumn are the natural peak seasons for fires. Certain plants and animals depend on these fires, including the fire beetle, which flies to a blaze site so it can mate and lay its eggs in the fiercely hot conditions needed for hatching.

OPPORTUNISTS
Very flexible in terms of what they eat, coyotes soon start scavenging in recently burned areas. Their howls, yips, and barks are often audible at night.

FIRST ARRIVALS
Lizards are the first creatures on the scene after a fire. You may spot them hunting returning insects and basking on still-warm branches.

1 After a fire the chaparral is charred and seemingly dead, yet the renewal process has already begun. Seeds start to germinate in the warm ash and a variety of creatures soon come to forage in the newly created open areas.

2 Encouraged by winter rains, green shoots emerge through the ash, and shrubs regenerate from roots and stumps. Deer and rabbits return to graze on new growth, followed by predators such as coyotes.

TRACKING WILDLIFE

As animals return to the changed landscape, their tracks become visible in the cooled ashes of the fire. Coyote and fox prints are common, but the large, rounded paw marks of a mountain lion or cougar are more elusive. Birds make tracks too—ground-hunters, such as roadrunners, prefer open, burned areas where they can see their prey more easily.

FRONT

COYOTE
PAW PRINTS

HIND

LOST IN THE FIRE
Some animals inevitably perish in the flames. This coyote skull may have belonged to an older or injured animal unable to flee.

ADAPTED FEET
Part of the cuckoo family, roadrunners are well known for sprinting across open ground in pursuit of reptiles. Their feet are flexible enough to allow them to perch, and they nest in bushes, relying on the regeneration of shrubs.

GROUND FEEDERS
Quail move around in small groups, keeping in touch with each other with low clucking sounds.

SHRUB DWELLERS
Pack rats depend on mature shrubs, in which they build untidy nests from plant stems and twigs.

3 The first summer after a fire, you can see well-established ground plants. While mature shrubs may not have survived, a new generation starts to replace them, attracting ground-feeding birds and small mammals.

4 Within three or four years the vegetation has recovered well. Maturing shrubs will eventually shade out the smaller plants that appeared immediately after the fire.

FORAGERS
Listen for noisy, inquisitive scrub-jays as they hunt for acorns, seeds, bugs, and lizards in new growth.

Heat-loving plants

Fires bring both death and life to the plants of the chaparral. The clearance of thick and aging vegetation offers a lifeline to long-dormant seeds and bulbs in the soil below. Some species rely on the intense heat of a fire to spark their germination. These so-called "fire followers" make a colorful, but temporary, display in the spring after a fire, while regenerating shrubs such as manzanita are more permanent features.

WILDFIRES

Fires can occur either naturally through lightning strikes or, unfortunately, as a result of accidental or deliberate human activity. Flames can sweep across the chaparral faster than a person can run, often causing loss of human life and property. Such sites should always be visited with caution and careful preparation.

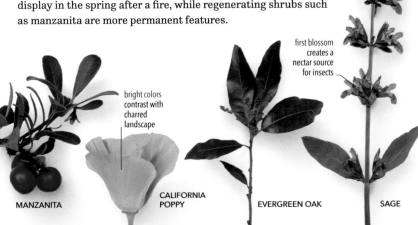

bright colors contrast with charred landscape

first blossom creates a nectar source for insects

MANZANITA

CALIFORNIA POPPY

EVERGREEN OAK

SAGE

Grassland

The endless, rolling prairies of North America, and flower-rich meadows of New England all have an enduring appeal—perhaps because they remind us of African savannas, our own species' primal home. They are all open and warm habitats that are highly productive, supporting a large number of herbivores, and in turn, a range of carnivores, from mountain lions and wolves to foxes and coyotes. Meanwhile, at ground level, the constant grazing gives non-grass species a chance to flower and prosper, and with them, insects. For all these reasons, grasslands are a great foraging ground for naturalists.

Tallgrass prairie

The tallgrass prairie ecosystem once dominated most of the midwestern US and adjacent Canada. It is dominated by tall grasses that may grow 10 ft (3 m) tall. Big bluestem and Indian grass tower over many wildflowers, such as coneflowers and blazing star. Fire and grazing by American bison once kept trees and shrubs from taking over. Sadly, this unique habitat was mostly converted to farm and grazing lands.

INDIAN GRASS

AMERICAN BISON

Grasslands

The wide open spaces of the world's grasslands are dominated by herbaceous plants and grasses, and kept in their natural state by grazing, fire, and long spells of dry weather. Most are home to large herds of herbivores.

Shortgrass prairie

Shortgrass prairie covers about 300,000 square miles (800,000 sq km) stretching from New Mexico north to Alberta, east of the Rocky Mountains. It is home to more than 300 species of bird, of which at least two dozen are birds of national concern. The two most dominant grasses are blue grama and buffalo grass, which grow to only 10 in (25 cm) tall, in part because of the low annual rainfall.

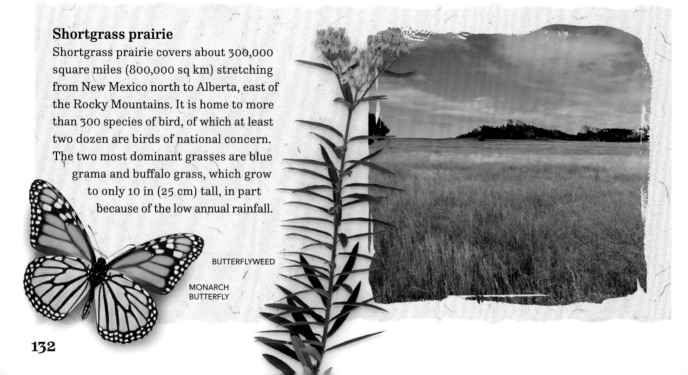

BUTTERFLYWEED

MONARCH BUTTERFLY

Eastern meadows

Meadow plants commonly grow along roadsides and in fallow farm fields where the soil is undisturbed. Meadows can also grow where the soils are too thin for trees and where succession dries former marshland. Eastern meadows are often dominated by cold-season grasses such as timothy and orchard. Native goldenrods and asters are also common.

EASTERN
MEADOWLARK

GOLDENROD

Managed fields

Grassland birds such as Bobolinks, Savannah Sparrows, and meadowlarks can thrive in habitats that are actively managed by people. Airports, hayfields, reclaimed strip mines, and landfills, as well as other agricultural lands, can provide essential habitat by replicating the conditions that grassland birds require. Care must be taken not to mow during the nesting season or use pesticides and herbicides.

AIRFIELD

UPLAND
SANDPIPER

In the grass

A variety of smaller habitats within grassland support interesting insects and invertebrates, all of which thrive among the rich diversity of plants.

Life in the wild

Insects live in all layers of the grassland, from the turf that is kept cropped by rabbits and other grazers, through the tangled jungle of grasses and herbs, up to the flowering heads of taller plants, where many beetle species can be found. Each species has its own special requirements and many live within a surprisingly small area. Some are fiercely territorial, defending their patch against intruders, while others are more nomadic, constantly on the move to find food or a mate. When exploring grassy slopes and banks, look closely for ground-foraging beetles and spiders' webs among the grass stems. Also check for snails that thrive on chalky grassland soils and don't forget to look up—the air will be full of butterflies, day-flying moths, hoverflies, and bees.

SPOTTED BEETLE

SINGING INSECTS

Male crickets and grasshoppers use their body parts to "sing." Crickets rub their wings together, while most grasshoppers chafe their hind legs against their forewings. This is known as stridulation and is the characteristic sound heard in grasslands during warm weather. Its purpose is to attract potential mates, who detect the singing via special receptors.

hind leg acts as a rasp | forewing creates noise

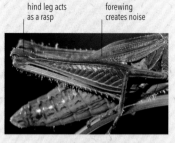

GRASSHOPPER

NIGHT LIGHT
Glow-worms can be found worldwide in grassland, and are most visible after dusk. The flightless female attracts males with a light made by a chemical reaction within her body.

SPIDER RELATIVES
Look for harvestmen as they scramble through lower vegetation. They have no silk or venom glands (unlike spiders), so use their long legs to find and trap insects.

BUTTERFLY WATCHING

Although certain butterflies will fly in overcast conditions, most only come out in the Sun. The peak time for butterfly activity is mid-morning to mid-afternoon. Choose your site carefully: a sheltered location is best, with plenty of flowering plants to attract the butterflies and warm rocks and grassy banks where they can bask in the Sun. Try to get a close look at them as they rest.

BUTTERFLY

BUTTERFLY NET

Making mountains

Ants excavate tunnels and chambers in their nests to provide safety
from predators and places to store food and raise the next generation.
Granule by granule, ants build hills by taking individual sand and
soil bits in their mouths and moving them upwards to create hills of
excavated digging debris. Some ant hills are perfect circles, others
are large mounds, but each is a monument to the hard work of ants.

Some mounds are thought to channel sunlight into the nest, to help regulate the temperature

ANT FACTORY
Ant colonies may have
thousands of members,
each with a specific
job. Most are workers,
gathering food for
the queen and other
members of the colony.

USING A QUADRAT
To get a good idea of local plant
and invertebrate diversity drop
a sampling square, known as a
quadrat, randomly on the ground.
Note the number of plant and
ground-dwelling insect species
in each square of the frame.

STRIDULATING GRASSHOPPER
Different species of crickets and
grasshoppers make distinctive sounds
that often follow the same pattern—a
series of chirps repeated about every
two seconds. Use their song to track
down the elusive insects on grass
stems and flowerheads.

Grassland close-up

Grasslands around the world provide rich habitats for plants and insects. The species vary with location, but study the ground and grasses to see what you can discover.

GULF FRITILLARY BUTTERFLY

Look around flowering plants for butterflies— you may also see their pupae hanging from leaves, twigs, or stems.

SMALL COPPER BUTTERFLY

LARGE WHITE BUTTERFLY

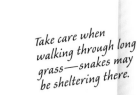

SILVER-SPOTTED SKIPPER BUTTERFLY

OX-EYE DAISY

A closer look through dense grass will reveal that it is also made up of wildflowers, which come into bloom in springtime.

Check grass stems for perching insects and invertebrates, such as grasshoppers.

TIGER BEETLE

Take care when walking through long grass—snakes may be sheltering there.

HARVESTMAN

TERMITE

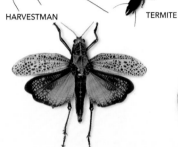

LARGE-HEADED GRASSHOPPER

PRAIRIE RATTLESNAKE

YELLOW CHAMOMILE

SAW WORT

BURDOCK SEED HEAD

COMMON SNEEZEWEED

TUFTED HAIR GRASS

YELLOW BEDSTRAW

MUSK THISTLE

BIG BLUESTEM

COUCH GRASS

WESTERN PRAIRIE FRINGED ORCHID

Life on the plains

With extreme weather and little in the way of shelter, wildlife living on the plains needs to be tough and resilient. Animals here spend most of their lives out in the open.

The great herds

The grassy plains of North America have historically been home to herds of plant-eating animals such as pronghorns and bison, which constantly move about in search of fresh pasture and water. Young calves must be able to run within minutes of birth so they can keep up with the others and avoid the predators that follow the herd, hoping to pick off the weak. In the past, the herds contained many millions of animals. While you can still see impressive gatherings of certain species, their numbers and the area they roam are greatly reduced.

GRASSLAND CONSERVATION

The flat, open nature of grassland makes it vulnerable to conversion for agricultural land. Crop farming and livestock ranches squeeze out wildlife, which comes under further pressure from urbanization and activities such as recreation and mining. Many grassland species are now endangered, so protecting the remaining undamaged habitats is vital.

PRAIRIE FARMING
Less than one percent of native prairie remains, largely due to commercial agriculture.

LOSING GROUND
Landfowl such as prairie-chickens struggle to survive where grassland is farmed.

ON THE MOVE
Farming and excessive hunting ended the grand migration of American bison. Today, small herds in a few parks are a reminder of this once mighty migration that shaped habitats through grazing.

LIVING SIDE BY SIDE
Pronghorns often wander the North American prairie in the company of bison—similar to the way in which African gazelles graze alongside wildebeest.

Refined predators

A healthy grassland ecosystem can support enough prey for predators to occupy specific niches. Different species have evolved in ways that help ensure that they are not often in direct competition. On the American Great Plains, for example, coyotes hunt small mammals from the ground, relying on their keen sense of smell and night vision combined with their stealth and pack hunting behavior. In contrast, Golden Eagles hunt alone and from above, using their keen sight to spot even small prey such as prairie-chickens and ground squirrels.

STALKING WOLVES
Wolves can hunt much larger animals, such as elk, when they hunt in packs. In this way, they share the risks and rewards of hunting meals for their family.

PRAIRIE FALCON
Prairie Falcons are fast-flying predators that hunt prairie dogs and ground squirrels by flying low across flat prairies.

BURROWING DOWN

Highly social prairie dogs are herbivorous rodents that live in colonies in the central and western US. They dig a system of underground chambers, tunnels, and escape routes, lining the chambers with grass to help insulate them. In deep soils their burrows can reach depths of more than 13 ft (4 m). The small humps outside burrow entrances—spoil heaps from the prairie dogs' excavations—provide elevation points from which the rodents can keep guard. Each colony is usually home to a mature male and his harem of up to four females.

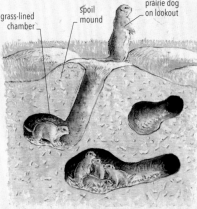

grass-lined chamber

spoil mound

prairie dog on lookout

STATE OF ALERT
Prairie dogs are native to North America and can often be spotted on lookouts outside their burrows. Their once vast territories have been hugely reduced, mostly due to prairie farming.

Mountain and hillside

Those of us with a hunger for wilderness gravitate to these environments because their slopes often have restricted cultivation, so they seem less "bruised" by the hand of people. But our perception of what appears natural is often skewed by idealized landscapes. If we really want to explore these habitats, let us revel in an exploration of the ecologies and behaviors of the unique assemblage of specialized plants and animals that live in these precipitous places: species for which the edge—and sometimes the void beyond—is a comfortable home.

Alpine tundra

This bleak, windswept habitat is covered in snow for much of the year and has a similar climate to the Arctic tundra. The plants that thrive here, such as purple saxifrage, grow close to the ground in thick mats and have small leaves to reduce water loss. Alpine tundra has few predators, making it a haven for animals that can endure the conditions, such as the ptarmigan with its thick, downy plumage. Ptarmigans grow white feathers in winter and brown in summer to camouflage themselves.

PURPLE SAXIFRAGE

PTARMIGAN

Mountains

The world's highest places present formidable challenges, with scorching days, fiercely cold nights, and some of the most extreme weather on Earth. Mountain plants and animals need to be superbly adapted to survive.

Rocky pinnacles

Even the bare rock of mountain pinnacles can support life. Freezing and thawing creates cracks in rocks, where you can find plants like mountain lupine growing. Mountain lions are well adapted to life in their namesake habitat, as these sure-footed big cats range the American mountains from Alaska south to the southern Andes. These adaptable cats can eat animals as large as bears and as small as mice.

MOUNTAIN LUPINE

MOUNTAIN LION

Forested peaks

Temperate deciduous forest dominates most mountains at lower levels, and it is replaced by coniferous forest higher up. Conifers are better adapted for the colder, windier, dryer habitats higher on the mountains as they shed snow with their springy branches and retain moisture in thick needles. Their evergreen needles can photosynthesize almost throughout the year. Squirrels such as Abert's squirrel are well adapted for life in the trees, as are birds that depend on conifer cones, such as crossbills.

SPOTTED CORALROOT

ABERT'S SQUIRREL

Volcano

If you visit an extinct or dormant volcano you will notice that the rich soils surrounding it host abundant life, but some specialists can live in areas with an active volcano. Forests and other plant communities colonize the lower flanks of volcanoes during inactive periods, providing habitat for many animals. Northern alligator lizards live in these volcano forests, venturing out onto sunny outcrops where they forage for insects. Likewise, Calliope Hummingbirds nest in open shrub habitats as high as the tree line at 11,000 ft (3,400 m).

CALLIOPE HUMMINGBIRD

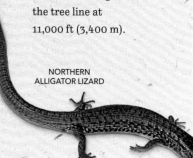

NORTHERN ALLIGATOR LIZARD

143

Living with your head in the clouds

Mountainous areas are home to a range of diverse habitats, with very specialized plants and animals exploiting every niche.

Mountain zones

Because of their vast range of elevations and temperatures, mountains have numerous microclimates, home to very different plant species. At the base of the mountain, a deciduous woodland gives way to a line of conifers, which thrive in the cold. Above this treeline, the alpine tundra, which receives intense sunlight and wind, is home to small-leaved, low-growing plants. In some sheltered areas of tundra, wildflowers take root, forming alpine meadows. The tundra finally merges into the scree and rock of the higher slopes, where only lichens grow.

TREE LINE
Strong winds, shallow soil, and dry conditions restrict trees to lower elevations, creating a distinct "tree line".

CAPTURING MOISTURE
Rock surfaces are difficult places to capture water, especially at high elevations where there is little rainfall and where water is locked in ice and snow much of the year. Rock tripe (a lichen), solves this problem by holding water that condenses on its leathery leaves. Like other lichens, it is a mutualistic association of a fungus and green alga. The fungus provides a structure for the alga, which produces food through photosynthesis. When rock tripe becomes saturated, it may change from crusty brown to plump green. It is sometimes used as a famine food when all else is unavailable.

Life on high

HIGH FLYERS
Bumblebees are becoming more generalist feeders as high-elevation flowers are impacted by climate change.

MARMOTS
Large rodents of the squirrel family, marmots hibernate through the winter in large burrow systems. They have a loud, piercing whistle.

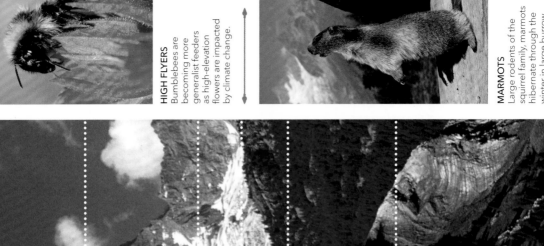

SUMMIT/NIVAL

GLACIER

ICE FALL

ALPINE

ALPINE MEADOW

SUBALPINE

MOUNTAIN CAPRIDS
Nimble and sure-footed, caprids such as Dall sheep live on steep slopes and rugged ground, where they can outrun predators.

MOUNTAIN BUTTERFLIES
Only seen briefly in the summer, the coronis fritillary lays its eggs near violets; caterpillars overwinter without eating, then feast on fresh leaves in spring.

MOUNTAIN TOADS
Yosemite toads spend most of their year underground. They emerge as soon as snow melts in the spring and see the light of day for just 4 months each year.

Life at high altitude

Life above 9,800 ft (3,000 m) has the added challenge of a lack of oxygen. Mountain animals like the pika and some migrating birds, such as bar-headed geese, have various adaptations to get around this problem. They have more efficient hemoglobin in their blood, and special sacs that direct air back through the lungs before it is exhaled, to extract as much oxygen as possible. These adaptations allow mountain animals to live normal lives in as little as one third of the oxygen found at sea level.

LIVING THE HIGH LIFE
The pika has a thin pulmonary artery wall, to allow more efficient uptake of oxygen into the blood.

GETTING AROUND THE MOUNTAIN ZONES

The most important thing to remember about exploring the mountains is to be prepared. The weather is not only more severe, but it can change very suddenly and catch you unaware. Always tell someone where you are going and when you will be back, take a map and compass, and keep abreast of weather forecasts. It is also important to know your limits: set a time by which you need to turn back in order to make it back down safely before dark. Unless you are an experienced mountain climber, it is not advisable to attempt hiking in steep or rocky terrain outside of marked paths.

HAVE FUN UP HIGH
Hiking or mountain biking are great ways to get around the mountains, but always remember to stick to designated paths.

Mountain plants

Mountain winters are long and severe; the short summer months bring an explosion of color as plants rush to grow and flower while they can.

Life above the treeline
The small alpine plants that grow above the treeline have adapted to low temperatures and humidity, frost and ice, increased winds, and a short growing season. Where there is enough soil, tussock grasses, shrubs, and low trees dominate—larger plants with bigger leaves cannot tolerate the desiccation caused by the high winds. Some plants in this zone have tough, hairy leaves; this reduces moisture loss and minimizes the effects of frost and ice. Others have special red pigments that can convert the Sun's light into heat.

MOUNTAIN LAUREL
This shrub grows on rocky mountain slopes. The leaves are retained from year to year and are quite toxic, which prevents them from being eaten by passing animals.

RHODODENDRON
Despite their huge success as garden plants around the globe, the rhododendron is an alpine plant with most species originating in the Himalayas. Rhododendron flowers attract scarce mountain pollinators with a spectacular array of colors—white, yellow, pink, scarlet, purple, and blue. In cold conditions, the leaves of certain species roll in on themselves creating a cigar shape. As it gets colder they roll even tighter, protecting themselves, and reducing water loss.

Mountain meadows
Look around you in the mountains and you will see that habitats often occur in a patchwork. This is due to prevailing winds, exposure to the Sun, hillside location, soil consistency, and underlying rock type, all factors that affect plant growth. Alpine meadows grow in the most favorable habitats, where sediments from weathering rocks create soils capable of sustaining grasses and wildflowers. Most of them store up energy to last them through the harsh winters and flower briefly. Many are dwarfed and stunted by their environment.

RECURRING BLOOMS
Some meadow flowers, such as the Indian paint brush, are perennials, meaning that a new plant grows from the existing root every year.

RED
HELLEBORINE

LESSER
BUTTERFLY
ORCHID

Keeping a low profile
Maintaining a low profile is a common strategy for plants above the tree line. If you kneel down for a closer look you will see that many of them grow in a creeping fashion, creating thick cushions or mats that are woven tightly together to provide a trap for precious soil blown around by the wind. By hugging the ground they are less exposed to the elements and they also provide shelter for insects and small animals. In turn, the insects help pollinate their protectors.

SHADY BLOOM
A classic alpine flower, the rock jasmine flourishes in the cold, in partial shade, and in rock crevices.

LOW-GROWING PLANTS
Each plant species requires its own special growing conditions. At this elevation, wind limits the growth of nearly all woody plants, favoring low-growing perennials.

Scaling the heights

Mountain mammals inhabit a precarious environment. However, they are protected by its remoteness.

Survival in the mountains requires athletic sure-footedness and an ability to survive in one of the most extreme habitats in the world. In return, the environment offers protection, a potential lack of competition, and even an escape from parasites and biting insects. For example, Dall sheep migrate to higher altitudes in the summer months to escape black flies. Mammals that rely on the mountains are highly adapted and therefore particularly at risk from the effects of climate change. As temperatures increase, they are forced higher and higher up the slopes and may eventually have nowhere left to go. The best way to see mountain mammals is with a good pair of binoculars. Find a safe, comfortable spot with a good view and slowly scan the mountainside. Look for any sudden movement; you may spot a bighorn sheep or mountain goat balanced on a knife-edged ridge.

GOLDEN EAGLE

Golden Eagles are at home in mountains throughout the northern hemisphere. They catch prey as large as baby mountain goats, but usually eat smaller mammals such as coyotes, foxes, marmots, and ground squirrels. They can spot prey the size of a marmot while soaring over their mountain domain with wingspans up to 7.5 ft (2.2 m).

Golden Eagles have such keen eyesight that they can spot prey from a mile away.

SURE-FOOTED SHIFTERS
Rocky Mountain goats have hooves with sharp rims for lodging in small footholds. Two rubbery pads on the base of the cloven hoof provide improved traction.

Mountain close-up

Mountain wildlife varies geographically, but you'll also notice a change in plants and animals as you move from one mountain zone to the next.

COULTER PINE NEEDLES

A line of conifers marks the highest point at which trees can grow.

AMERICAN LADY BUTTERFLY

Mountain butterflies migrate to higher elevations daily, returning to the lower slopes at night.

COLORADO HAIRSTREAK BUTTERFLY

COULTER PINE CONE

PINE CONE AND SEEDS

SLATE

ORNATE CHECKERED BEETLE

Mountain insects and spiders seek shelter among low-growing plants.

LICHEN

Rocks and fossils provide a glimpse into long-ago changes in Earth's geology.

SCAPHITID AMMONITE

COMMON WASP

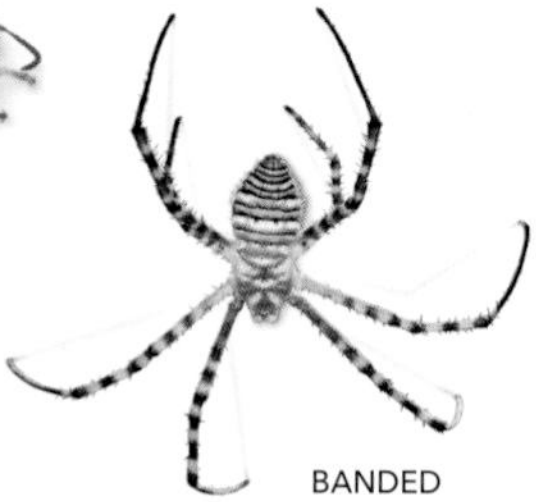

BANDED GARDEN SPIDER

WHITE GRANITE

RED GRANITE

GRANITE WITH LARGE CRYSTALS OF QUARTZ, MICA, AND FELDSPAR

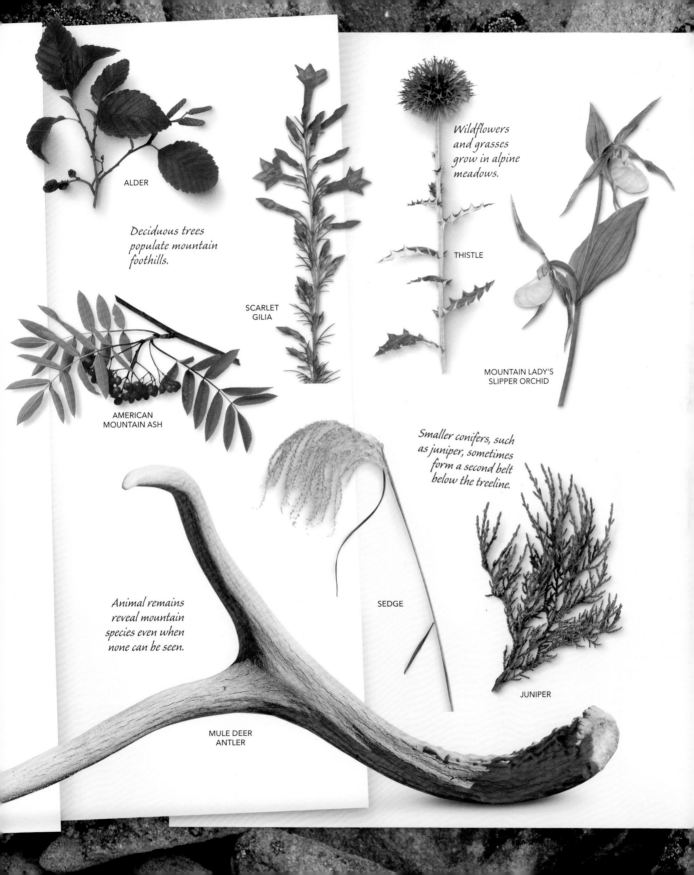

ALDER

Deciduous trees populate mountain foothills.

SCARLET GILIA

Wildflowers and grasses grow in alpine meadows.

THISTLE

MOUNTAIN LADY'S SLIPPER ORCHID

AMERICAN MOUNTAIN ASH

Smaller conifers, such as juniper, sometimes form a second belt below the treeline.

Animal remains reveal mountain species even when none can be seen.

SEDGE

JUNIPER

MULE DEER ANTLER

INDIANA
BAT

Life in the underworld

Caves are particularly prevalent in limestone mountains, formed by chemical action and erosion. The conditions inside are usually fairly constant, and they provide shelter for a multitude of unusual creatures.

Cave dwellers

Animals that live within caves fall into three categories. Troglobites live their whole lives in caves and never come out. Troglophiles, such as the cave salamander, favor caves, but may also live elsewhere. Trogloxenes use caves for shelter or for certain parts of their life cycle, but also venture out into the light. Classic trogloxenes include many bat species that roost and hibernate in caves.

CAVE VISITORS
Some animals end up in caves by accident, perhaps swept in by flash floods. Frogs have been found deep underground, apparently thriving!

STALACTITES AND STALAGMITES

Look around a cave and you might notice what look like stone "icicles." These are formed by acidic water, carrying dissolved limestone, dripping through the roof of the cave. Some of the dissolved minerals are left behind and eventually form stalactites, which hang from the roof of the cave, and stalagmites, which grow up from the floor where the drips land. This process may take tens of thousands of years, and the two may eventually connect as a column.

ANCIENT STALACTITES AND STALAGMITES

SPIDERS
Some cave-dwelling spiders are thought to be photophobic—averse to light.

MOTHS
While many moths overwinter as pupae, some, such as the herald (pictured) and tissue moths, hibernate as adults in caves.

CAVE ARTHROPODS
Arachnids such as this pseudoscorpion do well in cave environments. Unlike true scorpions, they do not have a tail with a stinger.

EXPLORING CAVES

Caving (spelunking) is one of the most exciting realms of nature exploration. Often a tiny entrance will lead to vast rooms. However, caves can be very dangerous places—it is easy to lose your footing on loose or uneven rock, and heavy rain can lead to flash floods. Make sure you're fully prepared, and check weather conditions before embarking on a caving expedition. If you are new to caving, only attempt it with an experienced guide.

Creatures of the deep

The world's deepest, darkest places are inhabited by some of the strangest-looking animals on the planet. These creatures have adapted to live in the darkness and have evolved to suit their surroundings with useless eyes, extended tactile limbs, antenna for feeling their way around, and an increased sensitivity to air pressure and temperature. Because food and oxygen can be scarce underground, troglobites often have low metabolisms and long lifespans. Some cave crayfish can live to be over 100 years old.

CAVE CRAYFISH

WINDOW TO THE WORLD
While much of the underground world is barren, cave entrances are a veritable haven for life—sheltered and safe, but with easy access to the outside world.

PLANTS

The cave systems themselves are too dark to support plant life, but cave entrances are often alive with shade-loving plants, known as sciophytes. Sheltered from the wind, they thrive in the moist conditions.

JEWELWEED

HERB ROBERT

WOOD SORREL

Lake, river, and stream

There is an almost incomprehensible range of scale in these habitats. Some lakes are sea-sized, and some massive rivers invisibly merge with oceans, yet they also vary throughout their latitude and altitude, as well as in response to the environment beyond their banks. No matter what the location, however, the thirst for a freshwater lifestyle has led to a wonderful richness of species—and for many of us, the humble garden pond forms a perfect doorway to the discovery of this abundance. Lie on your belly beside a stream and you can peer into the process of metamorphosis, marvel at a web of life linking predators, prey, and plants, and simply enjoy a range of species very alien from yourself.

Upland streams

These turbulent, rocky waterways flow quickly in some places, but most have quieter stretches as well. Waterfalls and runs are interspersed with pools, which are home to stonefly and caddisfly larvae, as well as small fish. Birdlife includes Spotted Sandpipers and diving specialists, such as dippers. Few plants may grow in the fast water itself, but ferns and mosses cling to stream banks. Pickerel weed and arrowhead may grow in the slower moving water.

AMERICAN DIPPER

Lakes, rivers, and streams

Freshwater habitats are some of the richest in terms of wildlife. The animals and plants that live in them vary, not only according to geography, but also to water chemistry and the speed of water flow.

Lowland rivers

Lowland rivers flow more gently than upland streams, and host a greater range of species. Plant life often grows thickly in the water and on the banks. Mayflies can be seen swarming around the water and laying their eggs on its surface. Mammals, such as beavers, build dams made of small tree trunks, branches, and mud. They then build their lodges and raise their kits in water made still by these dams.

MAYFLY

NORTH AMERICAN BEAVER

Ponds

Ponds are usually abundant with nutrients, such as nitrogen and phosphorous, and often full of plant life. Many ponds are cut off from streams or rivers, and the animals that live in them are often either seasonal visitors or are introduced. Most insects, including some species of water striders, have wings.

CANADIAN PONDWEED

WATER STRIDER

Lakes

Lowland lakes have abundant nutrients that have washed downstream and accumulate in bottom sediments. These lakes support many animals, including Mallards, dragonflies, and bottom-feeding fish, such as catfish, that use their whiskerlike barbels to smell and feel for food in the murky lake bottom. Upland lakes contain fewer nutrients and fewer species of fish. However, diving birds such as loons and mergansers make these lakes their home.

MALLARD

DRAGONFLY

Swamps, bogs, and fens

These waterlogged habitats are found in both upland and lowland areas. A swamp is a wetland with continuous water cover and the ability to support woody plants and trees. Bogs have acidic, peaty soil, while fens are neutral or alkaline and support more plant life than bogs. Such vegetation includes mosses, sedges, and reeds. Wildlife inhabitants range from frogs, snakes, and waterbirds to animals as large as alligators in the swamps of North America.

PURPLE GALLINULE

AMERICAN ALLIGATOR

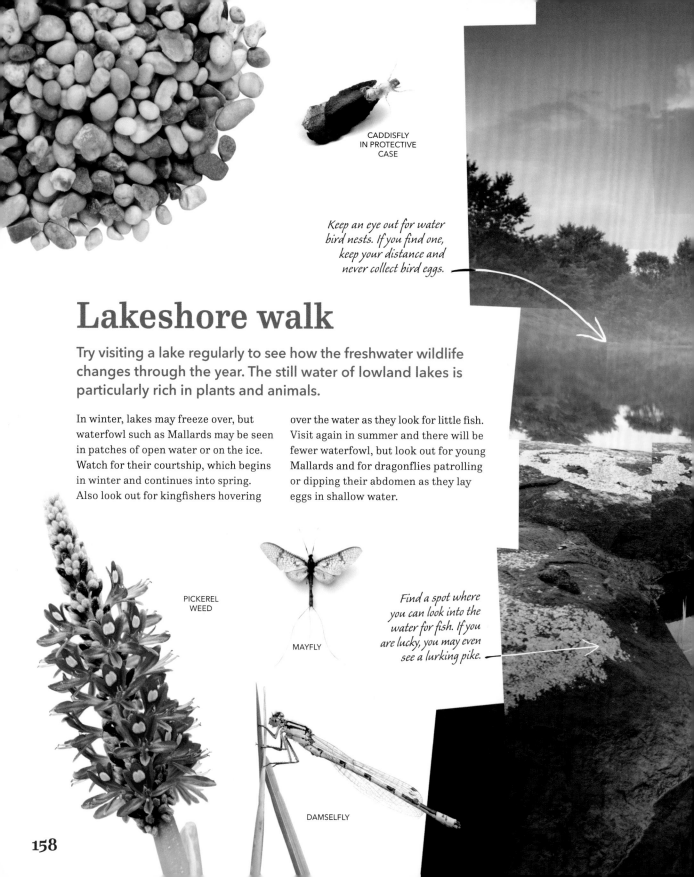

CADDISFLY
IN PROTECTIVE
CASE

Keep an eye out for water bird nests. If you find one, keep your distance and never collect bird eggs.

Lakeshore walk

Try visiting a lake regularly to see how the freshwater wildlife changes through the year. The still water of lowland lakes is particularly rich in plants and animals.

In winter, lakes may freeze over, but waterfowl such as Mallards may be seen in patches of open water or on the ice. Watch for their courtship, which begins in winter and continues into spring. Also look out for kingfishers hovering over the water as they look for little fish. Visit again in summer and there will be fewer waterfowl, but look out for young Mallards and for dragonflies patrolling or dipping their abdomen as they lay eggs in shallow water.

PICKEREL
WEED

MAYFLY

Find a spot where you can look into the water for fish. If you are lucky, you may even see a lurking pike.

DAMSELFLY

EASTERN
PONDHAWK

Check the surface
for damselflies and
dragonflies laying
eggs. Mating
damselflies may be
seen on waterside and
emergent vegetation.

Take a closer look at
aquatic plants and
you might see a
dragonfly perched
on a stem or leaf.

159

Life of a river

From small feeder streams to vast coastal estuaries, rivers carve the landscapes through which they flow.

Stream to river

Many rivers are born in higher areas of land, or uplands. Rainwater, melting snow, and water oozing out of bogs trickles into streams. As they flow downhill, these streams meet other streams and a river is formed. Farther downstream, a river may join other rivers. Some rivers begin in the lowlands; their water comes from natural springs that rise from subterranean water tables. Most rivers make their way to the sea, or into a lake, changing their character—and the animals and plants that depend on them—along the way.

Upland streams and rivers

Nutrients, such as phosphorus and nitrogen, are harder to come by in these bubbling, rocky waters than in the lowlands, so you will see fewer plants and animals here. But keep your eyes open for dippers—these short-tailed birds "dip" under the water, searching for food.

SPOTTED SANDPIPER
Spotted Sandpipers often nest along the shore of streams and rivers, where they build a simple nest to cradle their four speckled eggs. They eat tiny invertebrates.

Middle reaches

Here, notice the calmer water, intermittent rocky stretches, and a greater variety of plant and animal species. Try to see diving ducks, such as the merganser—a duck with serrated bill edges that help it grip slippery fish. On sandy, muddy, or gravely sections, look for the white flowers of common water-crowfoot, an aquatic perennial, floating on the water's surface.

BOTTOM-DWELLER
A sleek, silvery fish with a large, sail-like dorsal fin and colorful body markings, the Arctic grayling searches Alaskan riverbeds for larvae and other food.

BRINGER OF LIFE
In an otherwise arid habitat, rivers make all the difference for many plants and birds that are limited to river stream banks.

FLYING JEWELS
Damselflies often occur along the edges of streams and rivers where they hunt smaller flying insects.

FISH-WATCHING

Fishermen often wear polarizing glasses to make it easier to see fish in the water. Try wearing a pair to help you see what's living in your local rivers. Similarly, polarizing filters for camera lenses will help you better record what you see.

POLARIZING LENS

Lowland rivers

Nutrient-rich lowland rivers typically support more species than upland rivers, and these are the rivers most of us know best. The type of species that live in and around them is influenced by chemistry—more alkaline waters can be especially rich. Pollution from farming or sewage plants can reduce the diversity and number of species a river supports.

COTTONMOUTH
Also known as water moccasin, this poisonous snake lives near permanent swamps and lakes of the southeastern US, where it eats mostly fish, small mammals, and amphibians.

PATIENT HUNTER
You will often see long-legged birds, such as this Great Blue Heron, waiting or slowly wading, while looking for fish to eat.

Estuaries

Large rivers flow into the sea at estuaries. At low tide, mudflats are loaded with tiny snails, crustaceans, and other invertebrates that provide rich pickings for shorebirds (see pp.204–205). Estuaries are not always easy to explore; it's best to watch from the edges.

EXPERT FISH-CATCHER
Double-crested Cormorants are skilled fishers on estuaries and elsewhere. You can often spot them spreading their wings to dry off after a dive.

LIFE CYCLE OF A SALMON

Atlantic salmon lay their eggs in gravel on stream bottoms and riverbeds. The fish that emerge stay in fresh water for several years. Then they head downstream to the North Atlantic, where they remain for several more years. To spawn, they leave the sea and head back upriver. Most return to their birth stream, using their sense of smell to help them find their way. Salmon usually spawn just once in their lifetime, but a minority repeat their journey, spawning up to four times.

INCREDIBLE JOURNEY
On their way to spawn, salmon jump over weirs and waterfalls, sometimes clearing heights of over 9¾ ft (3 m).

Riverbank

For the best riverbank experience, try a quiet walk, or just sit and watch—preferably when there aren't any other people around.

Wet and woody

The saturated soil of a riverbank supports an abundance of plant life, which in turn provides hidden, protected areas for insects and invertebrates to reproduce. Mammals, such as otters, also make the riverside their home, living in

WILLOW
There are many willow species, and some trees are hybrids. Telling them apart isn't easy.

well-hidden underground "holts" within the dense vegetation. Willow and alder trees can be seen along riverbanks. Alders are the only broadleaved trees with cones, and their seeds provide food for many birds. Weeping willows, with their drooping branches, are easy to spot in any season. The leaves of many native willows are eaten by caterpillars, which are important foods for song birds.

ALDER
Long male catkins (flower clusters) hang from alders in winter, while shorter cone-shaped female catkins can be seen in spring.

Riverbank-dwellers

Rivers mean fish, so predatory mammals thrive here. These mammals all have various adaptations for life at the riverside, such as webbed feet and whiskers to help them navigate through murky waters. You may see an elusive beaver. It's unusual to see a beaver because they are most active at dawn and dusk, but evidence of beaver activity is hard to miss. Look for beaver lodges in ponds and gnawed trees.

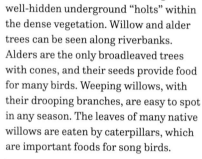

SKILLED BUILDER
Beavers are expert tree-fellers: just one family can cut down several hundred trees in a single winter for dams, lodges, and food.

Riverside fishers

Fish-eating birds have two main methods of hunting—stalking and diving. Herons stand patiently, or stalk, when hunting. Fish are their main prey, but they will also eat amphibians, reptiles, and insects. Kingfishers perch, watch, then dive in to grab a small fish.

QUIET HUNTER
Heron species vary in size, but all use the "stalk-and-stab" or "stalk-and-grab" approach when feeding.

fish swallowed head-first

ragged crest

RAPID DIVERS
You may spot birds, such as this Belted Kingfisher, hovering over the water. It dives at full speed to catch a fish, then bangs it on a branch before swallowing.

1 ADULT BREAKS FREE
The nymph hauls itself out of the water and the new adult damselfly breaks out of its final larval exoskeleton.

2 FLUID ENTERS WINGS
Contractions pump body fluid into the new adult's wings, to give them their full form.

3 MATURE ADULT
A damselfly may take more than a week and a half to become fully mature and ready to mate.

LIFE OF A DAMSELFLY

Damselflies and dragonflies spend most of their lives under water. Eggs are laid by adults and develop into fiercely predatory aquatic larvae, or nymphs. To grow, these larvae must shed their skin; they may do this more than 10 times before emerging as adults. Some spend 5 years under water. Adults may live less than 2 weeks, but some survive for 2 months.

EASTERN NEWT
The red eft is the land stage of the eastern (red-spotted) newt. Efts change to a green-backed stage with a paddle-shaped tail when they return to water as adults.

NIGHT-HERON
This Black-crowned Night-Heron is the world's most common heron species. It feeds mainly between dusk and dawn on a varied diet, ranging from fish and reptiles to bats and small birds.

WEBBED PREDATOR
All freshwater otters eat fish as their main food, but some will prey on birds, small mammals, or frogs. The webbing between their toes helps make them superb swimmers.

AMERICAN WATER SHREW
At 6 in (15 cm) in length, the water shrew is the largest long-tailed shrew in North America. It lives in mountain streams, where it dives under water in pursuit of small fish and invertebrates.

Water birds

Swans, geese, ducks, and grebes are just some of the fascinating birds you may see on larger areas of open freshwater.

Waterfowl and other birds

Wetlands attract all types of birds; many come to feed, others to nest and raise their young within the dense vegetation. Some of the most common birds are known as "waterfowl," a group that includes swans, geese, and ducks. However, this is not the only group of birds to live in this habitat; others include storks and herons. Diversity is the name of the game here—some species build floating nests, others nest in tree holes. Some eat fish, while others feed on invertebrates or plants.

TAKING OFF
Some water birds, such as this Trumpeter Swan, need plenty of space for takeoff. Watch them run over the water's surface to help attain the required momentum for flight.

long, slender neck

AGGRESSIVE SHOW
Birds like the Mute Swans make threat displays, including wing flapping and "busking"—a behavior in which a swimming and standing bird pulls back its neck and lifts its wings.

UPENDING
Many water bird species have long necks to allow them to reach underwater plants far below the surface, especially when they upend, a behavior known as dabbling.

SWAN FOOD
Some waterfowl also feed by skimming the surface of shallow water and sieving food and water through filters in their bills.

SNOW GOOSE
Snow Geese in North America come in two color forms, or "morphs"—this one is white, but the "blue" snow goose is mostly blue-gray.

BRANT
Brant are stocky sea-geese with long migrations from the Arctic to east and west coasts of North America, where they eat algae, snails, and mussels.

Geese

Geese may have webbed feet like ducks and swans, but they are adapted to eat plants on land. Their bills suit their tough vegetarian diet, and they walk well because their legs are centrally located underneath their bodies. Like swans, male and female birds look alike. Usually they mate for life, breed in the far north, migrate in family units, and winter further south. In some areas, however, Canada Geese can be seen all year round. You will often see geese flying in the "V" formation, which is also characteristic of ducks, a behavior that helps the flock save energy during migration by benefiting from lift from the birds in front of the line.

WHITE-FRONTED GOOSE
The Greater White-fronted Goose breeds in Alaska and northern Canada and then migrates to southern US and Mexico. Many feed on agricultural crops such as rice, soybeans, and grains in winter.

white patch at base of bill

orange legs and feet

Ducks

Ducks can be divided into divers and dabblers. The Mallard is a dabbler, mergansers and scaup are divers. Diving ducks propel themselves underwater to feed. To help them swim, their legs are positioned towards the rear, which makes walking awkward. You are less likely to see divers on shallow water than dabblers, which typically skim for food at the surface of shallow waters, or a little lower when they upend. Dabblers' legs are positioned further forward, so walking is easier. Male ducks in breeding plumage are easier to identify and distinguish from females. However, when males molt their flight feathers, they grow a more cryptic "eclipse" plumage and may look similar to the females.

reddish-orange hooked bill

COMMON MERGANSER
These fish-eating diving ducks frequent rivers and lakes, where they nest in tree cavities. Their bills have unique, toothlike points that help them hold fish.

WOOD DUCK
This North American bird nests in tree holes. The drabber, mainly brown female looks very different from the showy male with its patterned head, shiny green crest, and multicolored plumage.

RAISING YOUNG
As is typical among dabbling ducks, this female Mallard has sole responsibility for looking after her ducklings. The male probably departed when she was brooding her eggs.

Grebes

Grebes are striking birds. Males often resemble females, although some species are sexually dimorphic—the males and females look very different when they are not in breeding plumage. A grebe's feet are set at the back end of its body, making them superb divers but vulnerable on land. They have lobed toes rather than webbed feet. Floating nests are common, and adults transport their chicks on their backs. It is unusual to see a grebe fly, although most can.

chick rides on its parent's back

WESTERN GREBE
This North American water bird has a strong, sharp bill that it thrusts forward to stab prey.

COURTSHIP DISPLAY
The courtship of the Western Grebe starts with the "rushing ceremony," in which the pair perform a stylized dance. Ceremonies such as this help to synchronize the bird's behaviors before nesting.

WETLANDS FOR BIRDS

Access to good quality freshwater is vital for birds that are wintering, breeding, and migrating. Audubon is aiming for a 20 percent increase in the area of wetlands that are protected or managed for birds and other wildlife in the US. In the Florida Everglades, it aims to reestablish colonies of wading birds, including American Flamingos that have been displaced. Other key areas include the Great Lakes, the Delaware River watershed, the Great Salt Lake, Salton Sea, the Colorado River Basin, and the Mississippi River Delta.

On the surface

Look carefully at the water in freshwater habitats; the surface can be alive with a variety of creatures.

Animal adaptations

The water surface is an unusual and fascinating microhabitat that is inhabited by a variety of specially adapted animals. Water striders live up to their name by walking quickly across the surface film; their long legs distribute their weight over the water. They feed on animals that have fallen in and become trapped. Water snails also move across the surface film, but they cling to it from beneath the water. Water boatmen and beetles use the water surface as a temporary filling station, taking on air before and after diving into the water.

SURFACE INHABITANTS
Some animals, such as this backswimmer, have special adaptations like long legs and sensitive water-repelling hairs to help them move on water.

SEMIAQUATIC SPIDER
The European raft spider has water-resistant hairs on its legs to enable it to detect vibrations and run over the water surface after its prey.

TRANSPARENT FLEA
There are many water flea species; all are crustaceans. Some use their branched antenna as oars to swim around under the water surface, filtering microscopic food particles out of the water.

SENSITIVE HAIRS
Water-repelling (hydrophobic) hairs prevent water striders from getting wet and sinking, making walking on water seem effortless. These insects are common and easy to spot—look carefully for the tiny depressions their feet make on the water surface.

TESTING SURFACE TENSION

The water surface is like a very thin, transparent film that is strong enough to support a small amount of weight before it gives way—this is called surface tension. Soap bubbles clearly show the surface layer of a liquid. You can test surface tension with a simple experiment. Put some water in a bowl, take a small sewing needle, and try to float it on the surface. If you are having problems, try floating a small piece of tissue on the water and putting the needle on top of it—it might be easier if a small part of the needle projects over the edge of the tissue. Push the tissue down and away from the needle and, with practice, the needle should float, supported by surface tension. Animals such as water striders and fishing spiders are very light and their long legs allow them to use surface tension to walk on water.

back legs used to change direction

middle legs provide thrust

front legs used for seizing prey

Surface predators

Insects that don't normally live on water, such as flies, can become caught on the surface if they fall in. This is good news for water striders, whirligig beetles, water crickets, and fishing spiders that all hunt for food at the surface level and can move rapidly across the water to catch their prey. Backswimmers also hunt at the water surface, but attack their prey from beneath the water.

NASTY BITE
Backswimmers should not be handled—they can bite. These predators sense vibrations on the water's surface and attack fish and tadpoles with their stabbing "beak."

OPPORTUNIST
Water measurers catch mosquito larvae that live beneath the water; they also eat insects that are trapped on the surface.

PREDATORY FLY
Some long-legged flies (family Dolichopodidae) are brightly colored; they live on the surface film and feed on small insects.

SPEED SKATING
Whirligig beetles whizz in circles on water. Their eyes are divided to see predators and prey both above and below the water surface.

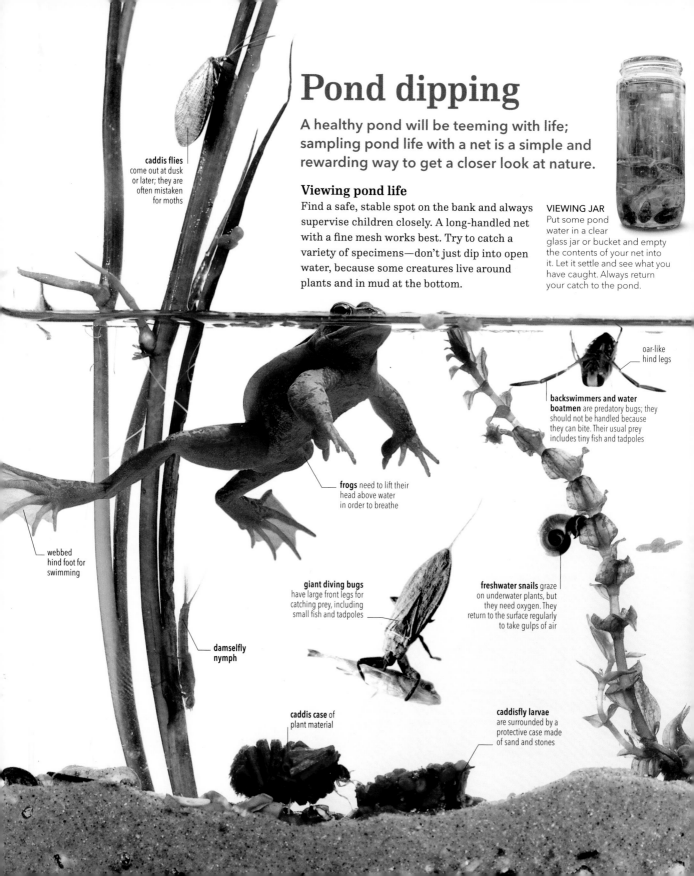

Pond dipping

A healthy pond will be teeming with life; sampling pond life with a net is a simple and rewarding way to get a closer look at nature.

Viewing pond life

Find a safe, stable spot on the bank and always supervise children closely. A long-handled net with a fine mesh works best. Try to catch a variety of specimens—don't just dip into open water, because some creatures live around plants and in mud at the bottom.

VIEWING JAR
Put some pond water in a clear glass jar or bucket and empty the contents of your net into it. Let it settle and see what you have caught. Always return your catch to the pond.

caddis flies come out at dusk or later; they are often mistaken for moths

oar-like hind legs

backswimmers and water boatmen are predatory bugs; they should not be handled because they can bite. Their usual prey includes tiny fish and tadpoles

frogs need to lift their head above water in order to breathe

webbed hind foot for swimming

damselfly nymph

giant diving bugs have large front legs for catching prey, including small fish and tadpoles

freshwater snails graze on underwater plants, but they need oxygen. They return to the surface regularly to take gulps of air

caddis case of plant material

caddisfly larvae are surrounded by a protective case made of sand and stones

A COURTSHIP DANCE
Red-spotted newts live in North American wetlands and ponds. During the breeding season the female is lured in by the male's spots and fanning movements.

Breeding season

If you visit a pond during the April and May breeding season and shine your flashlight into the shallow water at night, you might be lucky enough to see courting newts. These newts return to the water to breed each spring but do not spend their whole lives in a pond. You may be able to pick out a courting male, as he is typically more colorful than the female. He uses his tail to waft pheromones (chemical signals) through the water to the female and then drops a spermatophore (sperm packet) nearby to fertilize her eggs.

Tadpole development

The transformation from frog eggs to froglets is fascinating to watch and is an activity you can encourage. The shallow, unpolluted water of a garden pond is ideal for raising tadpoles. Keep the pond well vegetated to provide them with food and places to hide.

1 TADPOLE JUST HATCHED
Tadpoles emerge from their eggs after 30–40 days. They begin by eating the surrounding spawn, then feed on algae. You can provide them with chopped lettuce in ice cubes.

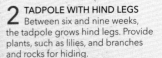

2 TADPOLE WITH HIND LEGS
Between six and nine weeks, the tadpole grows hind legs. Provide plants, such as lilies, and branches and rocks for hiding.

3 TADPOLE WITH ALL LEGS
By week 11, the tadpole's front legs are fully developed. Provide plenty of rocks, or a sloped piece of wood, so that they are able to climb out of the water.

4 FROGLET
By week 12, metamorphosis is complete. The froglet will now eat small invertebrates. It could be two or three years before the frog breeds.

fringes on legs propel beetle through water

strong, grasping front legs

diving beetles are fierce predators that can be up to 1½ in (3.5 cm) long–their diet includes newts, frogs, and fish

dragonfly eggs

male sticklebacks are aggressively territorial and build nests to attract egg-laying females

throat and belly turn red in spring

dragonfly nymph

Swamps, bogs, and fens

If you want to encounter a variety of species in a truly wild setting, try spending some time in one of these fascinating wetland habitats.

Insect-eating plants

The best places to see carnivorous plants are waterlogged habitats, such as bogs, which are nutrient-poor because water cannot flow to, or from, them easily. These remarkable plants get the nutrients they need by catching insects. The "hairs" on a sundew's leaf have a gland at each end that secretes a sticky substance. Once an insect is caught, the edges of the leaf gradually curl over, and enzymes help break the insect down. Sundews aren't the only carnivorous plant in North American bogs. They also host other carnivorous plants such as pitcher plants (see p.160), cobra lilies, and venus flytraps.

WATER WORLD
You will find plenty of plants even in the soggiest swamp. Reed swamps are dominated by reeds and bulrushes, while cypress trees flourish in swamp forests.

DEADLY VARIETY
There are about 150 sundew species. The great sundew has a large range, and grows in habitats in North America, Europe, Japan, and Hawaii.

SMOOTH MOVER
Watch the edge of a freshwater cattail marsh and you might see a Sora. These small, long-toed rails can move easily through dense cover.

Marsh birds

Some bird species have adapted to life in marshes—wetlands dominated by plants such as grasses, sedges, and cattails. Many rails, such as the Clapper Rail, are surprisingly slim, enabling them to get through dense vegetation, and the plumage of bitterns provides great camouflage. Marsh Wrens weave their nest around cattail stems, and as the plants grow, the nest goes up with them.

pale olive-brown in color

NEST BUILDER
Male Marsh Wrens build many nests, apparently a habit that impresses females, who are more likely to pair with a male that has numerous nests to choose from.

SILENT HUNTER
Bitterns are in the heron family and breed in marshes. They move quietly around the water's edge preying on fish, amphibians, and insects.

PRODUCTS FOR PEOPLE

While reeds are still used for thatching in Europe, they aren't the only wetland plant to have been exploited by humans. Sedge is also used in thatching, and in some areas, peat is still used as a fuel. Cranberries were originally bog plants, but are now grown commercially in North America. The cranberry harvest involves beating the beds, and then gathering the floating berries for juice and food.

Wetland inhabitants

Swamps, bogs, and fens provide a home for many plants and animals. Those shown here are just a few of those you might encounter on a wetland visit. You won't find all of them at every site, of course, but if you go with open eyes and an enquiring mind you should see something special.

1 Venus flytraps obtain nitrogen by capturing live insects. Insect-eating plants are more common in bogs than other habitats.

2 The common reed is highly invasive in many North American marshes, crowding out native plants. It can grow to heights of 9¾ ft (3 m) or more. In bloom, it reveals purple flowers.

3 The cranberry plant is found in North America, Europe, and Asia. It has pink flowers and red berries, which are rich in vitamin C.

4 The yellow iris is a distinctive wetland plant that can dominate freshwater wetlands and shorelines, crowding out more wildlife-friendly plants. It flowers between June and August.

5 American toads move to swamps and other wet habitats in the spring to lay their eggs, then leave for higher ground for the rest of the year.

6 A resident of the eastern US, the venomous cottonmouth eats a wide range of prey, but frogs and fish are its usual food.

7 Marbled salamanders live underground in forests most of the year, but migrate in the fall to pools where the female lays 50–200 eggs.

8 American alligators live in the swamps of the southeastern US. An adult male can be more than 13 ft (4 m) long.

9 The Snipe is a wading bird that can open the tip of its long bill independently of the rest of it. The sensitive tip is used to feel for food.

BOGBEAN
This attractive plant is an emergent aquatic perennial with flower stalks and leaves held well above the water.

171

Coast

The interfaces between land and sea are among the richest habitats on the planet at any latitude, because the mix of the terrestrial and marine generates opportunities for an immense diversity of life. Combine this with a multitude of geological and geographical variables, as well as the resulting range of coastal types, and that diversity expands even further. From mudflats to mangroves, sand to pebble beaches, towering cliff-sides to tidal pools, there is a fabulous array of species living on the edge of land and sea. It's also the place where you can safely explore part of the marine environment without getting too wet!

Sand

Sand forms a range of habitat types. Specialized creatures inhabit tide-washed sand, drawing birds such as sanderlings in to feed on them, while dry sand can blow into vast dunes that, when colonized and anchored by plants such as American beach grass, form a rich but environmentally challenging habitat for wildlife.

SEA HOLLY

SANDERLING

Beaches

At the front line between land and water, beaches are created and shaped by the actions of the sea, which erodes and deposits sediment. The nature of a beach, however, depends on the geography and geology of the land nearby.

Rock

Waves are a potent force of erosion, wearing away even the hardest of rocks where they meet the sea. On one hand this creates cliffs, but the other result—a rocky beach at sea level—is equally dramatic and the source of endless exploration and inspiration for any naturalist. Each rock pool is like a miniature ocean, home to a variety of accessible marine life such as mussels, anemones, and seaweeds.

MUSSELS

WRACK

SEA-ANEMONE

Coral

The gleaming white sand of many tropical beaches is formed from the broken and bleached coral remnants of shallow-water reefs. At higher latitudes, similar types of beaches are built from crushed seashells and glacial deposits of sand. Both are local beach types that reflect local sources of sediment, as revealed by the shells and bits of coral that wash up on them. All host a diversity of birds; some, like terns, feed offshore and nest on shore.

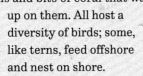

WHITE TERN

CORAL REEF

MUREX SHELL

Gravel

Gravel is also a product of erosion. Pebbles may be deposited as a border along an exposed coastline, sometimes thrown into ridges by storm waves. While the seaward zone supports annual plants, whose life cycle takes place in summer, more stable gravel supports drought-tolerant perennials such as beach peas or oyster plants. Ground-nesting birds, such as terns, thrive within the mosaic of pebbles and plants.

BEACH PEA

OYSTER PLANT

OYSTER
PLANT

*Find a patch of
sea buckthorn in autumn
and you may see birds
such as robins and cedar
waxwings gorging on the
energy-rich fruits to sustain
them on their migration.*

BUMBLEBEE

*Pollinating bees may be scarce
in such exposed habitats, so
large flowers are needed to
attract them. Watch and wait
to see what arrives.*

Beach walk

Bleak and windswept, a beach in winter resonates
with the cries of seabirds. Summer brings a whole
new set of sights, scents, and sounds.

Whether made up of coarse or fine sand, all beaches drain freely, and plants here must be able to cope with drought. Gently examine a beach plant's leaves and you'll find coatings of wax or hairs and succulent, fleshy stems—all part of the plants' adaptations to preserve water. Large, showy flowers attract pollinating insects, which lure in dragonflies and other predators from their freshwater breeding sites.

YELLOW HORNED
POPPY

COMMON GREEN
DARNER

VIPER'S
BUGLOSS

Scope out nectar-rich flowers, which may attract moths and butterflies. The nectar provides vital meals for these migrating insects.

RED VALERIAN

PAINTED LADY BUTTTERFLY

Tread carefully! Ground-nesting birds such as plovers lay their eggs directly on the beach, relying on camouflage for protection.

PLOVER EGG

SOW THISTLE

Delve into foliage, or search by flashlight at night, to find Insect larvae. Susceptible to drought and predation, they hide deep within the undergrowth.

Turning tides

A knowledge of tides is crucial to the exploration of coastal habitats, both for safety reasons and because tides affect everything that lives nearby or within them.

Understanding tides

As the Earth spins on its axis, each point on the planet's surface passes through two high tides every 24 hours. These bulges of water are formed by the gravitational pull between the Moon and the Earth. High tides occur twice a day at intervals that are a little over 12 hours apart, due to the Moon's orbit changing its position relative to the Earth.

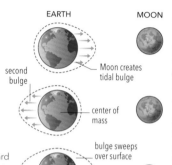

EARTH   MOON

second bulge — Moon creates tidal bulge

center of mass

bulge sweeps over surface

combined forces

MOON'S PULL
Once the Moon's gravity pulls a bulge of water toward it, a counterbalancing bulge forms on Earth's opposite side as the planet rotates.

READING A TIDE TABLE

Tide tables tell you when high and low tides occur on any particular day, and they normally give the predicted heights of those tides. Learn to use them—they could even save your life. But remember that tide tables are only predictions; both the timing and height of tides can be affected dramatically by weather conditions and atmospheric pressure, so remember to keep checking tides visually, too.

TIDE TABLES

4

3

4 Spray zone

This area beyond the tide's reach is still strongly influenced by the sea. Wind-driven salt spray means that the animals here, such as sea slaters, must tolerate a salty environment. On exposed coasts, the spray zone may extend hundreds of yards inland.

PERIWINKLE

3 Upper tidal zone

Survival in the upper tidal zone necessitates an ability to tolerate exposure to air and varying salt levels. In hot weather, seawater evaporates and becomes saltier; in wet weather it is diluted. A few species, including bladderwrack (rockweed), tolerate these extremes; others such as anemones retreat into tide pools.

BLADDERWRACK   ANEMONE

Tide cycle

In most places, the high to low tide cycle takes a little over 12 hours, but there are also longer-term tide cycles. At the full and new Moon, high tides are higher and low tides lower ("spring tides"), with "neap tides"—lower high and higher low tides—in between. And even longer cycles occur: the highest tides of all occur around the spring and autumn equinoxes.

STRANDED JELLYFISH
When a high tide recedes, it may leave behind some marine animals, like jellyfish.

Take a close look, but don't touch—beached jellyfish can still sting!

HIGH AND LOW TIDE
The constant ebb and flow of tides changes the land- and seascapes of our coastlines. Animals and plants in tidal zones must move or adapt to ever-changing conditions.

COASTAL STEWARDSHIP

Birds that feed and nest on beaches and barrier islands, including terns, plovers, and pelicans, are prone to human disturbance. Audubon trains volunteers to protect coastal nesting birds through beachgoer education, engaging with coastal communities, providing signage, and long-term monitoring of the birds' breeding success.

Audubon volunteers patrol the beach

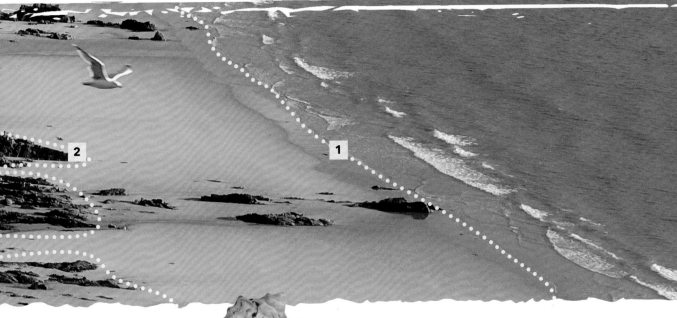

2 Middle tidal zone

In addition to constant wave action, the middle tidal zones are subject to alternate dousing with seawater and exposure to air. Brown seaweeds dominate this zone on rocky shores, and you may find animals such as crabs, whelks, and barnacles here.

DOG-WHELK

BARNACLES

BROWN SEAWEED

1 Lower tidal zone

Here, seawater dominates and wildlife adapts to having only short periods exposed to the air. However, wave action is constant, so the seaweed here is tough and leathery. Animals such as sandworms survive in burrows, and sea stars anchor themselves with tube feet.

SAND DOLLAR

Sand and gravel

Coastlines are shaped by the sea. Tides, waves, and currents erode, transport, and deposit sand, gravel, and rocks, sculpting diverse landscapes.

Cliffs are eroded by the action of the waves. Rocks are then worn down into ever smaller fragments, which are picked up by currents and transported along the shore until the strength of the current is no longer able to carry them. In this way, transported sediments are sorted into different sizes—the smaller the particle, the farther it has been carried from where it eroded. Each sediment type supports distinct habitats, and each habitat has a characteristic range of plants and animals.

LONGSHORE DRIFT
You can work out in which direction sediment was transported by the sea by looking for a build-up of material on one side of a sand spit of land or barrier.

Examine boulders on the upper shore for barnacles, taking care to avoid unstable rock surfaces.

pebbles are deposited in areas of high current strength, and can be thrown up into ridges by storm waves

rocks and pebbles are highly abrasive when carried by sea—rocky beaches are often devoid of life

BOULDERS
Angular chunks of rock that fall from a cliff gradually become rounded, worn down by the sea's continued erosive action, as happened to these boulders off the coast of Maine.

2½–½ in (64–16 mm) diameter

½–⅛ in (16–4 mm) diameter

SEDIMENT
Sorted into size classes by coastal currents, different sediments are deposited in different environments. The finest particles of all, called silt, are laid down only in the most sheltered conditions, such as in the lee of an offshore barrier or in the heart of an estuary, forming mudflats and salt marshes.

NATURE-BASED SOLUTIONS

Coastal birds are threatened by impacts of climate change, such as sea-level rise. Audubon's Coastal Resilience initiative aims to help coasts weather these shocks. This benefits millions of people who live close to the ocean, while also protecting and creating healthy habitats for those birds. Audubon supports natural infrastructure projects, such as rebuilding barrier islands in the Gulf of Mexico and on the South Carolina coast, restoring marshes in Long Island Sound, Chesapeake Bay, and San Francisco Bay, and reestablishing oyster reefs off North Carolina.

The Long-billed Curlew has the longest bill of any North American shorebird.

HABITAT LOSS
Rising sea levels have already reduced the Long-billed Curlew's intertidal feeding grounds.

small holes in rocks hold water and organic matter, which allows invertebrates to move in

sand is the foundation of some of our best-loved habitats—dunes for wildlife and beaches for recreation

SPIT
Sand and gravel extends as a spit across the mouth of an estuary.

4–2 mm diameter

2–0.125 mm diameter

DUNES
Carried first by water and then blown by the wind, sand can pile up and form large mobile dune systems, such as the Dune du Pilat in France.

BLACK SAND
Sand is the same color as its parent rock. Black sand beaches are formed from volcanic rock.

Between the tides

Tide pools are a window into a rich underwater world of marine life, otherwise visible only to divers or snorkelers.

Anything you take out of a tide pool should be put back.

STAYING SAFE
Take care on the shore. The rocks can be slippery, and the tide pools deep, sometimes hidden by seaweed. Always keep an eye on the tides.

Types of tide pool
Tide pools of all shapes and sizes are revealed when the tide recedes. Deep pools, with overhangs and crevices, have more niches for different plants and animals, and provide shelter from the waves. Shallower pools are easier to investigate, but contain a more restricted range of life.

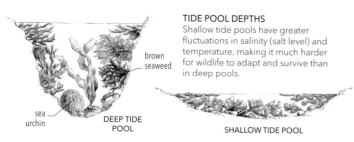

brown seaweed

sea urchin

DEEP TIDE POOL

SHALLOW TIDE POOL

TIDE POOL DEPTHS
Shallow tide pools have greater fluctuations in salinity (salt level) and temperature, making it much harder for wildlife to adapt and survive than in deep pools.

Life in a tide pool
Every tide pool is a marine microcosm, home to plants and animals, both predators and prey. The mini-dramas of everyday life and death play out before your eyes, as you peer into the pools at low tide. But it pays to be well hidden—you will find much more by exploring among the seaweed fronds and holdfasts, under the boulders, and deep into crevices. Watch the rocks closely as some animals, such as crabs, are masters of camouflage.

MAKING A VIEWER
Light reflecting off the surface of water and ripples caused by the wind can make it difficult to see what lies beneath. Sunglasses with polarizing lenses can help reduce glare, but a simple underwater viewer will reveal much more—especially in bright conditions.

1 Take a plastic ice-cream container and cut out the bottom with a sharp craft knife.

2 Carefully cover any sharp edges with strips of waterproof tape, such as duct tape.

3 Tightly roll plastic wrap over the bottom of the container and fasten it in place with an elastic band.

4 Put the covered end of the viewer just under the water's surface, and peer through it.

Survival strategies
Pools of water at low tide protect marine animals from drying out in the air, allowing them to survive higher up on the shore than would otherwise be the case. But animals on the menu of predators such as starfish must take other defensive measures, including living at the edges of the pool where these predators cannot reach—at least not until the tide comes in.

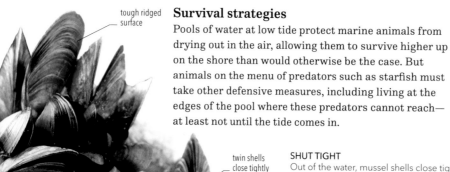

tough ridged surface

twin shells close tightly

SHUT TIGHT
Out of the water, mussel shells close tight to protect the animal inside. However, this behavior is no defense against the stabbing bill of an oystercatcher.

DRAWING IN
The stinging tentacles of anemones only come out underwater. At low tide, they are withdrawn into the round, jellylike body.

some red seaweeds attach to rocks or kelp at lower tide pools

rockweed covers rocks at low tide; its gas-filled sacs allow it to float on the sea surface at high tide

limpets withstand crashing waves by clinging firmly to rocks

Tide pool inhabitants

STARFISH
Starfish feed on mussels and other bivalves, pulling the shells apart with their multitude of sucker feet.

STICKLEBACK
Male sticklebacks build a nest and guard the eggs and young.

PRAWN
With a translucent body, a prawn blends into its background—until it moves.

HERMIT CRAB
Hermit crabs protect themselves by squeezing their soft bodies into empty seashells.

SEA URCHIN
Although mainly subtidal, sea urchins may be found in deep, lower-shore pools.

shell covered in spines

crabs shelter, scavenge, and hunt in deep tide pools

marine snails graze on algae upon the surface of rocks

starfish roam tide pools in search of prey

TIDE POOL NICHES
Each part of a tide pool is home to something. Look around the edges for limpets and barnacles, in deep water for anemones and fish, or among seaweed for crabs.

anemones are fiercely territorial, stinging those who get too close

LIMPET SCARS

When the tide comes in, limpets glide over rocks, grazing on algae. Unable to tolerate exposure to air and vulnerable to predation by birds, they return to their home patch as the tide falls. Repeated "sticking" by the limpet creates a shallow depression, or scar, on the rock—visible long after the animal has died.

circular depression left by limpet

Look for limpet scars at the edges of tide pools.

Shorebirds

Wherever you are in the world, some of the greatest concentrations of bird life can be found along shorelines, attracted by abundant food.

Shoreline specialists

Birds gather wherever there is food. The twice-daily tides that wash our shores bring in nutrients that support a rich and diverse food chain. At the top of this food chain are birds. As the tide retreats, wading birds and gulls throng the shoreline probing beneath the surface for invertebrates. Many waterbirds breed along the coast—sometimes in vast colonies—while others make use of shorelines as part of their annual migrations.

STIFF COMPETITION
To reduce competition for food resources, different bird species vary in their body parts and behaviors so that each has its unique feeding niche.

Gulls

The generalists of the bird world, gulls feed upon a vast range of foods including fish, earthworms, carrion, and fast food waste. Their stout bills and robust digestion allow them to feed opportunistically, which makes many gull species highly adaptable. The name "seagull" is quite inappropriate: they are found almost everywhere, from city rooftops—in effect, artificial cliffs—to the open oceans.

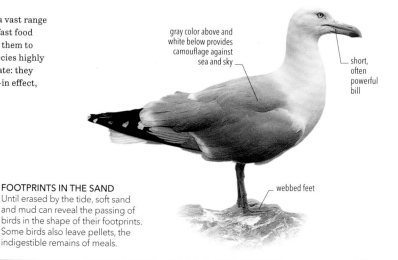

gray color above and white below provides camouflage against sea and sky

short, often powerful bill

webbed feet

FOOTPRINTS IN THE SAND
Until erased by the tide, soft sand and mud can reveal the passing of birds in the shape of their footprints. Some birds also leave pellets, the indigestible remains of meals.

black cap

like most terns, Sandwich Terns have long wingtips

long, pointed bill

short legs

IN FLIGHT
A forked tail, acrobatic flight, and long, pointed wings, have given rise to the terns' nickname: "sea-swallows."

Terns

Built for precision flying, terns feed by hovering, then plunge-diving on their fish prey, caught with the daggerlike bill. Food is carried back to the chicks until they can fly, so breeding colonies stay close to rich feeding grounds. When not raising young, terns stray farther out to sea. The Arctic Tern (see near left) has the longest migration of any bird, flying an average of 1.5 million miles—equivalent to three round trips to the Moon—in its lifetime.

Wading birds

A combination of long bill and long legs makes wading birds well adapted to feeding on invertebrates in soft mud. But the whole story is far more complex—different bill lengths and shapes provide access to different foods, while longer legs allow feeding in deeper water. Wading birds congregate mostly outside the breeding season, and especially in high tide roosts when their feeding grounds are unavailable.

IN FOR THE KILL
The oystercatcher's bladelike bill can pry open bivalve mollusks including mussels, clams, and as you might guess, oysters.

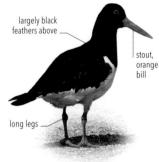

largely black feathers above

stout, orange bill

long legs

OYSTERCATCHERS

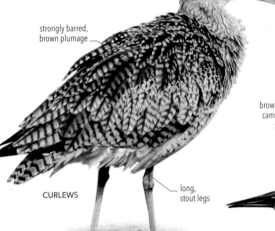

small black eye

long, pointed bill

strongly barred, brown plumage

long, stout legs

CURLEWS

sleek, slender body

straight bill

SANDPIPERS

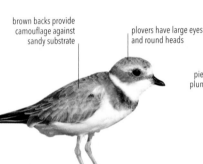

brown backs provide camouflage against sandy substrate

plovers have large eyes and round heads

PLOVERS

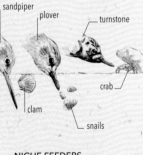

piebald plumage

thin, upcurved bill

very long legs

AVOCETS

HOW WADING BIRDS FEED

The length of a wading bird's bill is a factor in determining its diet. Some use visual clues to find their prey, picking at surface food, turning over stones, or probing siphon holes in the sand. Others rely on touch, often using a regular "sewing-machine" action and specialized muscles that allow them to open the tip of the bill, even while it's deep in the mud, to capture their prey. Watch carefully—often the bird will bring its food to the surface to wash it, giving us the chance to see exactly what it is eating.

FEEDING HOLES

curlew · godwit · oystercatcher · sandpiper · plover · turnstone

crab

clam

cockle

snails

lugworm

NICHE FEEDERS
Bill shape and length, leg length, and feeding techniques have evolved to give each wading bird family its own feeding niche, allowing outwardly similar species to coexist in the shoreline habitat.

Seal colony

Although they spend a lot of time in the water, all seals need to come ashore to breed, and many gather in colonies.

Seals and sea lions both belong to a group of aquatic, warm-blooded mammals called pinnipeds. Pinnipeds live part of their lives in water and part on land—their flippers and streamlined torpedo-shaped bodies make them well suited for diving and moving gracefully in water. The group is split into three families: walruses, eared seals, and true seals. True seals include the harbor (or common) seal, which is widespread in the Northern Hemisphere. In the North Atlantic, harbor seals often form mixed colonies with gray seals; however, the two species have different characteristics. Courtship and mating by harbor seals takes place in the water; they come ashore to rest and pup. The pups can swim as soon as they are born, so breeding colonies can reside on sand banks and flat beaches. In contrast, gray seal colonies are more active and mating takes place on land. Bulls fight to secure the best beach areas and the most females. Since gray seal pups cannot swim for the first few weeks of their life—until the first white coat is shed—they are born on rocky islets or pack ice, above the reach of tides.

VISITING A SEAL COLONY

Seal colonies can often be easily seen from land or sea, but take care when viewing them so as not to cause disturbance. Pups may become separated from their mothers if a colony is spooked. Each species has a distinct breeding season: harbor seal pups are born during the summer months, while gray seal pups tend to be born in winter. However, timing varies across their geographical ranges, so get advice from local experts.

BOAT TRIP
Seal colonies provide an attraction for many ecotourism initiatives. Approaching by boat allows close viewing with minimal disturbance.

GRAY SEALS
Gray seal pups remain safely out of reach of the tides for several weeks after birth, but storm waves may sometimes wash them out to sea.

Beach close-up

Walk along a tideline anywhere in the world and you'll find shells and other remains of marine fauna and flora, which have washed ashore or drifted in from the ocean.

DRIFTWOOD

STONE

GOOSE-BARNACLE

Stones are smoothed by the sea— some contain fossilized remains.

SPONGE

PEBBLE

SCALLOP SHELL

AMMONITE FOSSIL

Shells are abundant on some beaches; many more may lie buried beneath the sand.

WINKLE SHELL

MERMAID'S PURSE

SAND-DOLLAR

LIMPET SHELL

MUSSEL SHELL

WHELK EGGS

OYSTER SHELL

RAZOR-SHELL

STARFISH

SEA BEAN

*Despite their strong
holdfasts, seaweeds
are often torn from
rocks by rough waves*

*Partial or whole
skeletons and egg
cases from sea
animals are often
washed ashore or
dislodged from
tide pools.*

BROWN
SEAWEED

RED SEAWEED

GREEN
SEAWEED

CUTTLEFISH
SKELETON

SEA-URCHIN TEST

CRAB

JELLYFISH

Sandy beach

Sand is an inhospitable habitat for many plants and animals. All dune inhabitants must have adaptations to cope with these conditions.

How a dune forms

Onshore winds pick up dry sand from the beach and blow it inland. Out of reach of the tide, sand mounds can be colonized by drought-tolerant plants—their roots help stabilize the surface, while their shoots interrupt the wind flow, leading to further buildup of sand. This process continues until dunes are formed, sometimes more than 325 ft (100 m) high in favorable locations.

SANDY HOME
Mounds of vegetation interspersed with bare sand create microhabitats in which many animals thrive.

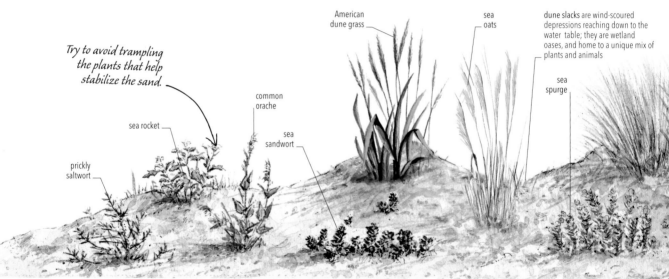

Try to avoid trampling the plants that help stabilize the sand.

prickly saltwort

sea rocket

common orache

sea sandwort

American dune grass

sea oats

sea spurge

dune slacks are wind-scoured depressions reaching down to the water table; they are wetland oases, and home to a unique mix of plants and animals

Embryo dune

Low dunes on the seaward-facing fringes are colonized by salt-adapted annual plants, which can complete their life cycles rapidly between the upheavals caused by storms.

PRICKLY SALTWORT

SEA ROCKET

Foredune

A short distance from the high tide line, a range of creeping plants can get a roothold. Most of these have fleshy leaves for storing water in hot weather, and waxy leaf coatings or silvery hairs to reflect intense summer sunlight.

SEA SANDWORT

SEA OATS

GULF RESTORATION

The 2010 Deepwater Horizon oil spill killed about 1 million birds in the Gulf of Mexico. This coastline is home to several birds. Audubon monitors and builds shelters for the species found here, such as these Least Tern chicks. They work with other agencies to conserve beaches where birds breed and restore nearby saltwater marshes.

Dune builder

With its almost unlimited ability to grow both horizontally and vertically through depositing sand, American beach grass forms the backbone of most large coastal dune systems. To survive drought, it has wax-coated leaves that roll up in dry weather, reducing the loss of water from its stomata ("breathing holes") on the upper surface of its blades.

tough, wiry leaves have very sharp points

tiny hairs retain moisture

rolled-up leaf

CROSS SECTION

STABILIZER
A unique combination of adaptations makes American beach grass the primary coastal dune-building plant throughout the world.

extensive creeping root system

Dune dwellers

Unlike plants, animals can move or hide to avoid summer droughts. Reptiles, insects, and snails, for example, shelter in the tussocks of American beach grass, where they can take advantage of shade and trapped moisture. Amphibians, such as spadefoot toads, bury themselves in moist sand, and sit out the drought until the rains return. Ghost crabs burrow in the sand year-round.

EASTERN SPADEFOOT TOAD

ATLANTIC GHOST CRAB
The sand-colored ghost crab's name comes from its ability to disappear quickly into the sand.

beach sunflower

American beach grass

seaside goldenrod

sand fescue

sea bindweed

Yellow dunes

American beach grass adds stability to foredunes, promoting further dune growth. Other largely drought-tolerant plants may follow, but yellow dunes still have a high proportion of bare sand. A lack of organic matter creates the sand's color.

BEACH SUNFLOWER

SEA SPURGE

SEASIDE GOLDENROD

Gray dunes

More mature dunes are stable enough to support a greater diversity of plants, and sometimes extensive patches of lichens. Dead leaves and other organic matter incorporated into the sand give it a grayish color.

BEACH PEA

Coral reef

The largest structures made by living organisms, coral reefs support a vast number of species, yet they are one of Earth's most fragile habitats.

Reef formation

Coral reefs are formed by groups of invertebrates called polyps, which deposit a hard outer skeleton of calcium carbonate as they grow. Corals get some nutrients from the water, but obtain as much as 90 percent from algae called zooxanthellae. These algae live in coral tissues and use photosynthesis to convert sunlight into carbohydrates. This process limits the growth of reefs to areas where sunlight can penetrate the water, mainly in the tropics.

FAN

flexible surface

BRAIN

branchlike "limbs"

tentacles extend to feed

BRANCHING

CORAL TYPES
Coral comes in many forms, but all have simple nervous and muscular systems and develop a rigid calcium carbonate skeleton.

Living together

The vast number of species living in close contact on the reef has led to a variety of interesting and useful relationships. Symbiosis is a process where two organisms interact, often over a source of food. Mutualism is a kind of symbiosis where both animals benefit, as in the examples below. In commensalism, one animal benefits while the other is barely affected.

CLEAN SWEEP
Bluehead wrasse feed on individual zooplankton and also clean parasites from larger fish.

GARDENER FISH
The dusky farmerfish actively removes other algae to create gardens of its favorite. This alga benefits from the weeding and only grows in its territories.

EXPLORING REEFS

Diving or snorkeling over tropical reefs with their incredible diversity of life, such as the barrier reef of Belize, can feel like flying over a rain forest. However, coral reefs are remarkably fragile, and any foreign substance or material that breaches the coral's protective mucous membrane can compromise an entire coral head that may have been alive for hundreds of years. Take great care not to handle corals, and certainly never remove any part of the reef as a souvenir.

Temperate reefs

Some of the world's most spectacular reefs are actually found in cold, temperate waters, where vividly colored sponges, soft corals, and other marine creatures anchor themselves onto rocks and other hard structures. In addition, giant kelp forests provide stunning habitats for marine wildlife. The kelp itself can grow as much as 20 inches (half a meter) per day—one of the world's fastest-growing plants.

SLY SWIMMERS
Seahorses inhabit seagrass beds and coral reefs. Slow movers, seahorses swim in an upright position, allowing them to easily hide behind vertical corals and grasses.

curled tail for gripping plants and rocks

UNDERWATER FORESTS
The giant kelp beds that grow in temperate oceans resemble sunlit forests. Their dark corners are full of life, which provides food for seals and otters.

Tropical reef species

BANDED CORAL SHRIMP
Adults live in coral caves and may live with their mate for years, usually not moving more than half a meter from home.

ATLANTIC WHITE-SPOTTED OCTOPUS
This night-feeding octopus is often followed by predatory fish that eat scraps from its meals.

RED CUSHION SEA STAR
These sturdy sea stars live in depths of more than 100 ft (30 m) as adults, but frequent shallow sea grass beds when they are young.

STOPLIGHT PARROTFISH
These parrotfish use their teeth like plates to scrape algae from coral and other hard surfaces.

CORAL REEF LIFE
Coral reef nooks and crannies are home for thousands of different fish, such as these sergeant major fish. They also provide an infinite hunting ground for animals higher up the food chain.

Limestone

Usually pale gray or yellowish in color, limestone is a very variable rock, due to the variety of ways in which it was created. Although often hard, leading to erosion structures such as platforms, it is vulnerable to weathering by acid rain. Many types of limestone contain the fossilized remains of animals that inhabited the prehistoric seas when the rocks were not yet formed.

WAVE CUT PLATFORM

LIMESTONE

Cliffs

Wherever rocks meet the sea, cliffs evolve. Their size and slope are dictated by the rock type. Erosion features such as caves, arches, and stacks reflect weaknesses in the rock that are more vulnerable to wave impacts.

RED SANDSTONE

Sandstone

A common sedimentary rock in which grains of sand are visible, sandstone ranges in color from pale whitish to red, or even green. Sandstone cliffs often show layers that allow you to track the environmental conditions present during deposition. Erosion acting upon sandstone cliffs may create natural sculptures, including caves.

SANDSTONE CAVE

Granite

Granite was formed by the cooling of molten volcanic rocks beneath the Earth's surface. This extremely hard, crystalline rock contains minerals that give it distinctive colors. Because of its makeup, it erodes very slowly, which is why granite cliffs are often stepped and well-vegetated—usually with few sheer drops and often featuring large, rounded boulders.

STACK

WHITE GRANITE

Volcanic

Throughout Earth's history, volcanic lava flows have solidified into a range of blackish rock types, commonly including basalt. The crumbly (friable) rocks in places of recent volcanic activity, such as the Canary and Hawaiian islands, form some of the most impressive barren cliff landscapes in the world. In such places the first stages of colonization by flora and fauna may be visible.

VOLCANIC ROCK

BLOW HOLE

Cliff colony

Sea cliffs, especially in northern temperate and Arctic regions, are often home to large colonies of seabirds. Here, their nests are relatively safe from predators.

nest of mud and seaweed

adult Black-legged Kittiwake incubating its eggs

Living on the edge

Cliffs provide an excellent location for seeing large numbers of different seabirds in summer. They provide a wide range of niches for seabirds to use as breeding sites, from the cliff top to just above tide level. Different seabirds prefer different niches, but all share one common requirement: the need to be close to the sea, the source of much—if not all—of their food.

STICKY NESTS
Seaweed, mud, and bird droppings (guano) create a nesting platform for gulls, such as Black-legged Kittiwakes.

POINTED EGGS
Long thought to prevent them rolling off ledges, the pointed shape of Common Murre eggs actually improves their ability to stand up to impacts from crash-landing adults.

pointed tip

Sea watching

You can use the elevated position of cliffs to scan the ocean for birds and marine mammals, such as porpoises. Watching the sea takes patience, as much of the time there may be little to see. Make sure you have a sheltered viewing spot, warm clothing, and good binoculars. The rewards will come when you spot something, perhaps a frenzy of gannets diving on a school of fish or a spouting pod of whales.

COASTAL VISITORS
Dolphins passing close to the shore can be seen from cliffs and other promontories.

Watch birds from a boat to avoid disturbing them.

BIRDWATCHING
Viewing cliff birds requires great care. Be sure to remain behind any safety fences, or better yet, take a boat trip to view the spectacle from below.

GANNET COLONY
Gannets live in large colonies. The safest spots are in the center; younger birds may be pushed to nest at the edges where gulls prey on eggs and chicks.

What nests where

JAEGARS
Some seabirds keep the same mate for many years. Some jaegars have dark and light color morphs, but they are the same species.

SUSTAINABLE FISHING

North American seabirds have declined by 70 percent since 1950, largely because the fish—especially sardines and herring—on which many depend have been overfished. Audubon launched Project Puffin (now the Audubon Seabird Institute) in 1973 to advocate for the long-term sustainability of fisheries to benefit seabirds such as puffins (seen here with wildlife photographer Derrick Z. Jackson), razorbills, and terns, as well as dolphins and whales.

ATLANTIC PUFFINS
Puffins nest underground in crevices or soil burrows. Both parents incubate eggs and bring home food, but the father usually stays at home to protect the chick.

COMMON MURRES
Lining cliff ledges in close-knit ranks, Common Murres and Razorbills find safety from predatory mammals and birds such as large gulls and ravens.

RED-FACED CORMORANTS
Cormorants build their nests on narrow ledges, and both parents feed the young until they are about 2 months old.

197

Cliff close-up

The wildlife found on cliffs varies depending on location and the geological makeup of the habitat. Most cliffs will have low, matted plantlife, while sandy cliffs facing the Sun are rich in insects.

Lichen thrives on rock faces exposed to sunlight and sea spray.

ROSEROOT

South-facing cliffs suit abundant flowering plants, but the harsh, dry atmosphere favors those with narrow or thick leaves that help to retain moisture.

CLADONIA LICHEN

COLT'S FOOT

SHEEP'S FESCUE

EASTERN PRICKLY PEAR CACTUS

SISKIYOU LEWISIA

SEA LAVENDER

RED ANT

PAINTED LADY BUTTERFLY

RED ADMIRAL BUTTERFLY

Insects and snails feed on plants and some make their homes in the loose soil.

LICHEN-COVERED ROCK

WILD COLUMBINE

BULBLET FERN

BANDED SNAIL

North-facing cliffs are cool, moist, and shady— ferns and other plants with broad leaves take root in crevices.

FOSSILS IN LIMESTONE

AMMONITE FOSSILS

BIRD'S FOOT TREFOIL

EBONY SPLEENWORT

Rocks can reveal the remains of sea life that lived millions of years ago.

Estuary

Where a river meets the sea, the resulting estuary becomes a fluctuating mix of fresh and saltwater. Interlaced with a range of other wetland types, such as salt marshes and mudflats, this mosaic of shallow, open water channels can harbor underwater sea-grass meadows, providing food for waterbirds and vital protected habitats for creatures such as sea horses and other fish.

COMMON
SEA HORSE

EEL
GRASS

GRAY MULLET

Coastal wetlands

On low-lying coastlines, the boundary between land and sea is blurred by the presence of coastal wetlands. Influenced by salt water and tidal movements, they make up some of the richest wildlife habitats in the world.

Salt marsh

Where a mudflat surface is exposed for a sufficient part of the tide cycle, salt-tolerant plants take hold to form salt marshes, providing swathes of color as they bloom during the summer months. Due to their deep tidal creeks, salt marshes aren't easily accessible to people, which adds to their attraction to birds, such as gulls, and other wildlife species.

LAUGHING GULL

SEA-
PURSLANE

SEA LAVENDER

Mudflat

Extensive mudflats, washed by every tide, are at the heart of many coastal wetlands, and are home to a vast range of invertebrates, including mollusks such as cockles and clams. These in turn attract wading birds such as sandpipers when the tide is out, as well as fish when the tide floods in. Largely featureless, apart from shallow creeks and pools, mudflats play host to some remarkable concentrations of species on a global scale.

HUDSONIAN GODWIT

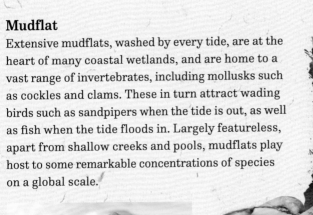

COCKLE SHELL

Mangroves

The tropical counterpart of salt marshes, mangroves are found in sheltered, muddy tidal waters. These swamps are formed when salt-tolerant trees gain a roothold. Many fish and crustaceans such as crabs rely on the shelter of their root systems and the upper branches provide feeding and breeding sites for water birds, reptiles, and other animals, protected by a natural moat.

MANGROVE CRAB

SALTMARSH SNAKE

Tidal marshes

Washed by the highest tides, salt marshes are dynamic habitats of low-lying coastlines, abounding in specialized plants and animals.

Salt-marsh strategies

Salt marshes are nature's own sea defenses, protecting the land by absorbing the energy of the sea like a sponge. All the plants within these marshes must be able to thrive in salty water. Many have desalination cells, which strip salt from the water, leaving fresh water for the plant's use. Other plant adaptations include some way to get rid of excess salt—you can see the crystals of excreted salt on their leaves—and succulent leaves in which to store available fresh water.

MARSHLAND SAFETY

Deep creeks and pools, soft mud, and the relentless tides, can make exploring a salt marsh treacherous. Luckily, salt marshes are flat, so much of their fascinating wildlife can be viewed from the safety of nearby higher ground, with the aid of binoculars.

STAND TOGETHER
Local knowledge is invaluable. Walking with a guide is the safest way to explore marshes.

Submergence marsh

Each tide brings in a fresh supply of silt. As this silt is deposited, the mud surface rises, and eventually plants begin to germinate and colonize. The lower submergence marshes are washed by every tide, but plants like spartina (cord grass) have air spaces in their tissues that allow them to survive the time they spend underwater. Animals here include fish and crabs, which take advantage of the rich food supplies.

STRIPED BASS
Salt marshes support spawning and nursery areas for many fish species, including bass, which move in at high tide.

BLUE CRAB
Marine creatures such as crabs remain in the marsh at low tide, taking refuge in tide pools or burying themselves in the mud.

Emergence marsh

Midlevel marshes are covered by the higher tides of the monthly cycle (see pp.178–179), so salt is an ever-present challenge, which is why salt marshes are rarely as diverse as their freshwater counterparts. But many salt-marsh plants have attractive summer flowers, such as the vibrant, purple blooms of sea lavender. These plants in turn attract insects.

GROUND BEETLE
Some insects, such as beetles, live in leaf litter on the marsh surface.

Salt marsh birds

Regular soaking by the tides prevents birds from breeding on all but the highest-level marshes. Above the reach of summer tides, however, wading birds and gulls nest, sometimes in large colonies. In winter, many species of birds use all areas of the salt marsh—which makes it a great place to view them from a safe distance in a car or blind. Wading birds roost on high marshes and feed on fish and invertebrates in the muddy creeks; ducks and geese graze on aquatic plants, and finches and sparrows feed on the abundant supply of seeds produced by salt marsh plants.

MARSH DABBLER
Many ducks, such as this Green-winged Teal, head for salt marshes in winter, where they graze and dabble for the nutritious, oil-rich seeds.

WETLAND FISHER
Even at low tide, the network of creeks and pools in a salt marsh provide very rich pickings for birds like herons and egrets, such as this Great Egret, which feed on crustaceans and fish.

ARROWGRASS
The fleshy leaves of sea arrowgrass can be distinguished from true grasses by their sweet, aromatic scent when crushed.

Upper marsh

Above the level of all but the highest tides, the upper marshes are often dominated by low shrubs. Infrequent tides followed by evaporation in sunlight can produce extremely high salt concentrations, so most plants have fleshy leaves that can store water and help buffer the effects of salt at their roots. Insects such as grasshoppers are common here.

SEA LAVENDER
Sea lavender's colorful flowers provide nectar for monarch butterflies fueling up for their Gulf crossing.

BUSH CRICKET
Safe from the risk of frequent flooding, a wide range of insects can be found in the upper marsh zone. Some, like the bush cricket, are almost invisible in the green foliage.

Mudflats

Found in sheltered areas, such as estuaries, mudflats are made up of very fine silt particles deposited by sea and river water.

How mudflats form

As soon as the silt (see p.180), settles out, plants begin to colonize it. First, microscopic algae called diatoms start to grow on the surface, helping to "glue" the silt particles together and make it more stable. The seeds of salt-tolerant plants, carried by the tides, can then germinate. Their roots provide additional stability to the mud, and their shoots help slow down water movement, which means that even more silt is deposited when the sea washes over it.

MUDDY MOSAIC
Estuarine mudflats form an intricate mosaic with water channels and salt marsh.

LIFE IN SALT WATER
Glasswort is well-adapted for life in salt water; its fleshy, cylindrical stems store fresh water.

What to spot

At first glance, mudflats may seem bleak and devoid of life, but a closer look reveals an abundance of marine creatures and plants. This rich habitat is reliant on twice-daily tides that supply the mudflats with food as well as fresh silt. Even when the wildlife is not visible, it is often possible to see evidence of their activities, such as worm casts and feeding tracks. If you decide to visit a mudflat, keep an eye on the sea and be careful not to get cut off by the rising tide (see pp.178–179).

1 Gulls and other water birds that feed on the flats leave their tracks in the soft mud.

2 A gull pellet contains the indigestible remains of its last meal—handle with care and be sure to wash your hands after touching it.

3 Cockles and other filter-feeding shellfish form dense beds on the surface or in the top layer of mud.

4 In shallow water, fan-worms extend a crown of feathery feeding tentacles from their rubbery mud tubes.

5 The shells of mussels are attached by strong threads to stones and other hard structures buried in the mudflats.

6 Dog whelks leave feeding tracks as they move over the surface, feeding on dead organic material.

7 Algal mats provide food for grazing water birds and snails.

8 Mud-snails are tiny but numerous and provide miniature morsels of food for throngs of wading birds.

9 Lugworms live in a u-shaped burrow in the sand, drawing food in at one end, and excreting waste (casts) from the other end.

10 Lugworms feed on organic matter within mud and sand.

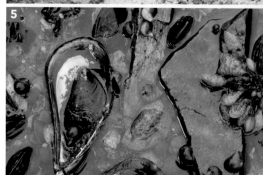

What lies beneath

To get a true picture of mudflat life, you cannot just look at the surface. Buried in the mud, sometimes at considerable depth, are a variety of burrowing and tube-dwelling invertebrates. Some filter food from the sediment, while others prey on the animals around them. They stay in their burrows, where they are protected from drying out when the tide recedes, and only show themselves at the surface of the mud when it is covered with water. At high tide, they are preyed upon by fish, but at low tide wading birds take their toll. The length of wading bird bills determines the range of prey available to them (see pp.184–185).

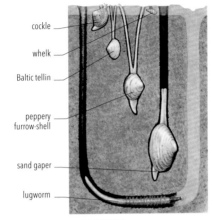

cockle
whelk
Baltic tellin
peppery furrow-shell
sand gaper
lugworm

BURROWERS
Each type of burrowing animal lives at a particular depth within the mud.

CLAM WORM   BLOODWORM   RIBBON WORM

BURROWING MUDSHRIMP

MUDDY DWELLERS
Whether pushing through the mud or inhabiting a tube, the hidden creatures within a mudflat add complexity to a hugely diverse ecosystem, as productive as any other habitat on Earth.

SIEVING FOR LIFE

To fully appreciate the richness of mudflat life, you need to get your hands dirty. Dig up a small sample of mud with a trowel and put it through a series of strainers, starting with the largest mesh. This will retain the larger shells and lugworms, while a finer mesh will hold back periwinkles and smaller worms. Even mud that has passed through both strainers will still have life in it, including larvae and nematodes that are only visible through a microscope.

CLEAN SWEEP
A large sieve, small strainer, and brushes are basic tools to help tease apart and identify specimens.

Mangroves

Mangrove swamps are dominated by a range of salt-tolerant trees that grow in relatively sheltered estuarine conditions.

Trees from several families have adapted to living with their roots in salty water. Although not closely related, these species are all called mangroves. Each displays one or more of a set of adaptations, including breathing tubes in the roots, impermeable root surfaces to limit salt uptake, and the ability to excrete excess salt through their leaves. These adaptations have enabled mangroves to flourish in places where few other plants could survive. Mangrove swamps host a vast range of wildlife, both above and below the water. Depending on the region—mangroves are found in the Indian, Atlantic, and Pacific oceans—Scarlet Ibises, proboscis monkeys, and mangrove snakes may be found breeding or feeding above the waterline, while the underwater zone harbors numerous crabs, oysters, and other crustaceans and mollusks, often important as food sources for local communities. The sheltered water among mangrove root systems makes them important nursery areas for many types of fish and other animals that then spend their adult lives out at sea.

FRAGILE HABITAT

Despite their extensive root systems, mangroves are vulnerable both to human influences—pollution, shrimp farming, and coastal development—and to natural erosion by the force of the sea. However, where they do survive, their ability to absorb wave energy plays a vital role in protecting coastal settlements from storm waves and tsunamis. Boardwalks and boats are the safest way to visit mangroves without harming them.

MANATEE
Large, slow moving, aquatic herbivores, manatees are found in mangrove swamps in the Atlantic. The closely related dugong inhabits coasts from East Africa, through southeast Asia, to Australasia.

CROCODILES
These are the world's largest living reptiles. They often occur in salt water where they find cover and food (especially fish) among mangroves. American crocodiles occur from south Florida through much of South America.

All at sea

Most of the oceans' depths have never been explored, but you can watch many species from the surface of Earth's last great wilderness.

Exploring the big blue

Over 70 percent of the world's surface is covered by seas and oceans, which have an average depth of over 2 miles (3 km). Most ocean depths are beyond the reach of all but the most specialized submarine, but you can explore coastal seas—both above and below the waves—with relative ease. Many types of animal life are within easy reach of the seashore, and taking a boat trip can provide an insight into the lives of seabirds, seals, whales and dolphins, and other mammals such as sea lions and sea otters. Under water, diving or snorkeling can bring you into contact with another experience—ocean wildlife—and give you a totally different, more intimate encounter with many types of marine animals.

SWIM WITH DOLPHINS
Dolphins are naturally inquisitive and highly intelligent mammals, and may approach visitors in their environment.

BOAT WITH A VIEW
Take a ride in a glass-bottomed boat in areas with clear seas, and you can get a close-up view of sea life.

FINS AND TAILS

The shape and marks on the dorsal fins of cetaceans allow scientists to recognize individual animals. The challenge is to identify species by fin profile as they surface to breathe. The very tall dorsal fin of an orca is unmistakable, as is the curved back of a humpback and its tail silhouette before a dive. Porpoise sightings, however, are more fleeting; look for a straight, leading edge to their dorsals instead of the curve of a dolphin's. Narwhals lack a dorsal fin, but their tails have a distinct notch in the middle.

ORCA (KILLER WHALE)   BOTTLENOSE DOLPHIN

HUMPBACK WHALE   NARWHAL

WHALE-WATCHING
An encounter with any type of whale is unforgettable. In this orca pod, you can see the huge dorsal of an adult male.

Taking the bait

Many marine animals rely on speed to escape predators, but small fish such as anchovies or sardines gather in schools for protection. Large schools can also form at an upwelling, where smaller fish gather to feed on plankton. Just like large flocks of birds, a school of fish can move as one, whirling and changing direction so rapidly that it is difficult for a predator to pick off any one fish. However, when many predators come together, the odds change, and a wildlife spectacle unfolds as the school changes from a safe haven into a "bait ball." In this situation, attackers strike from all sides; the fish are driven toward the surface by dolphins, whales, or sharks, where they are picked off by waiting seabirds, such as gannets.

DIVING GANNETS
Plummeting from a great height, gannets can penetrate deep into the water to spear their prey.

dark back and upperwings

BAIT BALL
Clumps of fish such as sardines attract predators from above and below— sharks, tuna, whales, and diving birds.

STRANGER TO THE GROUND
Most albatross species spend almost their entire lives at sea. Laysan Albatross sometimes appear off the coast of California.

SAVE OUR SEAS

Modern fishing methods, climate change, and pollution are stripping oceans of life and upsetting their natural balance. We can take practical steps to lessen our impact on the oceans by keeping beaches clean, supporting marine sanctuaries, and safely disposing of harmful pollution.

POISONOUS OIL
Oil spills destroy the waterproofing on seabird feathers and the fur of seals and otters, then poisons them as they preen or clean themselves. It also affects the entire food chain.

DANGEROUS GARBAGE
Any garbage in the sea is gathered by currents. The North Pacific gyre, about twice the size of Texas, contains millions of tons of plastic—toxic to marine life.

Tundra and ice

Freezing temperatures present life with
challenges. Combine these with high
altitudes, drought, and long periods without
sunlight, and you have one of the most
challenging environments on Earth. Yet if
there are resources available, no matter how
sparse or apparently remote, life will reach for
them and adapt to take advantage of them.
The barriers of glacial cold, unremitting
darkness, and thin air have been breached by
a guild of specialists that thrive where we
would shiver to a fatal standstill. And of
course, the fate of these remarkable
communities is now threatened as these
fragile habitats succumb to climate change.

The Arctic tundra

The treeless Arctic tundra is a great place to see wildlife such as elk, musk ox, and polar bears—best done from the comfort of a guided tour.

What is the tundra?

The Arctic tundra is a vast landscape north of the tree line (see pp.160–161), extending through Canada, Alaska, Siberia, and Scandinavia. It is a habitat shaped by extreme cold. For much of the year, it is snow-covered, dark, and windy. Soil in this region, called permafrost, is almost perpetually frozen. This limits the growth of roots, so the only plants that survive there are small shrubs, mosses, and lichens. In summer the upper permafrost melts, transforming the tundra into a marshy bog that supports a host of wildlife.

SOLID GROUND
Permafrost is soil that remains below the freezing point of water. Plant life blooms in summer when its upper layer thaws.

What you might encounter

Since few animals can tolerate the cold, windy conditions, the tundra is a place of relatively low biodiversity. However, you may see caribou (also called reindeer) and musk ox grazing on small plants and lichen. Predators include Arctic foxes and wolverines, and smaller animals include Arctic hares and lemmings.

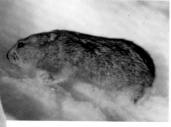

ICE SURVIVOR
Lemmings survive the cold by burrowing underground. They are a vital food for Snowy Owls and other Arctic predators.

SUMMER VISITOR
Polar bears aren't just creatures of the ice. In summer they move into the Arctic tundra, where they are sometimes seen on wildlife tours.

ARCTIC REFUGE

Protected since 1960, parts of the Arctic National Wildlife Refuge in Alaska are now threatened by drilling for oil and gas, which could have a devastating impact on the area's wildlife. Birds migrate from six continents to breed here in summer. It is also vitally important for mammals. Audubon is campaigning to give stronger protection to the refuge, especially the Coastal Plain, which is most vulnerable to fossil fuel extraction.

ARCTIC PLAIN

ANIMAL SANCTUARY
Nearly 200,000 caribou raise their young in the Arctic National Wildlife Refuge, which is also home to gray wolves and polar bears.

What to see in the summer

Winters are cold, windy, and harsh, but the tundra in summer is a transformed landscape. Long days of almost 24-hour sunlight warm the topsoil, melting the surface layers and turning the environment into a lush, boggy marshland where many plant species can grow. Summer is a good time to see animals that migrate to this region to avoid predators as well as to feed on abundant insects and fish. Caribou are just one of the migrant species, roaming many hundreds of miles to graze on the summer plant life. You can also see birds such as Snow Geese, which gather in massive flocks, raising their goslings in the marshlands.

FLOCKS RETURN
Snow Geese arrive on the tundra in summer, ready to lay eggs and raise their young. They feed on tundra vegetation in such large flocks that they sometimes deplete the habitat used by many other species.

SILENT HUNTER
Snowy Owls prey on small animals such as lemmings. With no trees available, the owls make their nests on the tundra ground.

Even the Snowy Owl's huge talons are feathered to help it cope with the cold.

SUN FOLLOWER
The Arctic poppy is a miniature version of its relative in temperate regions. Its tiny flowers turn their heads to follow the Sun.

WATCH OUT FOR MOSQUITOES

We may think of mosquitoes as warm-weather insects, but the summer tundra teems with them. Because tundra is flat with frozen permafrost below, meltwater from the surface has nowhere to go. Stagnant puddles are warmed by 24-hour sunlight, making them ideal for mosquito larvae. This is good news for waterfowl, which feed on the larvae, but bad news for human visitors, who are plagued by the blood-sucking insects. Take your mesh insect netting and repellent!

Arctic fox

In the tundra the change between seasons is extreme; the animals that live there must adapt to survive.

The Arctic fox lives in some of the coldest parts of the planet. The fox stores heat within its body; with its stout legs, short muzzle, and small rounded ears, little surface area is exposed to the cold. However, its chief adaptation for dealing with the icy Arctic winters is its fur. The Arctic fox is the only member of the dog family to change the color of its coat with the seasons. In spring, the fox is tawny brown but as winter comes, thick white hair grows in. It has one of the densest fur coats, and the hairs of its winter coat are almost double the length of its summer coat hairs, and the thick, deep fur provides warmth. Every part of the animal's body is covered in fur—even the pads on the soles of its feet, helping it walk on ice. The fox's color change blends it with the white of the environment. This allows it to sneak up on prey and avoid larger predators. The Arctic fox has such sharp hearing that it can hear a small rodent rustling beneath the snow—the better to pounce upon it.

SEASONAL FUR

Both hunter and hunted animals employ similar strategies to avoid detection. Arctic foxes prey upon Arctic hares, although the hare's large size makes them intimidating game. By blending in with its surroundings, the fox can stealthily approach its quarry. Similarly, the hare's white coat helps it avoid its predators, which also include Arctic wolves and Snowy Owls.

CAMOUFLAGE COLORS
The Arctic hare in winter (left) and summer (right). In winter the hare's white coat usually blends in with the snow, helping it avoid the eyes of predators.

HIDE AND SEEK
In winter the thick coat of the Arctic fox turns white, blending in with the snow and ice. This camouflage helps it sneak up on rodents, birds, and occasionally, ringed seal pups.

Life on the ice

The Arctic is among Earth's last wildernesses. Although Arctic areas are changing fast, wildlife thrives there.

Visiting the ice

Visiting a polar region can be the most exciting trip you ever make, yet due to the sensitive nature of these fragile environments, tourists must respect them. Many Arctic destinations, such as coastal Alaska, Baffin Island in Canada, or the west coast of Greenland, are best seen from the water; the best time to visit is from May to September. Remember that these are remote, pristine, and extreme locations. Listen to your guide, respect the animals and the ice, and you can have some of the most memorable wildlife encounters of your life.

DISTANCE FLYER
Arctic Terns winter in Antarctica, but breed in the Arctic, so may travel up to 25,000 miles (40,000 km) a year.

What you will see

In the Arctic, expect to see whales, walruses, and, if you're lucky, polar bears. While the last are top predators with little fear of people, cautious encounters from a safe distance can be magical. Ivory Gulls feed on any carrion they leave behind. With luck, you may see a beluga whale or a narwhal around the edge of the ice, where thousands of auks and other seabirds dive for fish.

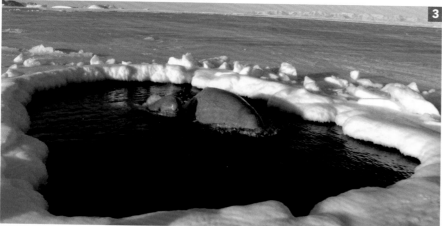

1 Ivory Gulls are the world's northernmost nesting birds. As climate change causes ice to melt, they cannot shift their range further north.

2 Walrus can weigh 3,000 lb (1,360 kg)—the weight of a small car—and dive to a depth of 300 ft (90 m), where they rely on their whiskers to help them find clams and sea cucumbers.

3 Belugas are one of the so-called Arctic "ice whales." They travel long distances beneath the ice, using holes and cracks to surface and breathe.

What to pack
1. Binoculars, for spotting birds and whales.
2. Sunscreen to protect your skin—the ozone layer is thin at the poles.
3. Sunglasses to cut glare reflected from the ice.
4. Camera to record what you see.
5. Warm clothing, especially for hands and feet.

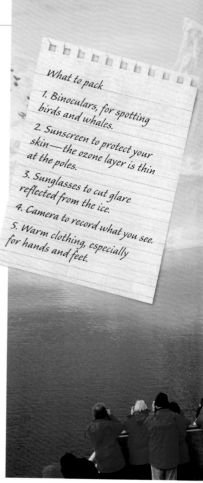

POLAR CRUISE
Most polar trips include a cruise to see the beautiful and ever-changing natural sculptures carved by the ocean from floating ice.

LIFE UNDER THE ICE

In the Arctic, the foundation of the food chain is made up of billions of tiny crustaceans called copepods and krill, which feed on even tinier organisms under and around the ice. They provide food for seabirds, seals, and whales.

KRILL

EARTH'S VITAL ICE

Climate change is drastically affecting polar regions, which must be conserved for all species—not just those that live there. Average Arctic temperatures have risen at twice the rate of those elsewhere, while the Antarctic Peninsula has risen to five times the average. This has profound implications for the planet. An increase in the Earth's temperature causes icebergs to melt, raising sea levels. The Greenland ice sheet is the area scientists consider most at risk: if it melts, sea levels could rise by up to 23 ft (7 m), bringing flooding to many coastal areas.

Dovekies breed in the Canadian high Arctic. Scientists have shown that their diet has changed as Arctic sea ice has retreated.

Ice structures

Ice occurs in very different forms on land and in the ocean. On land, centuries and millennia of snowfall, layer upon layer, builds into glaciers and ice sheets that can be miles thick. In the Arctic, ice sheets and glaciers can flow directly into the sea, where they "calve" icebergs—floating mountains of ice. Ice also forms when the sea itself freezes, but this results in much less substantial "sea ice." Sea ice is only up to a few feet thick and is often thinner than that. Sea ice attached to land is called "fast ice" while "pack ice" floats freely, carried by wind and currents.

90 percent of an iceberg lies under water

HOW ICEBERGS FLOAT

Ice floats because it is less dense than water, thanks to open spaces formed between the hydrogen molecules when water is frozen.

MELTING ICE

Pack ice (above, right) refers to a body of drifting ice, which is carried along by wind and surface currents. Icebergs (below) are carved by the sea and Sun into various organic shapes and sizes.

Glossary

Abdomen
In mammals, the part of the body between the thorax (chest) and pelvis; in insects, the hind section of the body behind the thorax.

Adaptation
The evolution of features within a species or population, improving fitness for life in a particular habitat.

Agro-forestry
Cultivation of trees as a crop, for lumber, pulp, or other products, such as palm oil.

Algae
Simple organisms, the most complex being seaweeds, lacking structures of plants such as roots and leaves.

Arctic
The region around the North Pole, north of the Arctic Circle at 66° 33'N.

Biodiversity
The total variety of living things, including species and subspecies.

Biome
An ecosystem, or community of plants and animals, living in particular geographical and climatic conditions.

Botany
A branch of biology specializing in the study of plants.

Cambium
A layer of cells within stems and roots of plants whose growth gives an increase in girth.

Chlorophyll
Green pigment in plants, vital in extracting energy from sunlight.

Chrysalis
Pupa, a life stage in insects and moths between larva and adult.

Climate change
A gradual change of global climatic balance, natural or artificially induced.

Cocoon
A silky protective casing produced by some caterpillars.

Colony
A grouping of breeding animals in a specific site, for social stimulation or protection.

Commensal
A lifestyle relationship between two organisms, to the benefit of one with no harm to the other.

Compound leaf
Leaf split into several leaflets.

Contour
Line on map (or, imaginary, on ground) joining points of the same altitude.

Cyclone
An area of winds rotating inward to "fill" a central area of low pressure; also a name for tropical storms in the Pacific and Indian oceans.

Dabbling
The taking of water, debris, seeds, and tiny organisms into its bill by a surface-feeding duck; water is expelled with its tongue, and food is retained.

Debris
Assorted mixture of material washed or fallen from above: from hillside rocks to fine soil and plant material in tree bark cavities.

Deposition
The laying down of suspended items washed along in a current.

Dorsal
On the upper part of the body; view from above.

Ecosystem
Complete assemblage of living things, from soil organisms to higher plants and animals, living in particular conditions and geographical area.

Enzyme
Protein produced by living organisms, helping speed up chemical reactions.

Epidermis
Outer layers of the skin.

Epiphyte
A plant growing on another plant without parasitizing it.

Evergreen
Having leaves all year, which are shed and replaced more or less continually, not seasonally.

Fern
A plant with vascular system, roots, leaves, and stems, but reproducing by spores instead of flowers.

Filter-feeder
An animal that takes a mouthful of water containing minute food and expels it through a filter, retaining the food, for example whales with "whalebone" or baleen plates instead of teeth.

Fragmentation
Past extensive distribution of plant or animal, now reduced to small, isolated, or remnant areas, through climate change or human action.

Fresh water
Water from rain, in lakes, rivers, marshes, and aquifers, with low concentration of dissolved salts and minerals (these increase through brackish to salt or seawater).

Friable
Crumbly and easily broken down.

Fungus
Plantlike organism that does not create its own food with chlorophyll, lacking any green pigment, typically feeding on remains of dead plants and animals.

Gall
Growth on plant leaf or twig in response to attack from parasitic insect, mite, fungus, or bacteria; parasite often identifiable by particular shape and color of gall.

Genus
A unit in scientific classification of living things, linking similar species—first of two-word "scientific name," for example *Homo* in *Homo sapiens*.

Germination
Period when seed or seedling emerges from dormant period, such as winter, to begin growth.

Gill
A structure that extracts oxygen from water, in fish or early stages of amphibian; also structure beneath cap of some fungi, containing spores.

Glacier
A mass of ice that becomes so heavy that it gradually "flows" imperceptibly downhill.

Greenhouse gas
Gas, such as carbon dioxide, that allows heat from the Sun to reach the Earth, but prevents it from radiating outward, hence increasing global temperature.

Gyre
A large-scale circulation of ocean surface currents.

Habitat
The amalgamation of features, such as soil, plants, animals, and local climate, in which a particular organism lives.

Harem
A group of females assembled and defended for reproductive purposes by one male.

Heliotropism
Movement of plant during the day, "following" the movement of the Sun.

Herbaceous
Plant that dies back to soil level in autumn and winter.

Hibernaculum
A structure made to give a safe site for hibernating reptiles and amphibians in winter.

Humidity
The amount of water vapor in the air.

Humus
Decaying vegetable matter in the upper layer of soil, giving it a dark brown or black color.

Hyphae
Long filaments of fungi, on or below ground, that form the mycelium; extracts and transports nutrients.

Lateral line
A line of sensitive cells along the side of a fish, able to detect sound and movement.

Leaflet
Division of a compound leaf, such as an ash leaf.

Lek
Communal display of males of some birds, such as prairie-chickens and Sage Grouse, to attract and impress females; also the name for the traditional site used for such displays.

Lichen
Organism formed by close liaison of a fungus and a green plant that takes energy from sunlight, such as a green alga.

Litter
Fallen leaves collecting beneath trees and shrubs, decomposing over several months.

Mantle
On a bird, feathers cloaking the upper part of the body; a bird of prey also protects its catch by "mantling," opening its wings over its food.

Meander
Wide, S-shaped bend or loop in a river; fast flow undercuts the outer edge of a bend while slower flow deposits gravel on the inner edge, gradually shifting a meander downstream.

Melanin
Dark pigment, for example in fur and feathers, giving darker, richer colors and black, and also adding strength to color.

Metabolism
The sum of all physical processes that take place in the body.

Metamorphosis
Marked and rapid change between life forms of certain groups of animals, for example from caterpillar to chrysalis to butterfly.

Microbe
Microscopic organism, or microorganism, almost invisible to the naked eye.

Midrib
Central stiff support of flat leaf.

Migration
A regular, often annual, large-scale movement of animals of a particular species, such as wildebeest and swallows, often in connection to seasonal changes in climate and food, or for breeding purposes.

Monsoon
Seasonal wind and associated rainfall, producing majority of annual rain in one short season: West African and Asian—Australian monsoon systems are the biggest.

Mycelium
Network of fibrous filaments, or hyphae, beneath a fungus, which collects nutrients.

Mycorrhiza
A close association between a fungus and roots of a plant, to the benefit of both.

Native
An organism in its natural geographical range, i.e. not introduced, either deliberately or accidentally, by human action.

Nymph
Stage in the life of some insects, looks much more like the final adult form than a typical larva.

Opposite
Describes leaves or leaflets arranged in opposing pairs on a stem.

Outer skeleton
A shell-like, structural outer layer of certain invertebrates.

Oxygen
Abundant, tasteless, colorless gas in the atmosphere, essential to life; also in water and other natural substances.

Palmate
Having leaflets emerging from a common point, such as those of Buckeye, or having webbed or partially webbed toes like a Semi-palmated Sandpiper.

Permafrost
Permanently frozen soil, often causing waterlogged ground when higher layers thaw out in summer.

Pheromones
A chemical signal between insects, for example laying a "food trail" or attracting a potential mate, often over remarkably long distances.

Photosynthesis
Extraction of energy from sunlight by chlorophyll in plants, and conversion to sugars and carbohydrates.

Pigment
A chemical material that influences the color of reflected light by absorbing various wavelengths.

Plankton
Assorted minute plants, animals, and bacteria living and drifting freely in upper layers of water.

Polar
An area close to the pole: an imprecise definition, but closer to the pole than "Arctic" or "Antarctic."

Pollination
Fertilization of plants as male pollen grains are transferred (by wind, insect, or bird) to female reproductive structures.

Precipitation
Water vapor coagulating in the atmosphere as its capacity to absorb water is reduced through changing pressure or temperature, to form rain, sleet, hail, or snow.

Prehensile
Mobile or capable of grasping, for example a prehensile tail that can be curled to grasp a branch.

Proboscis
Elongated structure from an animal's head, especially a tubular probe from an insect.

Pupation
Period in metamorphosis of some insects in which larval structures break down and adult features develop.

Saliva
A secretion from the mouth, serving as lubrication for swallowing food and also as "glue" to help create external structures, such as nests.

Scale
A small, rigid platelike structure growing from the skin, for protection and color, for example on fish or butterfly.

Sciophyte
A plant that can thrive in shaded areas.

Schooling
Fish living in groups, with a degree of collective action.

Sediment
Particles initially suspended in water, deposited as water velocity reduces or particles coagulate into heavier items.

Species
A basic unit in the classification of living things that groups together genetically similar individuals: members of a species interbreed and produce fertile offspring recognizably of the same species.

Spinneret
Organ of a spider that spins its silk fiber or web.

Stipe
The stem of a typically toadstool-shaped fungus.

Substrate
Underlying rock or subsoil beneath the soil.

Symbiosis
Arrangement in which two or more organisms live inextricably and closely linked.

Temperate
A broad area between more extreme tropical and Arctic climates, without marked extremes of temperature or rainfall.

Thermals
"Bubbles" of rising air, produced as areas of bare or light-colored ground warm the air above them in strong sunshine; never produced over water.

Thorax
The part of the body between the head and the abdomen.

Topsoil
Uppermost layer of soil in which decaying leaves decompose and from which roots of plants and fungi extract nutrients.

Transpiration
The loss of water vapor from leaves of plants.

Tropical
Area between the Tropic of Cancer and Tropic of Capricorn, extending across the equator, typified by high temperatures, lack of marked seasonality, and little change in length of days.

Understory
Shrub and sapling layer in forest or woodland that is below mature trees, but above the herbaceous layer.

Veil (of fungi)
Partial or universal veil encloses growing cap and stem; splits to leave remnant ring on stipe.

Volva
A bag or cup-shaped structure at the base of the stem of a fungus, a remnant of the veil.

Index

Audubon

The National Audubon Society protects birds and the places they need, today and tomorrow. Audubon works throughout the Americas using science, advocacy, education, and on-the-ground conservation. State programs, nature centers, chapters, and partners give Audubon an unparalleled wingspan that reaches millions of people each year to inform, inspire, and unite diverse communities in conservation action. A nonprofit conservation organization since 1905, Audubon believes in a world in which people and wildlife thrive. Learn more at audubon.org and by following the National Audubon Society on Facebook, Twitter, and Instagram @audubonsociety.

For more information about Audubon, including how to become a member:

National Audubon Society
225 Varick Street
7th Floor
New York, NY 10014

1-800-274-4201
www.audubon.org

Join Audubon

By becoming a member of the National Audubon Society, you'll join a community of people who care about protecting birds and the places they need, today and tomorrow. By becoming a member, you'll receive:
• The award-winning Audubon magazine. Savor the terrific blend of great reporting, photography, field guides, and more.
• A chance to get involved locally in one of the over 450 Audubon chapters. Go on birding walks and volunteer to protect local habitats. Learn more about our new college chapter program Audubon on Campus, reaching 150 campuses nationwide and growing.
• An opportunity to keep up with the latest news on birds and the places they live, including tips about how you can enjoy birds in your yard and community.

Acknowledgments

Dorling Kindersley would like to thank the following for their help in the preparation of this book: George McGavin for consultancy, Daniel Gilpin and Elizabeth Munsey for editorial assistance, Sunita Gahir for design assistance, Hilary Bird for indexing, Rakesh Kumar for the jacket, The Cotswold Store and Alana Ecology for supplying equipment, and Peter Anderson and Gary Ombler for additional photography. We thank all of the Audubon experts who contributed their knowledge to ensure this book represents the organization's mission: Audubon's Development Division, including Sean O'Connor, Chief Development Officer; Kevin Duffy, Vice President of Corporate, Foundation, Public, and Legacy Giving; Julisa Colón, Director of Brand Marketing; Holly Fairall, Manager of Brand Marketing; Audubon's Science and Conservation Divisions, including Geoff LeBaron, Director of the Christmas Bird Count; Brooke Bateman, Director Climate Science; Nicole Michel, Director Quantitative Science; Dr. John Rowden, Senior Director Bird-Friendly Communities; Chad Witko, Outreach Biologist; Marlene Pantin, Partnerships Manager of Plants for Birds; Audubon's Content Division, including Jennifer Bogo, Vice President of Content; Kristina Deckert, Art Director; Sabine Meyer, Photography Director; Melanie Ryan, Assistant Art Director; Camilla Cerea, Contributing Photo Editor; and Luke Franke, Network Photographer/Photo Editor.

The publisher would also like to thank the following for their kind permission to reproduce their photographs:

(Key: a-above; b-below/bottom; c-center; f-far; l-left; r-right; t-top)

1 Dreamstime.com: Alfio Scisetti (fcl); Harold Stiver (c). **2–3 naturepl.com**: Donald M. Jones / Minden. **4 Dorling Kindersley**: Frank Greenaway courtesy of Natural History Museum, London (tr); Jerry Young (cl).5 Stephen Oliver (br). **naturepl.com**: Donald M. Jones / Minden (tr). **6 Dorling Kindersley**: Peter Chadwick, courtesy of the Natural History Museum, London (tr); Neil Fletcher (bc) (fbl); Frank Greenaway courtesy of Natural History Museum, London (tc); Matthew Ward (tl) (br); Jerry Young (bl). **7 Alamy Images**: Bob Gibbons (r). **Dorling Kindersley**: Frank Greenaway courtesy of Natural History Museum, London (cr) (tc); Derek Hall (bl) (bc) (crb); Tim Ridley (tr); Matthew Ward (br). **8–9 Alamy Stock Photo**: Richard Levine. 9 Corbis: Gisuke Hagiwara / amanaimages. **10 Corbis**: Patrik Engquist (br); Frank Krahmer (c); Roger Tidman (tr). **Dreamstime.com**: Andreistanescu (bl). **11 Ardea**: Francois Gohier (cr/prairie dogs) (cra) (tr). **Corbis**: W. Cody (ca); Simon Weller (bl). **Dorling Kindersley**: NASA / Finley Holiday Films (br). **Getty Images**: Robert Postma (crb). **Photolibrary**: Shattil and Rozinski (cr/ferret). **12 Corbis**: Hans Reinhard (tc). **Dorling Kindersley**: Thomas Marent (crb). **Getty Images**: Colin Milkins / Photolibrary (ca). **12–13 Alamy Images**: WILDLIFE GmbH. **13 Alamy Images**: Rolf Nussbaumer (bl). Herbert Zettl (bc). **Dorling Kindersley**: Harry Taylor, courtesy of Natural History Museum, London (tl). **Dorling Kindersley: Dreamstime.com**: Jason Ondreicka / Ondreicka (cb). **Getty Images**: De Agostini (cl); Dr Sauer (ca). **14 Alamy Images**: All Canada Photos (cla). **Dreamstime.com**: Dennis Donohue (cla). **14–15 naturepl.com**: Jane Burton. **15 Getty Images**: Jeff Hunter (cr); Joel Sartore / National Geographic (tr). **16 Corbis**: E & P Bauer (bc). **Dorling Kindersley**: Frank Greenaway courtesy of Natural History Museum, London (clb). **Getty Images**: Christopher Furlong (cl). **16–17 Alamy Images**: Peter Arnold, Inc. **18–19 Dreamstime.com**: Lawrence Wee. **20 Corbis**: Paul Souders (tr); Hubert Stadler (br). **Getty Images**: Astromujoff (bl). **21 Corbis**: Theo Allofs (bl). **Getty Images**: Philip and Karen Smith (tr). **22 Corbis**: Mike Theiss / Ultimate Chase (crb). **Getty Images**: John Marshall (br). **23 Alamy Images**: Arctic Images (bc); blickwinkel (tl) (tc); Ashley Cooper (ca); Eddie Gerald (clb); NaturePics (c); Ken Walsh (bl). **Corbis**: Johnathan Smith; Cordaiy Photo Library Johnathan Smith; Cordaiy Photo Library Ltd (cb); Craig Lovell (cla). **24 Alamy Images**: Andy Arthur (tr); Ryan McGinnis (crb). **Dreamstime.com**: (cra). **Getty Images**: Jamey Stillings (br). **25 Alamy Images**: Ashley Cooper (clb); imagebroker (cl); Oleksiy Maksymenko (fcl). **Corbis**: Glowimages (c); Richard T. Nowitz (br). **Getty Images**: Arctic Images (cla); Jeff Foott (tl). **Science Photo Library**: Kenneth Libbrecht (tr) (cra) (fcra). **26 Alamy Images**: Hemis (c). **26–27 Corbis**: Peter Wilson. **27 Corbis**: Gene Blevins (bc). **Getty Images**: Alan R Moller (tr); Priit Vesilind / National Geographic (cr). **Science Photo Library**: J. G. Golden (ca). **28 Alamy Images**: WildPictures (cl). **Dreamstime.com**: Roman Ivaschenko (cr). **Getty Images**: Brian Stablyk (cb); Kim Steele (tr). **iStockphoto.com**: (br). **NOAA**: Carol Baldwin (bc). **Image courtesy of Oregon Scientific (UK) Limited**: (tc/bottom) (tc/middle). **29 Alamy Images**: Nepal Images (tc/top). **Corbis**: Jorma Jamsen (br); Tony Hallas / Science Faction (crb). **Getty Images**: Michael McQueen (cr). **Science Photo Library**: Garry D. McMichael (cl). **30 Corbis**: Larry Dale Gordon (cl). **Getty Images**: Jeremy Walker (cb). **30–31 Getty Images**: Tetra Images. **31 Alamy Stock Photo**: All Canada Photos (crb). **Audubon**: 2022 (bc). **Corbis**: Chen Zhanjie / XinHua Press (cla). **Getty Images**: Johnny Johnson (ca). **32 Getty Images**: Lew Robertson (bl). **32–33 Till Credner & Sven Kohle / allthesky.com**. **33 Alamy Images**: Peter Arnold, Inc (cr); Galaxy Picture Library (cb). **Corbis**: Roger Ressmeyer / Science Faction (cl). **34–35 Alamy Stock Photo**: LightField Studios Inc. **36 Dreamstime.com**: Mikhail Primakov (tr). **Magenta Electronics Ltd**: (cb). **SWAROVSKI OPTIK**: (crb). **Watkins & Doncaster**: (br). **Wildlife Acoustics, Inc.**: (bc). **37 RICOH Imaging Europe S.A.S**: (tr). **rspb-images.com**: Malcolm Hunt (tl). **40 Alamy Images**: Peter Titmuss (bc). **Dorling Kindersley**: 123RF.com: Aleksey Boldin (cr). **40–41 Getty Images**: Superstudio. **41 Getty Images**: Joel Sartore / National Geographic (c). **42 123RF.com**: cloud7days (bc). **Canon Inc**: (cl). **Dreamstime.com**: Audrius Merfeldas (clb); Dimitry Romanchuck (c); Audrius Merfeldas (cb); Joe Sohm (cra). **FLPA**: Yva Momatiuk & John Eastcott (crb). **Getty Images**: Gerry Ellis (tr). **Pentax UK Ltd**: (br/zoom). **Sigma Corporation**: (br/wide). **42–43 Corbis**: Peter Johnson (t); Gary W. Carter (b). **Getty Images**: David Maitland (cb). **43 Corbis**: Michele Westmorland (cla). **Dreamstime.com**: Brian Lasenby (br); Dan Rieck (crb); Slowmotiongli (tl). **FLPA**: Robert Canis (bc); David Hosking (cra); Roger Tidman (cb). **rspb-images.com**: Gerald Downey (crb). **44 Audubon**: 2022 (cra/image on iPhone). **Dorling Kindersley**: 123RF.com: Aleksey Boldin (cra, ftr/iPhone). **Getty Images**: Marc Romanelli (tr). **Marek Walisiewicz**: (bl). **Wildlife Acoustics, Inc** (ca). **45 Corbis**: Bob Krist (crb). **Marek Walisiewicz**: (c). **46–47 Alamy Stock Photo**: Nature Picture Library. **47 naturepl.com**: MYN / Clay Bolt (ca). **48 Alamy Images**: blickwinkel (cra). **Corbis**: Elizabeth Whiting & Associates (tl). **Getty Images**: Evan Sklar / Botanica (br). **naturepl.com**: Barry Mansell (cra). **49 Corbis**: Toshi Sasaki / amanaimages (tl); Owaki-Kulla (bl). 50 **Alamy Stock Photo**: Natalia Kuzmina (c). **Dreamstime.com**: Victor Chaika (cl).FLPA: Erica Olsen (cla). **naturepl.com**: John Downer (bc); Kim Taylor (crb). **Photolibrary**: Roger Jackman (bl). **51 Getty Images**: Tony Bomford / Photolibrary (cb). **NHPA / Photoshot**: Stephen Dalton (br). **52–53 Alamy Images**: Lawrence Stephanowicz. **54 Dreamstime.com**: Rinus Baak (c); William Wise (bc). **naturepl.com**: Laurent Geslin (tl). **55 Alamy** Stock Photo: B LaRue (bl). Audubon: 2021, by Luke Franke (tr). **Corbis**: O. Alamany & E. Vicens (tl). **Dreamstime.com**: Wirestock (c). **Getty Images / iStock**: jgareri (br). **Getty Images**: Raymond Blythe / Photolibrary (bc). **56 Alamy Stock Photo**: Adam Jones (c); Nature Picture Library (tr). **Dreamstime.com**: Steve Byland (bc); Gaysorn Eamsumang (cla); Gerald D. Tang (cra); Paul Reeves (br). **57 Corbis**: Gary Carter (crb). **Dreamstime.com**: Steve Byland (tc); Brian Kushner (ca); Steve Byland (clb). **Getty Images**: Paul E Tessier (cla); Sven Zacek / Photolibrary (cra). **58 Alamy Stock Photo**: Rosanne Tackaberry (cr). **rspb-images.com**: (bc). **59 Corbis**: Gary W. Carter (c). **Dreamstime.com**: Gerald Marella (tc). **FLPA**: Gianpiero Ferrari (bc); S & D & K Maslowski (bl). **60 Getty Images**: Visuals Unlimited (crb). **61 123RF.com**: danrieck (cr). **Alamy Stock Photo**: Jeff Lepore (tr). **Dreamstime.com**: Julie Feinstein (bc). **62 Corbis**: D. Robert & Lorri Franz (bl); Paul Taylor (ca). **FLPA**: David Hosking (crb). **63 Alamy Stock Photo**: Danita Delimont (crb); CarolDembinsky / Dembinsky Photo Associates (cra); John Glover (cl). **Dreamstime.com**: Suer27 (bl). **Getty Images**: Tier Und Naturfotographie J & C Sohns (crb). **Cara Tyler**: (bl). **64–65 Getty Images**: Steve Samples / 500px. **65 Alamy Stock Photo**: Brian Lasenby (bc). **Dreamstime.com**: Steve Byland (tc); Maryswift (crb); Brett Hondow (cra). **66–67 Dreamstime.com**: Sean Pavone. **68 Dreamstime.com**: Gualberto Becerra (bc); Flaviano Fabrizi (tr); Cheryl Fleishman (cra). **69 Alamy Stock Photo**: Rick & Nora Bowers (bc). **Dreamstime.com**: landewarphotography (bl); Gerald D. Tang (c). Kory D. Roberts (cl). **70 Alamy Images**: Nigel Cattlin (cl). **Corbis**: Joe McDonald (crb). **Dreamstime.com**: Melinda Fawver (bl).**Getty Images**: Wendy Shattil & Bob Rozinkski / Photolibrary (br); David Zimmerman (tr). **iStockphoto.com**: (cr). **naturepl.com**: Visuals Unlimited (clb). **71 Alamy Stock Photo**: Andrew Cline (cr); Don Geyer (bl); Photostock-Israel (cl). **Dreamstime.com**: Cristographic (br); Kcmatt (crb). **Getty Images**: Visuals Unlimited (clb). **72 naturepl.com**: Bruno D'Amicis (bl) (bc). **72–73 José Luis Gómez de Francisco**. **72 Alamy Images**: Neil Hardwick (ca). **Getty Images**: Brian Hagiwara (c); GK Hart / Vikki Hart (cr); Oxford Scientific / Photolibrary (cra); Paul Taylor (cl). **Science Photo Library**: Bjorn Svensson (tr). **72–73 Alamy Images**: flabCC. **73 Getty Images**: Anthony Bannister (tr). **74 Alamy Stock Photo**: Minden Pictures (c). **Corbis**: Tom Bean (cra); Joe McDonald (clb). **Dreamstime.com**: Paul Sparks (bc). **Science Photo Library**: Terry Mead (cla). **74–75 Dreamstime.com**: Sergey Rezinkin. **75 Alamy Images**: Nigel Cattlin (crb/springtail); Tom Joslyn (crb/dung fly). **Corbis**: PULSE (br). **Dreamstime.com**: Jeffrey Banke (cr); Paul Reeves (tr). **Getty Images**: Andrew Howe (c); Rodger Jackman / Photolibrary (bl). **76 Alamy Stock Photo**: Bruce Montagne / Dembinsky Photo Associates (tr). **Dreamstime.com**: Alian226 (cra); Le Thuy Do (bc). **77 Alamy Stock Photo**: WILDLIFE GmbH (clb). **Dreamstime.com**: Shirell Brucker (tl); Steve Byland (cla). **78–79 Dreamstime.com**: Maksershov. **80 123RF.com**: donyanedomam (tr). **Dreamstime.com**: Anton Foltin (br); Brett Hondow (cra); Bob Grabowski (bl). **Getty Images**: David Tipling (tl). **81 Alamy Images**: David Noble Photography (tl). **Dreamstime.com**: Robyn Mackenzie (bc); Sdbower (br); Wirestock (bl). **82 Dreamstime.com**: Pimmimemom (ca). **Getty Images / iStock**: Dole08 (bc). **83 Alamy Images**: imagebroker (tr); Stefan Sollfors (cra). **Dorling Kindersley**: Dreamstime.com: Olga Popova (br). **84 Alamy Stock Photo**: Tonia Graves (tl). **Dorling Kindersley**: Frank Greenaway courtesy of Natural History Museum, London (tr). **Getty Images**: Photolink (br); Visuals Unlimited (cr). **85 Getty Images / iStock**: aimintang (tc). **86 Getty Images**: Jozsef Szentpeteri / National Geographic (cla). **87 Corbis**: Karl Kinne (cra). **88 Alamy Images**: Simon Colmer and Abby Rex (tr). **Dorling Kindersley**: Rollin Verlinde (cra). **Dreamstime.com**: Wildphotos (cl). **89 Alamy Images**: David Crausby (tl). **Dreamstime.com**: Cvandyke (tr); Le Thuy Do (cr). **92 Alamy Stock Photo: blickwinkel (bl); Corbis**: Roger Tidman (tc); Visuals Unlimited (ca). **Dorling Kindersley**: Frank Greenaway courtesy of Natural History Museum, London (cla). **Dreamstime.com: Neil Letson (crb); Artem Stepanov (clb); Christian Weiß (cb); Pluc01 (bc); Dzmitry Zelianeuski (br). 92–93 Corbis**: Ashley Cooper. **93 Alamy Images**: blickwinkel (cl); **Dreamstime.com**: Neil Letson (bl). **Steve Kress**: (cb) (bc) (br). **94 Alamy Stock Photo**: Dorling Kindersley ltd (ca); Martin Shields (bc). **Dreamstime.com**: Chabkc (cla); Multik (c). naturepl.com: Staffan Widstrand (bl). **95 Alamy Images**: blickwinkel (cb); David Chapman (ca). **96 Alamy Images**: William Leaman (c). **Dreamstime.com**: Harold Stiver (bc). **97 Alamy Stock Photo**: William Leaman (c). Sharon Beals: (tc). **Dreamstime.com**: Sheila Fitzgerald (bc); Glenn Price (tr); Suebmtl (br). **Getty Images / iStock**: JackVandenHeuvel (bl). **98 Dreamstime.com**: Le Thuy Do (cra); Melinda Fawver (br). **naturepl.com**: Nick Hawkins (cl). **99 Dorling Kindersley**: Twan Leenders (bl). **Dreamstime.com**: Jason P Ross (bc). **100 Alamy Images**: Michael Griffin (bc). **Corbis**: Lothar Lenz (tr); Manfred Mehlia (cra). **Dorling Kindersley**: 123RF.com: somkku9kanokwan (br). **Getty Images**: Stephen Studd (cl). **naturepl.com**: Philippe Clement (bl). **101 Corbis**: David Chapman Natural Selection (cl); Fridmar Damm (cr); D. Robert & Lorri Franz (cra). **Dreamstime.com**: Jens Stolt (cb). **Getty Images**: Visuals Unlimited (clb). **102 Alamy Images**: David Hosking (tr). **Dreamstime.com**: Holly Kuchera (br). **Getty Images / iStock**: madsci (bl). **102–103 Getty Images**: Joel Sartore / National Geographic. **103 Alamy Images**: Peter Arnold, Inc (tl). Colin Seddon (br). **Science Photo Library**: GARY MESZAROS (bl). Shutterstock.com: Karel Bock (tc). **104 Corbis**: Frans Lanting (br). **Getty Images**: Charcrit Boonsom (tl). **105 Alamy Stock Photo**: Minden Pictures (cla). **Dreamstime.com**: Steffen Foerster (tr); Petr Simon (tc). **Corbis**: W. Perry Conway (cb); Ed Darack / Science Faction (b). **naturepl.com**: Gerrit Vyn (ca). **106–107 Alamy Images**: Louise A Heusinkveld. 106 **Dreamstime.com**: Daila Jansone (tl). **107 Alamy Stock Photo**: Stan Rohrer (tr). **Getty Images / iStock**: HHelene (crb). **108 Alamy Images**: Gay Bumgarner (br); Danita Delimont (cr); Rolf Nussbaumer (tr). **108–109 National Geographic Stock**: Michael Nichols. **109 Alamy Images**: Mary Liz Austin (cr). **Getty Images**: Philippe Bourseiller (tl); Michael Orton (c). **Science Photo Library**: MICHAEL P. GADOMSKI (tr). **110 Alamy Images**: A. P. (tr); Neil Hardwick (l). **113 Dreamstime.com**: Digitalimagined (bl). **114 Getty Images**: Peter Lilja (cl). **114–115 Alamy Images**: First Light. **115 Alamy Images**: Arco Images GmbH (tr). **Getty Images**: Bob Stefko (cra). **naturepl.com**: Oscar Dewhurst (cr). **116 Corbis**: Galen Rowell (bl). **116–117 National Geographic Stock**: Michael Nichols. **118 Dorling Kindersley**: Frank Greenaway courtesy of Natural History Museum, London. **118–119 Getty Images / iStock**: davelmorgan. **119 Dreamstime.com**: Johnbell (ca). **120 Alamy Stock Photo**: Andrew DuBois (cra). **Dreamstime.com**: Steve Byland (bl); Melinda Fawver (bc); Claire White (br). **121 Alamy Images**: David Boag (tr). **Corbis**: Nigel J. Dennis; Gallo (crb). **Dreamstime.com**: Ondřej Prosický (tc). **FLPA**: Gerry Ellis / Minden Pictures (clb). **Getty Images**: Panoramic Images (br). **122 Alamy Stock Photo**: Minden Pictures (fbr). **Dreamstime.com**: Steve Byland (bc); Smitty411 (c); Jay Pierstorff (br). **Getty Images**: Visuals Unlimited (cra); Tim Zurowski (tr). **123 Alamy Stock Photo**: Ron Niebrugge (bl); SuperStock (bc); Dennis Swena (fbl). **Corbis**: Tim Davis (fbr). **Getty Images**: Joel Sartore / National Geographic (c); Oxford Scientific / Photolibrary (cra). **Green-Witch.com**: Deben (ca). **124 Alamy Stock Photo**: Rick & Nora Bowers (cl). **Corbis**: James Randklev (br). **Dreamstime.com**: Kcmatt (c); Melani Wright (cr). **Getty Images**: Jason Edwards / National Geographic (tc); Pankaj & Insy Shah (cra). **125 Corbis**: George H. H. Huey (l). **Dreamstime.com**: Stephan Pietzko (c). **naturepl.com**: Jack Dykinga (cra). **126 Alamy Stock Photo**: Don Johnston_BI (tr). **Getty Images**: Mark Turner / Botanica (c); Jeff Foott (cl); Jason Edwards / National Geographic (br); Visuals Unlimited (bl). **127 Corbis**: Franck Guiziou / Hemis (c); Frans Lemmens (cla); Paul Souders (tc); Martin Harvey / Gallo (cb). **naturepl.com**: Richard du Toit (tl); Neil Lucas (bc) **128 Getty Images**: Wolfgang Bayer (tc); David McNew (cl); Paul Chesley / National Geographic (cla); Photolink (bc); Visuals Unlimited (cra). **129 Corbis**: Peter Reynolds; FLPA (tc). **Getty Images**: David McNew (cla) (cra). **Still Pictures**: David McNew (br). **130–131 123RF.com**: unitysphere.**131 Dreamstime.com**: Alfio Scisetti (ca). **132 Alamy Stock Photo**: blickwinkel (cra); John Sullivan (tr). **Corbis**: Frank Blackburn; Macduff Everton (br). **Dorling Kindersley**: Frank Greenaway courtesy of Natural History Museum, London (bl). **Dreamstime.com**: Ricardo Reitmeyer (tl). **133 Alamy Stock Photo**: Dennis K. Johnson (bl). **Dreamstime.com**: Le Thuy Do (ca); Corey Lefkowitz (tr); Paul Reeves (br); Brian Lasenby (cl). **134 Corbis**: Hans Pflefschinger / Science Faction (clb). **Dorling Kindersley**: Jerry Young (ca). **Getty Images**: Raymond Blythe / Photolibrary (cl). **naturepl.com**: Meul / ARCO (cra). **134–135 naturepl.com**: Kim Taylor. **135 Dreamstime.com**: Melanie Hobson (cla). **136 Alamy Stock Photo**: Eyal Bartov (bl). **Dreamstime.com**: Taviphoto (bc). **Getty Images**: Jody Dole (c). **137 Alamy Stock Photo**: Danita Delimont (bc). **Dreamstime.com**: Iva Vagnerova (tr). **naturepl.com**: Ingo Arndt (cb). **138 Alamy Stock Photo**: Prisma by Dukas Presseagentur GmbH (bc). **Corbis**: Tom Bean (cr). **Dorling Kindersley**: Jerry Young (tr). **Dreamstime.com**: Willfields (cla). **Getty Images**: Russell Illia (c). **naturepl.com**: Donald M. Jones (crb).**139 Corbis**: W. Perry Conway. **140-141 Getty Images / iStock**: TheBigMK. **141 Dreamstime.com**: Kwiktor (ca). **142 Corbis**: Andrew Brown; Ecoscene (tl); Pablo Corral Vega (bl); Tim Zuroswski (ca). **Dreamstime.com**: Ryan Deberardinis (bc). **143 Alamy Stock Photo**: All Canada Photos (bc); Michael Wheatley (tc); Audrey Taylor (ca); Nature Picture Library (br). **Corbis**: George Steinmetz (bl). **144 Alamy Stock Photo**: Michael Doolittle (bl); FLPA (br); Kevin Schafer (tl). **Corbis**: Roy Hsu (tr). **Getty Images**: Konrad Wothe (cr). **144–145 Alamy Images**: Art Kowalsky. **145 Alamy Images**: Andrew Darrington (cr). **Corbis**: George D. Lepp (tl). **Dreamstime.com**: Yuval Helfman (tc). **Gary Nafis**: (tr). **Getty Images**: (bl/cycling); DEA / A. Calegari (br); David Epperson (bl). **146 Corbis**: David Muench (cr). **Getty Images**: Visuals Unlimited (cl). **147 Shutterstock.com**: Bridget Calip. **148 Dreamstime.com**: Ivan Kokoulin (bl). **148–149 naturepl.com**: Sumio Harada / Minden.**150 Alamy Stock Photo**: Megan McCarty (ca); Nature Collection (cr). **Dreamstime.com**: Armando Frazão (crb); Paul Reeves (tc). **151 Alamy Stock Photo**: Nature Picture Library (tr); Lee Rentz (b). **Dreamstime.com**: Sgoodwin4813 (tc). **152 Alamy Stock Photo**: Minden Pictures (tr). **Dorling Kindersley**: Frank Greenaway courtesy of Natural History Museum, London (bc). **Dreamstime.com**: Wildphotos (ca). **152–153 Photolibrary**: Luis Javier Sandoval. **153 Dreamstime.com**: Pedro Antonio Salaverría Calahorra (tc); Le Thuy Do (bl); Le Thuy Do (bc). **Getty Images**: Stephen Alvarez / National Geographic (tr). **154-155 Getty Images / iStock**: marekuliasz. **156 Corbis**: Adam Woolfitt (br). **Dorling Kindersley**: Frank Greenaway courtesy of Natural History Museum, London (bc); **Dreamstime.com**: Frank Fichtmueller (bl). **Getty Images**: Paul McCormick (tr). **157 Dreamstime.com**: Ajdibilio (crb). **Getty Images**: Matt Cardy (tl). **158 123RF.com**: flobow (bc); leekris (bl). **158–159 Getty Images**: Tyler Gray. **159 123RF.com**: mariedaloia (tr). **160 Dreamstime.com**: Brian Lasenby (c). **160–161 naturepl.com**: Jeff Vanuga. **161 Alamy Stock Photo**: RooM the Agency (cra). **Dorling Kindersley**: Daniel Cox / Photolibrary (bc). **Dreamstime.com**: Hakoar (cr); Nflane (ca). **162 Ardea**: Tom & Pat Leeson (cr). **Corbis**: Kennan Ward (cb). **Getty Images**: Hauke Dressler (cl); Visuals Unlimited (crb); Dominic Harcourt Webster (tl). **162–163 naturepl.com**: John Cancalosi. **163 Dorling Kindersley**: Cyril Laubscher (cr). **Dreamstime.com**: Steve Callahan (tr). Robert Ivens (br). **164 Corbis**: Frans Lanting (cl); Roger Tidman (br). **Dreamstime.com**: Eric Dale (bl). **Getty Images**: Catherine Cedner (tl); Frank Krahmer (ca); Sven Zacek / Photolibrary (cra); Paul E Tessier (tc). **165 123RF.com**: karelbock (tc). **Alamy Stock Photo**: Monkey Business (br). **Dreamstime.com**: Rinus Baak (cb). **Getty Images**: Frank Krahmer (c); Purestock (tr). **166 Alamy Images**: blickwinkel (cl). **Getty Images**: Spike Walker (c). **166–167 Alamy Images**: Papilio. **167 Alamy Images**: Daniel Borzynski (bl). **Getty Images**: Oxford Scientific / Photolibrary (bc). **168 Alamy Images**: Brian Bevan (tr). Getty Images: Colin Milkins / Photolibrary (cr) (cb); Visuals Unlimited (tl). **169 Getty Images**: Bianca Lavies / National Geographic (tl). **170 Alamy Images**: blickwinkel (cra). **Corbis**: W. Cody (tr). **Dreamstime.com**: Randy Fletcher (crb); Brian Lasenby (clb). **Getty Images**: AFP (br). **naturepl.com**: Tom Vezo (bl). **171 Dreamstime.com**: Jason P Ross (ca); Jason P Ross (clb). **Getty Images / iStock**: Martin Leber (tl). **Getty Images**: Theo Allofs (bl); Jan Tove Johansson (cl); Harold Taylor / Photolibrary (cla); Visuals Unlimited (cb) (bc). **172-173 Getty Images**: Chris Axe. **173 Alamy Images**: Richard Murphy. **174 Corbis**: Arthur Morris (cra). **Getty Images**: Image Source (br); Jupiter Images (tl). **175 Alamy Stock Photo**: marek kasula (crb); Latitude 59 LLP (br). **Corbis**: Frans Lanting (tc); Michele Westmorland (cla). **Chris Gibson**: (bl). **176 Alamy Stock Photo**: Bob Gibbons (tl). **Dreamstime.com**: Melinda Fawver (bl). **176–177 Corbis**: Andrew Brown; Ecoscene. **177 Dreamstime.com**: Urospoteko (cra). **178 Alamy Images**: John Taylor (cra). **Dreamstime.com**: Sjöholm Dan (br); Manfred Ruckszio (bc). **178–179 Corbis**: Bertrand Riegel / Hemis. **179 Audubon**: 2021, Luke Franke (cra). Corbis: Eberhard Streichan (cl); Anthony West (tc); Adam Woolfit (cla). **Dreamstime.com**: Bddigitalimages (br). **Getty Images**: Laurance B. Aiuppy (bc). **180 Alamy Images**: Leslie Garland Picture Library (tr). **Getty Images**: De Agostini (clb). **181 Alamy Images**: Skyscan Photolibrary (cr). **Dreamstime.com**: Ivkuzmin (tc). **Getty Images**: Thierry Grun (br); Camille Moirenc (bl). **182 Alamy Images**: Lightworks Media (bl); Peter Titmuss (tr). **Getty Images**: Bob Pool (br). **183 Dorling Kindersley**: Frank Greenaway courtesy of Natural History Museum, London (br). **Dreamstime.com**: Witold Krasowski (cra). **184 Alamy Images**: Robin Chittenden (tr). **185 Dreamstime.com**: Moose Henderson (c). **Getty Images**: Rosemary Calvert (tc). **186 Alamy Images**: Nigel Housden (bl). Corbis: Ronald Wittek / dpa (bc). **186–187 Corbis**: Paul Darrow / Reuters. **188 Alamy Images**: David Chapman (br); photow.com (cra). **188–189 Dorling Kindersley**: Stephen Oliver (t). **190 Dreamstime.com**: Redwood8 (bc). David Harp / ChesapeakePhotos.com (br). **naturepl.com**: Juan Manuel Borrero (tr). **191 Alamy Stock Photo**: Hilda DeSanctis (bc); Ivan Kuzmin (cr). **Corbis**: DK Limited (cla). **Dreamstime.com**: Artmorfic (br); Dr Ajay Kumar Singh (bl); Mikelande45 (tr).**192 Alamy Stock Photo**: Danita Delimont (bl); Waterframe (crb). **Corbis**: Brandon D. Cole (br). **Dorling Kindersley**: Colin Keates, courtesy of Natural History Museum, London (ca). **Dreamstime.com**: Mirecca (bc). **Getty Images**: Stephen Frink (cra). **193 Dreamstime.com**: John Anderson (br); Seadam (l); Gerald Robert Fischer (tr); Seadam (crb). **naturepl.com**: Sergio Hanquet (cra). 194 Corbis: Destinations (bl); Chinch Grynziewicz; Ecoscene (tl) (tr). **195 Corbis**: Ashley Cooper (tr); Robert Pickett (bl). **Dorling Kindersley**: Colin Keates, courtesy of Natural History Museum, London (br). **196 Alamy Stock Photo**: Saverio Gatto (br); Stefan Huwiler (bl); Jerome Murray - CC (cb). **Getty Images**: Ghislain & Marie David de Lossy (cla). **196–197 Getty Images**: Christina Bollen / Photolibrary. **197 Alamy Stock Photo**: Minden Pictures (br). **Corbis**: Winfried Wisniewski (bc). **Derrick K. Jackson** (tr). **198 Dreamstime.com**: Jolanta Dabrowska (bc). **Getty Images / iStock**: bonchan (bl); douglascraig (cr). **199 Alamy Stock Photo**: JamesMundy, Nature's Ark Photography (ca) (cb); **Dreamstime.com**: Melinda Fawver (cla); Cathy Keifer (tc); Sgoodwin4813 (cra). **200 Alamy Images**: Michael Howell (bl). **Corbis**: Yann Arthus-Bertrand (tl). **Dreamstime.com**: Hakoar (bc). **201 Alamy Images**: Loetscher Chlaus (tr). **Corbis**: Demetrio Carrasco (bl). **Dreamstime.com**: Jason Ondreicka (br); Paul Reeves (cla); Helena Kivisto Vila (crb). **202 Alamy Images**: RWP (cl). **Corbis**: Chris Collins (bl). **Getty Images**: Sabine Lubenow (tr). **iStockphoto.com**: (cb). **Science Photo Library**: Nigel Cattlin (br). **202–203 Chris Gibson. 203 Alamy Stock Photo**: Mark Boulton (cr); **Roswitha Irmer (bc). Corbis**: Chinch Grynziewicz; Roger Tidman (tr). **Chris Gibson**: (bl). **Neil Hardwick**: (crb). **204 Alamy Images**: blickwinkel (cra). **Corbis**: Frank Blackburn; Ecoscene (cl); Raymond Gehman (br); Eric and David Hosking (tr); Robert Marien (crb). **Getty Images**: Ron Erwin (cla); Christopher Furlong (cr). **205 Alamy Stock Photo**: Derrick Alderman (c); Robography (clb). **Corbis**: Brandon D. Cole (cl); Roger Tidman (bl). Colin Keates, courtesy of Natural History Museum, London (br). **Getty Images**: China Foto Press (cla). **Chris Gibson**: (tl). **Science Photo Library**: Kjell B. Sandved (fcr). **Steve Trewhella**: (cb). **Shutterstock.com**: Andrew Balcombe (cr). **206 Getty Images**: Jeff Rotman (bl). **206–207 naturepl.com**: Jurgen Freund. **208 Corbis**: Paul A. Souders (c); Specialist Stock (cl). **208–209 Getty Images**: Johnny Johnson. **209 Alamy Images**: Thomas Hanahoe (tr); Michael Patrick O'Neill (c); Rosanne Tackaberry (bc). **Corbis**: Karen Kasmauski / Science Faction (crb). **Dreamstime.com**: Agami Photo Agency (cr). **210-211 Getty Images**: Scott T. Smith. **212 Corbis**: Galen Rowell (c). **Flickr.com**: Lisa Hupp / USFWS (bc). **Getty Images**: Paul Nicklen / National Geographic (clb). **212–213 Corbis**: Galen Rowell. **213 Alamy Images**: Arcticphoto (c); Karen & Ian Stewart (tr). **Getty Images**: Geoff du Feu (br). **naturepl.com**: Donald M. Jones / Minden (cr). **214 Corbis**: Steve Kaufman (br); Kennan Ward (bl). **214–215 naturepl.com**: Konrad Wothe. **216 Alamy Images**: Louise Murray (bl); WILDLIFE GmbH (br). **Dreamstime.com**: Agami Photo Agency (cl). Getty Images / iStock: KenCanning (c). **Getty Images**: Chris Jackson (tl). **216–217 Corbis**: Bob Krist. **Dreamstime.com**: Agami Photo Agency (tr). **Corbis**: Momatiuk-Eastcott (br); Paul Souders (cr).

All other images © Dorling Kindersley
For further information see: www.dkimages.com